Robot Wireless Control Made Simple with Python

Build Your Robot in 40 Days

This book is primarily directed at Microsoft Windows® operating environment.

Control Room uses Python language, runs on most operating systems.

The robot side uses the Atmel® ATMega328 chip.

H-Bridge and PWM are used for motor direction and speed control.

The chip programming uses the WinAVR GNU compiler for C.

Complete Source Codes for Python and C programs are provided.

Electrical diagrams and schematics provided.

Herb Norbom
First Edition

Where we are aware of a trademark that name has been printed with a Capital letter.

Great care has been taken to provide accurate information, by both the author and the publisher, no expressed or implied warranty of any kind is given. No liability is assumed for any damages in connection with any information provided.

Contents

Preface

Where do we come from?
A great question that many have answered and no one can prove, at least not now. For what is about to happen, that question will be very answerable, at least for awhile and for some. By the time you read this, artificial intelligence may be a reality, it is very close. Very soon the question may evolve to whose intelligence is artificial.

How long have I got?
Another question that has echoed through time and for which there is no answer. Even that question is about to change, at least for some. The question may become -- How long do you want? At first we will answer the question, later it will be well beyond our control.

Where am I going next?
Another common question, and for this one, the answer will evolve to – Wherever you can imagine.

Are we alone?
We are probably not alone, but if we are, not for long.

At what point would a 'thing' with artificial intelligence be considered alive? Could it have a soul?
My guess would be, who knows and how could you prove it either way?

Mission Statement

To be a reliable source of information for the various areas related to robotics. My goal is to provide professional advice and good standards. This book is aimed at the hobbyist. Over the years, I was frustrated, because the information I needed was so fragmented. The implementation of simple ideas required many days and many false starts. This book will straighten the path and provide bridges over some of the gaps. Some site reference links are provided where I found helpful information. This book is going down a specific path. The book is not a general reference source for Python, C, hardware or electronics. The book goes into just enough depth to accomplish the goal of building a working wireless controlled robot. For greater depth, the reader can consider more specific references on subjects of interest. My path in developing my robot, Max, has gone down many trails that I once thought to be promising and just didn't work. You may have shared some of my frustrations, spending days chasing something that just would not work as you wanted, or as knowledge permitted. In this book I am going to be able to give you a more direct path for the development of your robot. What is referred to as a day, generally took much more than a day. Most of the false starts have been eliminated; you will find some major changes to the code as our project evolves. I left a little trail of evolution so that you could enjoy finding better solutions. As you follow along, I hope you enjoy the journey and try as many side paths as your time permits. I will not intentionally mislead, or give false information. The reader is expected to carefully think out the actions I suggest and if something looks to be in error to adjust accordingly. I will not be responsible for any damages. I am always looking for enhancements and suggestions, your help is appreciated. I urge you to visit the web site at www.rymax.biz.

Project Goals

To provide a roadmap for you to follow down a specific path. This will include some description of my early less than satisfying results. The main components of our project are as follows:
- Control Platform running on the PC. This will be accomplished using Python
- Wireless communications
- Physical robot construction
- Robot electronics
- Camera and speakers

Some of the areas we are going to touch on to achieve our working robot are:
- Programming Languages – Python and C
- Python threading
- Python queues LIFO and Priority
- Python windows via Tkinter
- C – bit manipulation
- DOS commands
- Electronics – circuits and motor controls

- Robot hardware Microchips Atmega328p, Atmega168 and the H-Bridge
- Serial Communications between Python and a C program on the microchip
- Wireless communication to and from your robot
- A WiFi camera that is tied into our Python program
- Text to voice and wav file sounds on your robot

For this project your completed Robot will be remotely controlled from your PC. Python will be used to develop the control panel. The Robot, Max, will have two drive motors, an arm, a bumper and a camera with speakers. As you will see in the pictures and descriptions, an expensive beautiful robot was not my goal. Code shown in these examples may be freely used for your personal hobby enjoyment. Reference needs to be made to the source of the code as from RyMax, Inc. If you wish to use the code for resale, you must receive written permission from the author or RyMax, Inc.

Day One – Why Python?

The 'art' of programming can be fun, it is definitely time consuming. If you find yourself starting to dream of coding or solving problems while just relaxing, the bug has bitten you. Some of the things you are going to need must be searched for. I will point you in the direction I went and give you the reasons why. There are as many paths to take as you could ever imagine. Each decision point potentially closes some paths and opens many more. If you do not have high speed internet this journey is going to be much more difficult. With the advent of WiFi you should be able to find hot spots somewhere in your area.

You are going to need some level of knowledge or familiarity with command line instructions. I will provide some of what you need for Linux and Windows, while Apple users may find similar instructions useful, my expertise is not in that area – at all. Since you have made it this far, you have some interest. I am a programming nut and I will start there, but if you are an electronics nut, start there. These two disciplines are required, just hard to say which comes first, I think programming.

If you have never programmed you are going to have to catch up. Never fear, everybody else is still trying to catch up as well. There are a lot of FREE tutorials out there, take advantage of them. While you are working with them take notes on the key points so you can have a 'cheat sheet' for reference. Ok, fine with that, but where do you start? Even If you have never programmed before, I suggest you start with Python. We are going to be using a lot of Python. While I am sure everyone has their own favorite programming language and good reasons for it, at this point Python is my choice. As you learn Python you will gain insight into areas you are going to need to control your robot. There are several reasons for choosing Python, they include the following:

- Object Oriented – will flow with events rather than straight lines
- Not compiled, uses an interpreter – therefore, quick results while developing applications
- Runs on Windows, Linux, Unix, even Apple – it is portable
- There is lot of FREE information on the web about it
- Python is free
- There are a lot of free modules - you will need –for communication, etc.
- What you learn, program flow and structure will to some extent carry over to C, C++ or C#, or whatever language you evolve to

Yes, of course there are disadvantages, if you are going to do something for resale Python may not be the language for you. If you are here, you are probably not close to having anything to sell, so don't worry about that. Just because Python uses an interpreter do not think you are limited in terms of program size and complexity. With today's computer's Python will be fast enough for you. So I wore you down, now you may be wondering, where can I get Python and how hard will it be to install? You are in luck, I will give you two sites and it is not hard to install. But before that I suggest you think about which Python version. You of course need the version that runs on your computer's operating system, but with Python you need to consider the release version. As I mentioned earlier Python is free, and being free means there are issues to be aware of. Let's say you want to communicate with your robot over a serial communication port. A good thing, however the text to speech and the communication software were not available for the Python 3.x version when my development project started. So, what you would want to get is the <u>Python 2.7.2.5 version or later as long as 2.7</u>. Keep in mind that many operating systems come with Python pre installed; some will even have two versions. Check out your computer prior to going through the download effort. Another reason for version 2.7.x is that most of the on-line references are for it or older releases. The Python code in this book is Active Python® 2.7.2.5 which is based on Python 2.7.2.

Where to get Python

- www.activestate.com   The Community Edition as it is FREE. This is a great site, I suggest you go ahead and register on it. As you will see later, they have some great tools for downloading other modules that you may need.
- www.sourceforge.net is also a great site and it is a good idea to register here also. You can do searches for software modules. This site also has great download tools.

I like the ActiveState® site because it is very user friendly. I have found it easy to use for adding python modules. A general hint, unless you have a great memory and know what you are doing, use the defaults when installing programs.

Day Two – Hello World

You have installed Python 2.7.x and you are saying this is great, but now what? The answer is keep going, practice and learn to use the on-line tutorials. Go ahead and look at the Python Tutorial at www.docs.python.org. While this is good stuff, you may be overwhelmed quickly. Use your web browser search capabilities and as you look at the sites try to figure out what version of Python the examples are written in and what modules are loaded. I suggest you try some of the following sites:

- www.astro.ufl.edu
- www.sthurlow.com
- www.learnpython.org
- www.tutorialspoint.com/python/index.htm
- https://developers.google.com/edu/python
- http://anh.cs.luc.edu/python/hands-on/handsonHtml/handson.html

Before we write the first traditional program, we should go ahead and set up a few things that we are going to need. Another decision to be made is; how will you run Python? In running Python you can do it from the command prompt, I tend to call it the DOS prompt or DOS window or command line. Or you can run it from a GUI called 'Idle'. I am going to take you down the DOS path, because it is more of a nuts and bolts path. You will need to know DOS commands at some point. If you are working in a Unix/Linux environment, chances are that you are very familiar with command language.

From Windows you can get to the command prompt several ways:

- You can click on the 'Start' button and select 'Run' and enter '*cmd*' and press return. This will open a DOS window and should show you the current directory path.
- Or, if you have a 'Windows Key', press that key and the letter '*r*' together. This will bring up the 'run' window. Enter '*cmd*' and press return.

Python needs to be in your system's search path. Let's see if it is in yours. At the command prompt type *python* and press enter.

```
C:\Documents and Settings\Herb Norbom\work>python
ActivePython 2.7.2.5 (ActiveState Software Inc.) based on
Python 2.7.2 (default, Jun 24 2011, 12:21:10) [MSC v.1500 32 bit (Intel)] on win
32
Type "help", "copyright", "credits" or "license" for more information.
>>>
```
Exhibit1

It should bring up the Python prompt. You can exit the Python prompt by pressing Ctrl and z keys. If it does not work, chances are that Python is not in your system's search path. To check your search path, type *path*.

```
C:\Documents and Settings\Herb Norbom\work>path
PATH=C:\Program Files\AMD APP\bin\x86;C:\WinAVR-20100110\bin;C:\WinAVR-20100110\
utils\bin;C:\Program Files\Common Files\Microsoft Shared\Windows Live;C:\WINDOWS
\system32;C:\WINDOWS;C:\WINDOWS\System32\Wbem;C:\WINDOWS\system32\WindowsPowerSh
ell\v1.0;c:\Program Files\Microsoft ASP.NET\ASP.NET Web Pages\v1.0;C:\Program F
iles\ATI Technologies\ATI.ACE\Core-Static;C:\Program Files\AMD APP\bin\x86;C:\Wi
nAVR-20100110C:\WinAVR-20100110\utils\bin;C:\Program Files\Common Files\Microsof
t Shared\Windows Live;C:\WINDOWS\system32;C:\WINDOWS;C:\WINDOWS\System32\Wbem;c:
\Program Files\Microsoft SQL Server\100\Tools\Binn;c:\Program Files\Microsoft S
QL Server\100\DTS\Binn;C:\WINDOWS\system32\WindowsPowerShell\v1.0;c:\Program Fi
les\Microsoft ASP.NET\ASP.NET Web Pages\v1.0;C:\Program Files\ATI Technologies\
ATI.ACE\Core-Static;C:\Documents and Settings\Herb Norbom\Application Data\Pytho
n\Scripts;C:\Program Files\Atmel\Flip 3.4.3\bin;c:\python27;c:\python27\scripts

C:\Documents and Settings\Herb Norbom\work>
```
Exhibit2

You should see Python27, or whatever version you are running. Here you see it at the end. If it is not in your search path, there is a relatively simple way to add it to the path using the following command.

        Path=%path%; c:\python27

What this does is take your systems existing search paths and add c:\python27 to it. If you installed python using defaults this should work, if not, change it to match your installation. With this method each time you restart your computer, you will need to add this command. A little later we will look at putting the command in a script, or as I like to call them a batch file. You can also do a 'permanent' add which involves environmental parameters which I will not be going into.

Let us write the traditional program. Type 'python' at the DOS prompt. From the python prompt of >>> you will add the following.
>>> greeting ='Hello World'
>>>print greeting
Your screen should look similar to the following one.

```
C:\WINDOWS\system32\cmd.exe - python                                _□×
ActivePython 2.7.2.5 (ActiveState Software Inc.) based on
Python 2.7.2 (default, Jun 24 2011, 12:21:10) [MSC v.1500 32 bit (Intel)] on win
32
Type "help", "copyright", "credits" or "license" for more information.
>>> greeting='Hello World'
>>> print greeting
Hello World
>>>
```
Exhibit3

To exit a Python program press Ctrl + z

Day Three – Programmer's Notepad

Very quickly, you will see that you do not want to be typing all your commands into the Python prompt for every program. You would spend forever and a day and quickly quit, not to mention the errors that would creep in. What we need to do is save our programs in a file so that we have an easy way of changing the programs. To save the files we need what is referred to as an editor. There are a great many editors available, your computer probably has one and if you like you could use a word processor, as long as it can save your files in text format.

We are going to need some additional tools later, specifically a C compiler with libraries, so I am going to have you get the editor that comes with that package now. Go to http://winavr.sourceforge.net/download.html. Select download and follow the instructions. The version we are using here is WinAvr-2010 and is approximately 28.8Mb. The editor is called Programmer's Notepad.

We are going to be writing a number of programs and it can get very confusing where they are located. Also from a backup view point it is nice to have them in a separate directory, probably several. Let's make a separate directory now. Also, we will create a batch file that changes to our new directory and sets up the Python path.

Simple DOS commands

I am going to create a directory in the location where my '*cmd*' prompt opened. Adjust the following as needed for your system. Before we go any further, a few quick words on DOS commands. They can do damage, they are not very user friendly; they will destroy without asking twice. So make sure the command you enter is the command that you want and that you know what the command is going to do.

Simple DOS commands, execute from the DOS command prompt. Remember DOS is not case sensitive.

- Dir or dir   – This will give you the contents of the current directory
- Help   – all the commands that are available
- Help dir   – gives you all the options available with dir
- cd {dir name}   – change directory, you would add the directory name
- cd ../   – moves up the directory tree one level
- cls   –clear the DOS window screen

We are going to create a directory to store our programs. Call the directory 'work'.

   mkdir work   –this will create the directory

To see if the directory was created type 'dir w*' this should list your work directory and any other file or directory starting with 'w' the * is called a wild card.

```
C:\WINDOWS\system32\cmd.exe                                         _□×
C:\Documents and Settings\Herb Norbom>mkdir work

C:\Documents and Settings\Herb Norbom>dir w*
 Volume in drive C has no label.
 Volume Serial Number is B865-BE3A

 Directory of C:\Documents and Settings\Herb Norbom

11/10/2011  02:42 PM               174 WCFsetupPaths.bat
07/02/2012  07:04 AM                94 whiteLed.bat
07/03/2012  05:16 AM                89 whiteLedSlave.bat
02/18/2013  09:06 AM    <DIR>          work
               3 File(s)            357 bytes
               1 Dir(s)  18,172,108,800 bytes free

C:\Documents and Settings\Herb Norbom>_
```
Exhibit4

Batch or Bat File

Before we go to our new directory let's create a batch file that does several things.

- Loads the path statement for Python
- Changes to our new directory
- Lists the contents of that new directory

Our goal is to have a simple command that is easy to find and does things that we tend to forget about. We are going to use our new Programmer's Notepad to create the batch file. Note at this point we have created a new directory called 'work' but we have not changed to that directory. If for some reason you are not sure that you are in the correct directory, just exit the DOS command prompt. Click on the x or type *'exit'*. Call the DOS prompt back up if you did exit. Leave the DOS prompt window open for now. We now want to access the Programmer's Notepad. We will set up a shortcut for it.

- Click the Start Button and select all programs
- Find WinAvr-20100110
- Slide cursor open to Programmer's Notepad
- Right Click
- Select Create Short cut
- Grab the new icon and slide to desktop or cut and paste to desktop

From the desktop double click your new Programmer's Notepad icon to open it. We are going to create a simple batch file that we can execute from our DOS prompt. Type the following so that your screen looks like the screen below. Make any changes you need to get the correct path and for changing to your work directory.

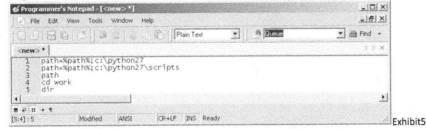

Exhibit5

Don't worry about the search word "Queue", just a left over search.

I have added one additional path statement, we will need later.   Prior to saving you will see this is set up as Plain Text. You can leave that, but we will save it as a bat file.

We want to make sure we save this file in the same directory that is opened when we run the 'cmd' to get the DOS prompt. Look at your DOS prompt and the directory and save this file to same directory with the name 'mypython27.bat'. Use the 'File' and 'Save As' menu items. Move to correct directory and enter the file name.

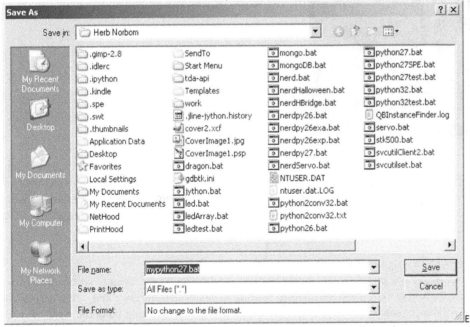

Exhibit6

After you have saved the file, note at the top of Programmer's Notepad you will see the full path and your program file name below the menu items. Worth noting you can have many files open under the Programmer's Notepad. I suggest you take a few moments to look at the options settings under the tool menu item. I like to see line numbers and the full path of the file.

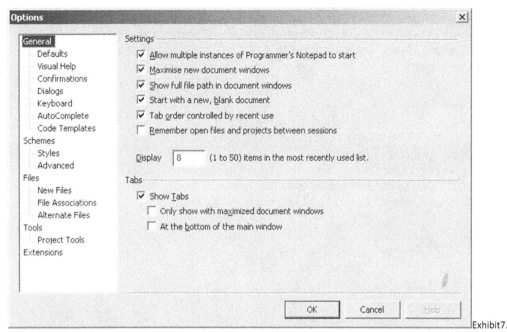
Exhibit7.

At this point we have created our 'mypython27.bat' file. The file sets our path and changes to our 'work' directory and from our work directory list the contents of that directory.

Before we run our new bat file, another useful DOS command, but more familiar to Unix/Linux users is 'ls', for list directory. Try the 'ls' command, you should see our new bat file mypython27.bat. Or use the more traditional dir. Try typing 'dir mypy*' using the wild card '*' to see all files starting with 'mypy'.

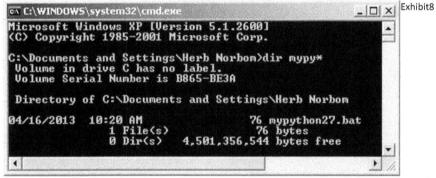
Exhibit8

Once we are sure the file is there let's see if it works. At the DOS prompt enter '*mypthon27*', leave off the .bat or include it if you like. While case doesn't matter, exact spelling does. If it did not run because you misnamed the file name, you can change the name from with Programmer's Notepad or your file manager. There is also a DOS command, 'rename'. Unless you are familiar with that DOS command skip it for now, or do some research before using. You should see something like the following screen. Go ahead and type 'path' at the DOS prompt and see if your Python paths have been added.

Let's put our traditional 'Hello World' program into a program file that we can modify and easily run.

In Programmer's Notepad Click on File and New, this will pop open a window that has a lot of file types. Select Python. Enter the following lines. A general hint or suggestion, Python is extremely sensitive to spacing issues or indents on a line. This may drive you crazy. The traditionalist in python will use the spacebar; I choose to use the tab key. My thumb would be numb if I used it all the time. Whatever method you choose STICK with it. Python will not like it if you mix and match spaces with tabs on the beginnings of lines. It is a good idea to get used to commenting your programs. This will help as your programs get more complicated. Two quick notes to consider, putting '#' before anything tells Python to ignore everything after the '#' until it hits a new line. I have found it easiest to just put the '#' on each line rather than getting into 'block' comments. Explore that as you like.

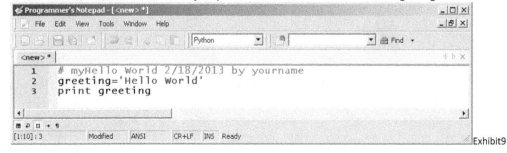
Exhibit9

Observe the above screen shot. We need to save our new Untitled <new>* program or file. To save the file, click on File and Save As 'myHelloWorld.py'. Note we want to save the file in our new 'work' directory.

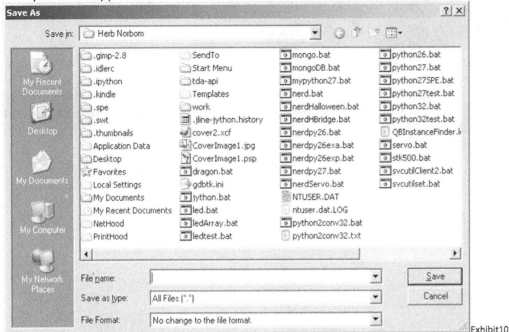
Exhibit10

You want to select our 'work' directory and then type in the correct file name. Double click 'work' and then enter our program name, let's use myHelloWorld.py and Press Save.

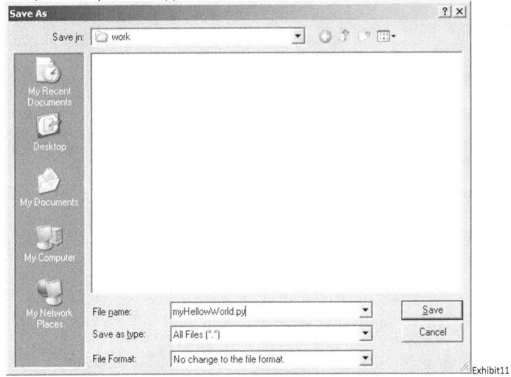
Exhibit11

We now need to satisfy ourselves that the program works. Run our program from the DOS prompt. Make sure we are in the correct directory and that our program is there. Type the command 'ls' or 'dir' to see your file.

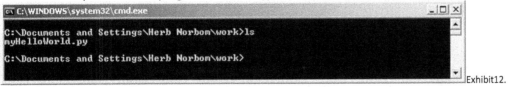
Exhibit12.

Run the program with the following command at the DOS prompt.

Python myhelloworld.py   Remember case doesn't matter to DOS.

Exhibit13

You now have the basic tools to write and execute programs written in Python. Use the on-line tutorials and you will be amazed at how quickly your knowledge and the complexity of your programs grow. Let's try one more program to introduce the concept of Python modules. Python comes with a lot of modules.   Many more are available on-line, more on that later.   Let's write a program that introduces a new module. In Programmer's Notepad select NEW and then Python from the menu File. Type the following Python code. Save the file in our work directory as 'timeDelay.py'.

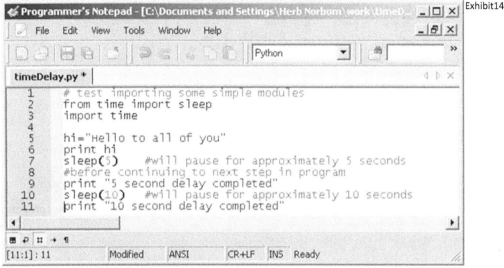

Exhibit14

Some comments about the program:
- Imported a module called time
- From the module time we imported sleep
- Note the comments placement

With Python there are a number of choices to importing modules. See Exhibit 15 for other import options. Make changes in your editor and save the program. Run the revised program.

Hint.   If you are not familiar with DOS, you can press the up arrow key to repeat a command. If that doesn't work, type in 'doskey' and see if that lets you use the up arrow key.

The program still works as shown in Exhibit15.

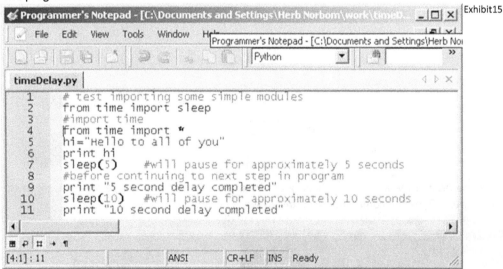

Exhibit15

BUT, if I try the changes shown in Exhibit16 I get an error message.

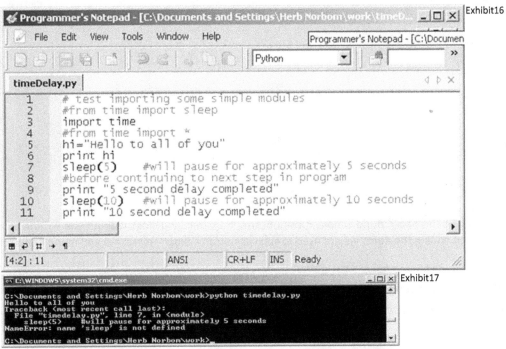

How you load the modules will impact the amount of memory your system uses. While not too critical for us at this point you should be aware of limits and resources your program consumes.

Day Four – Tkinter Module

I hope you have been going on line to find tutorials and to write a bunch of programs yourself. Many can be copied and pasted into the Programmer's Notepad, saved and then run without any changes. While copying and pasting is a fine exercise, you will find many programs will not work. Remember Python is very sensitive to spacing, and that can be a big problem with copying programs. Second, Python has a number of versions, and the example programs sometimes do not tell you what version they were written for. Third, there are a number of standard modules and a great number of custom modules that must first be downloaded and installed for Python to work with them. Fourth, I know for myself that I learn quicker if I type in the program myself. Try more tutorials.

Going through tutorials you may have seen references to GUI's or windows type interfaces. Python has a number of options in this area. For now we will stick with the standard interface that is included with Python 2.7.x on some operating systems, the Tkinter module. If you need to upgrade your version of Python or are missing a module see DAY - Twenty.

We are going to program a simple GUI (Graphical User Interface). In the Programmer's Notepad open a new Python worksheet.

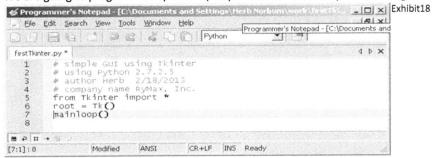

Type in the above example substitute names, dates and your appropriate comments. It is a very good idea to include items like which Python version this program is developed under, dates, and a brief message about what the program does. The three lines that are not commented out are all that is needed to produce a window.

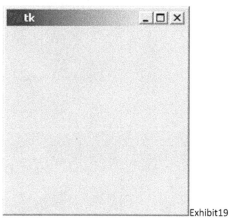
Exhibit19

Notice that Tkinter and Python are handling all the background actions, position, size, min, max and close without you writing any code. This is all great but of little use without adding the items we are used to such as buttons, labels, messages and menu items to name a few.

As with Python there are a number of web sites devoted to Tkinter. Some are listed below:

- http://infohost.nmt.edu/tcc/help/pubs/tkinter/web/index.html
- http://www.tkdocs.com/tutorial/windows.html
- http://pages.cpsc.ucalgary.ca/~saul/personal/archives/Tcl-Tk_stuff/tcl_examples/
- http://effbot.org/tkinterbook/
- http://www.pythonware.com/library/tkinter/introduction/hello-tkinter.htm
- http://www.tutorialspoint.com/python/python_gui_programming.htm
- http://www.beedub.com/book/2nd/TKINTRO.doc.html

There are a number of reference sites, just type into your search browser 'tkinter examples' or 'tkinter tutorial' for more sites. You can spend a lot of time in this one area alone, we are going to cover the basics and that will take some time. In the program, firstTkinter.py, shown as Exhibit18, it is important to understand at a high level what is going on. The tools and background programs to make Tkinter work are brought into memory by the import. The statement 'root=Tk ()' creates or forms the root window, sometimes called the master. The statement 'mainloop()' is what actually runs everything above that line and actually displays the window.

Let's add a title to the window.

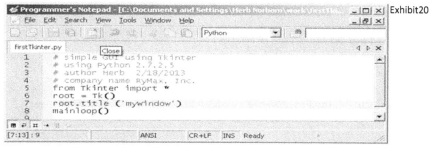
Exhibit20

That one change results in the following window.

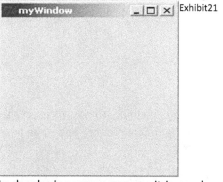
Exhibit21

In developing your programs it is good practice to learn the standards and to use them. I have to admit, do as I say not as I do, applies a lot. But a good practice is to format your programs so they can be called by other Python programs and run as modules. To do this we need to add some new lines to our program.

Exhibit22

While we only added the one line we have introduced the very important line spacing requirements of Python. In my case, I inserted a Tab before each of the last three lines. The standard would probably be to add two to five spaces vs. a tab. Try your program both ways. On one line only put three spaces and see what happens. For Python programming standards, a good site is http://www.python.org/dev/peps/pep-0008/ .

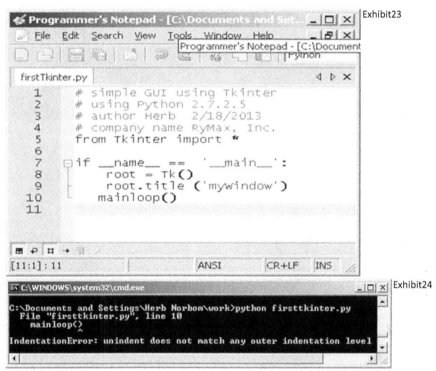
Exhibit23

Exhibit24

As you can see spacing is critical to Python. Hint. As you can see I have included a lot of screen shots in this document. Under windows it is easy to do. Make the window you want the screen shot of the active window. Then press Alt and Print Screen keys together. Go to where you want the screen shot to appear and paste or Ctrl v. If you want the whole screen, do as above only press the Print Screen Key.

Day Five – Tkinter Widgets

Within Tkinter there are a number of very useful and powerful subroutines or called programs that are referred to as 'widgets'. Let's add a button widget to our example. A good tip is to use the save as function for major changes to the program.
Great to have a button that doesn't do anything, but I am sure you would like something else.

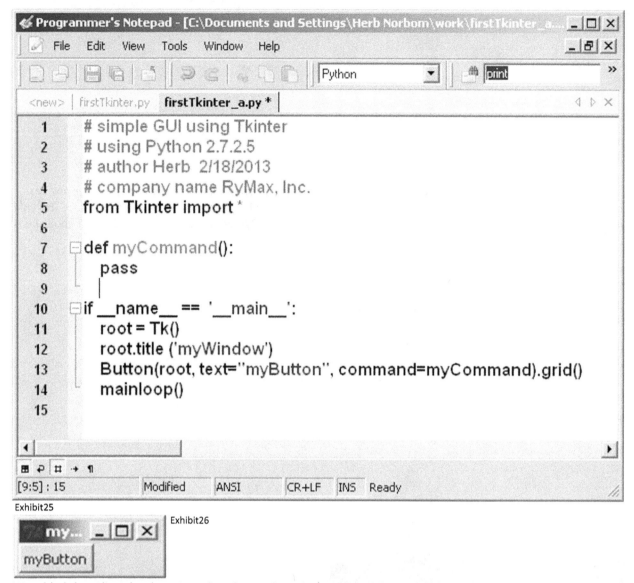

Exhibit25

Exhibit26

We added three lines but have introduced a number of new items to be considered. The actual 'Button' line has a structure to it. The widget name is Button; we want the button to appear in the 'root' window. The text of the button will be 'myButton'. If the button is pressed the program will run the procedure 'myCommand'. Grid is a whole concept by itself. For now, just know we need it there or the button will not display. When you press the button, click on it with the mouse and you will see it depress, then bounce back. The program ran the procedure we specified. In our program, as we are just developing it, nothing happened as we used the 'pass' statement to just run and return. The 'pass' statement is from our view point just a place holder that does nothing. But it is perfect to use while developing functions. HINT. If you position the mouse over the edge you should see a two sided arrow. Left click the mouse and hold, pull or push to resize the window. Did you notice how the window became smaller when we added the button? Put a '#' sign in front of the line 13, save the program and rerun. Tkinter tries to outguess you in giving window sizes. Take the '#' sign out and re-save the program.

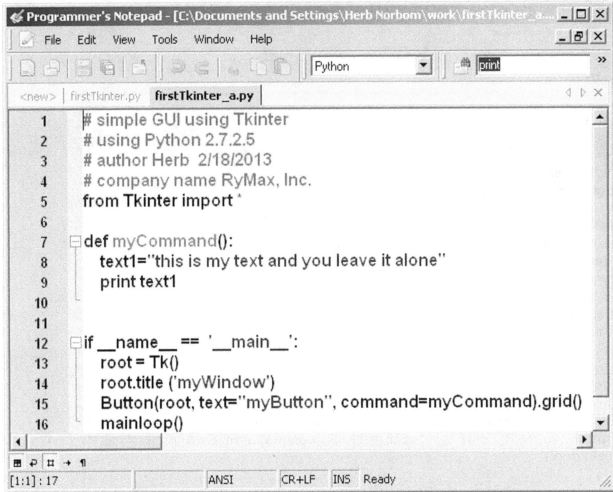

Exhibit27

I took the pass statement out and defined a string variable text1 and assigned the words shown in the example. Now when you run the program, press the button, the message is shown in the DOS command window.

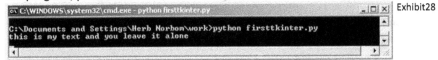
Exhibit28

Note the program is still running, just waiting, press the button again. Remember Ctrl + z to exit.

Tkmessagebox and If Statement

Let's add a second button for exiting the program. This button will also introduce some formatting options. We are also going to introduce the 'tkMessageBox'. And the infamous "if statement", not to mention the quit option.

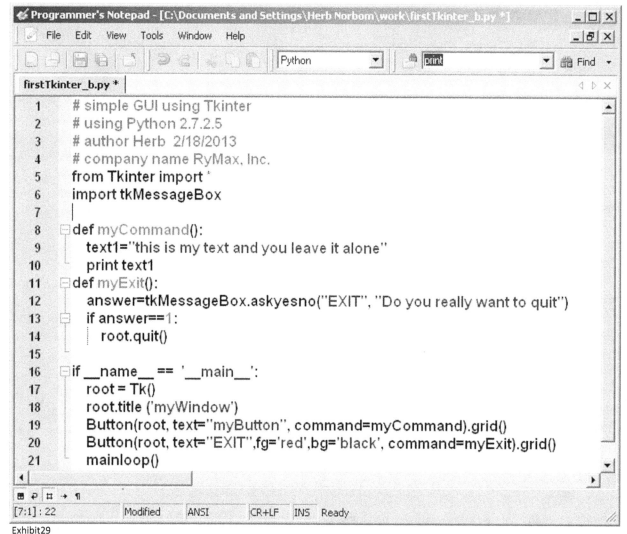

Exhibit29

Notice the following new items:

- We imported the tkMessageBox while case doesn't matter in DOS, it matters here in Python.
- We have the response to our tkMessageBox.askyesno captured in the variable answer. We can then use the 'if statement' to evaluate and decide which action to take.
- In our 'if statement' notice that answer==1:   has two '=' symbols, very important, we are evaluating a response not assigning a value.
- In the format of the tkMessageBox.askyesno ("Exit", "Do you really want to quit?")   The first portion is the title of the tkMessageBox; the second portion is the question to display. The program knows to display the Yes or No buttons. The program assigns a 1 to answer if 'Yes' pressed and a 0 if 'No' pressed.

Note, if you click on 'No' the program keeps running.

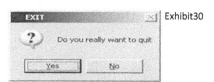
Exhibit30

- There are a number of different standard message boxes including: showinfo, showwarning, showerror, askquestion, askokcancel, askyesno, and askretrycancel.

Hint. As you progress you are probably going to open multiple windows. The main window or 'root' can be considered the 'parent' of the 'child' windows, when you close the root window the program will automatically terminate all the child windows.

While we are on the 'if statement' it is worth showing a few more tips. You can have multiple if statements. In the following example I have added 'return' after each one. What that means is when the 'if statement' is satisfied the program will return to where the function was called from. In this program there are only two 'correct' values for our variable 'answer'. If neither condition is satisfied something is wrong and a message is printed on the console. While this is a very simplistic logic check it is very important that you as a programmer develop a feeling for things that can go wrong in your program and methods of handling them.

Let us use the 'Save As' and now call our program 'firstTkinter_c.py'. A good idea as your programs get more complex is to have different versions of them that are easily identified as the same program.

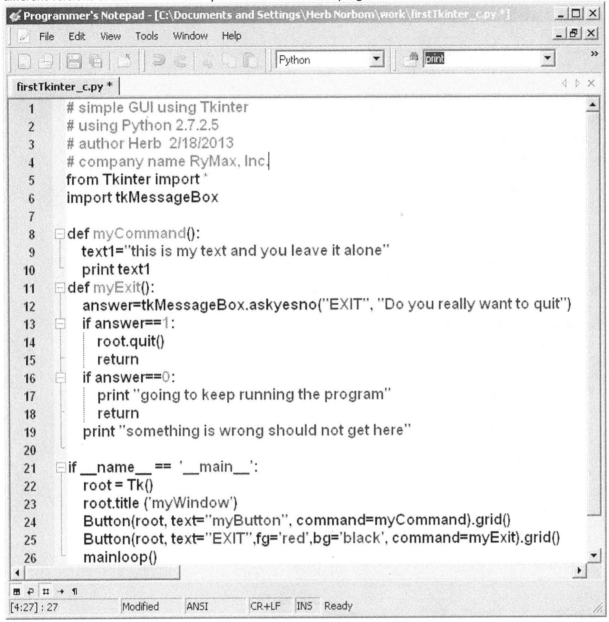

```
1    # simple GUI using Tkinter
2    # using Python 2.7.2.5
3    # author Herb  2/18/2013
4    # company name RyMax, Inc.
5    from Tkinter import *
6    import tkMessageBox
7
8    def myCommand():
9        text1="this is my text and you leave it alone"
10       print text1
11   def myExit():
12       answer=tkMessageBox.askyesno("EXIT", "Do you really want to quit")
13       if answer==1:
14           root.quit()
15           return
16       if answer==0:
17           print "going to keep running the program"
18           return
19       print "something is wrong should not get here"
20
21   if __name__ == '__main__':
22       root = Tk()
23       root.title ('myWindow')
24       Button(root, text="myButton", command=myCommand).grid()
25       Button(root, text="EXIT",fg='red',bg='black', command=myExit).grid()
26       mainloop()
```

Exhibit31

Try commenting out the returns by placing a '#' symbol in front of them, and run the program, select 'No' on the Exit button.

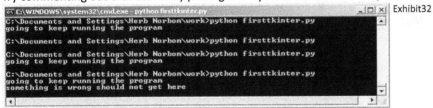
Exhibit32

Day Six – Python Error Handling

I think we need to go a little deeper into Python error handling before getting very deep into the programs. What we started at the end of the last day is a beginning, but when we get an error it would be nice to have a little more information. For a simple message try making some minor changes to the program. See line 20 Exhibit33.

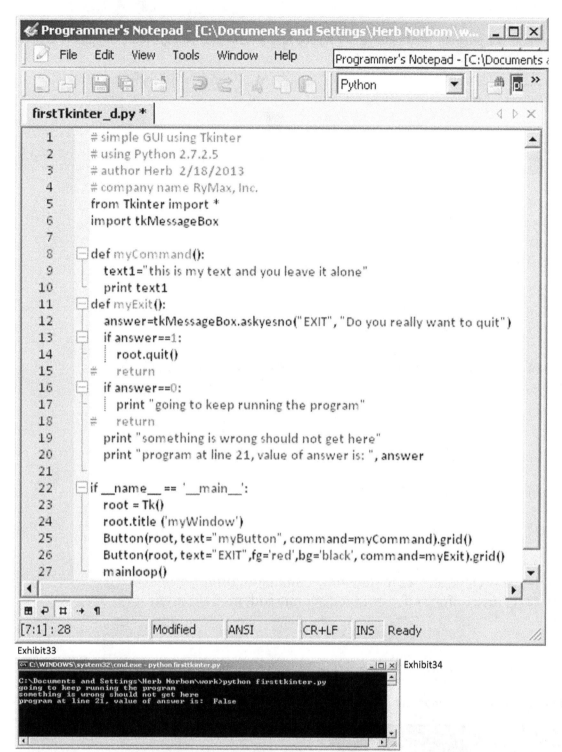

Exhibit33

Exhibit34

When I ran the program I selected 'No' from the 'tkMessageBox'. The program continued on as I have left the 'return' lines commented out. Then it printed the message. The value of the answer is 'False' and maybe not the '0' you expected. This brings up another programming concept of switches; "off" and "on" or the binary system of 0's and 1's. A '1' means 'on' or 'True'. The opposite, '0' means 'off' or 'False'. Later on we will return to a better means of reporting and handling error messages. We have jumped around a little, so let's do a little more. In Python you are not locked into what 'type' you first define a variable as. Try some examples, first make answer =9 and see what happens. See line 13 Exhibit35.

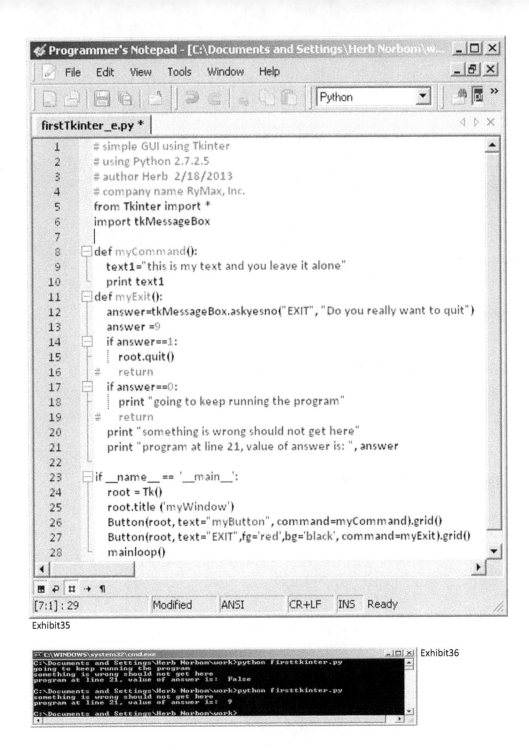

Exhibit35

Exhibit36

Now try making 'answer' equal a string, see line 13. Exhibit37 "My answer is no".

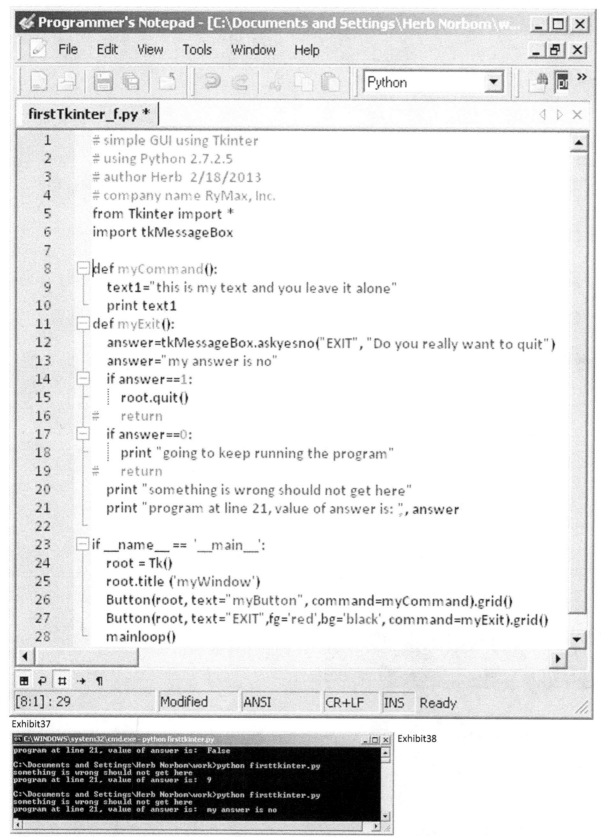

```
1    # simple GUI using Tkinter
2    # using Python 2.7.2.5
3    # author Herb  2/18/2013
4    # company name RyMax, Inc.
5    from Tkinter import *
6    import tkMessageBox
7
8    def myCommand():
9        text1="this is my text and you leave it alone"
10       print text1
11   def myExit():
12       answer=tkMessageBox.askyesno("EXIT","Do you really want to quit")
13       answer="my answer is no"
14       if answer==1:
15           root.quit()
16   #     return
17       if answer==0:
18           print "going to keep running the program"
19   #     return
20       print "something is wrong should not get here"
21       print "program at line 21, value of answer is: ", answer
22
23   if __name__ == '__main__':
24       root = Tk()
25       root.title ('myWindow')
26       Button(root, text="myButton", command=myCommand).grid()
27       Button(root, text="EXIT",fg='red',bg='black', command=myExit).grid()
28       mainloop()
```

Exhibit37

```
program at line 21, value of answer is:  False

C:\Documents and Settings\Herb Norbom\work>python firsttkinter.py
something is wrong should not get here
program at line 21, value of answer is:  9

C:\Documents and Settings\Herb Norbom\work>python firsttkinter.py
something is wrong should not get here
program at line 21, value of answer is:   my answer is no
```

Exhibit38

In Python you can change what type the variable is just by assigning a value of the type you want. This is good until you forget and mess yourself up.

Day Seven – Tkinter Label and Entry Widgets

In Tkinter there are a number of widgets, but I wanted to consider the 'Label' and the 'Entry' widget for some quick examples. We are going to use the 'Entry' widget to enter a value from the keyboard and the 'Label' widget to display the value in our window.

We will also print the value at the DOS command window. I am going to keep using our firstTkinter.py program but I will remove the line where the answer was assigned a string value.

Python Class

```python
# simple GUI using Tkinter
# using Python 2.7.2.5
# author Herb 2/18/2013
# company name RyMax, Inc.
from Tkinter import *
import tkMessageBox
class defaultClass:
    def __init__(default,myResponse):
        default.myResponse = myResponse
myC = defaultClass( 'got none' )

def myCommand():
    text1="this is my text and you leave it alone"
    print text1
def myExit():
    answer=tkMessageBox.askyesno("EXIT", "Do you really want to quit")
    if answer==1:
        root.quit()
#       return
    if answer==0:
        print "going to keep running the program"
#       return
    print "something is wrong should not get here"
    print "program at line 21, value of answer is: ", answer

def myInput():
    temp= myC.myResponse.get()
    print temp
    Label(root, text =temp).grid()

if __name__ == '__main__':
    root = Tk()
    root.title ('myWindow')
    Button(root, text="myButton", command=myCommand).grid()
    Button(root, text="EXIT",fg='red',bg='black', command=myExit).grid()

    myC.myResponse=StringVar()
    myC.myResponse_entry=Entry(root, textvariable=myC.myResponse).grid()
    Button(root, text="print input",fg='red',bg='white', command=myInput).grid()
    mainloop()
```

Exhibit39

We have added some new concepts to make the data collection and transfer to functions easier. Consider adding a 'class' method whenever you need to share data with various sections of the program. The 'class' definitions are extremely important, the better you understand them the more professional and useful your programs become. They are easier to understand than they look if you think about their parts and how the program flows. While you define the 'class' you don't call it or really reference it directly. The 'class definition' is similar to the import function. Python interprets and sets up the class BEFORE it gets down to the main loop where the program runs.

The main parts are:

- class   – tell Python what you are building
  - defaultClass: – tell Python the name of the class (Name it whatever you want ideally something meaningful as a description to help you remember what you are doing. Don't make it too long as you will be typing it a lot.)
  - def __init__(default,myResponse): – this is probably the most confusing line, (Use names with some meaning as I described above) I think of "default" as the data name or object and "myResponse" as the attribute of the object, but I am sure there are better ways.
    - the first section def __init__ – tell Python to define and initialize the parts, notice there are two underscores '__' on either side of init
    - default   – tell Python the first part of the data name
    - myResponse   – tell Python what the data elements are, you will generally end up with a list, each item separated by a comma
- myC = defaultClass ('got none') -- this is probably the next most confusing line, (Name as you like, just remember what I described above and of course use that name.)
  - myC   – tell Python the data front end 'name' that you are going to reference throughout the program.
  - =defaultclass   – tell Python that for 'myC' in this class, we are going to assign the following values to the data variables
  - ('got none')   – tell Python that the first item described in the line immediately above this getting assigned the string variable text   'got none'

Class adds extra functionality in the background, making your job much easier. Hint, for more information look at http://www.sthurlow.com/python/lesson08/ .

To help in this important area I am going to start a fresh program called lesson02.py and add some additional data to the class structure and clean up the program a bit. You can take your existing program which is open in the Programmer's Notepad and click on File and Save As. Enter new name, I will be using 'lesson02.py'. Then make the changes to the new program.

```python
1    # using Python 2.7.2.5  using Classes
2    # author Herb 2/18/2013  company name RyMax, Inc.
3    from Tkinter import *
4    import tkMessageBox
5    class herbClass:
6        def __init__(herbData,myResponse, second, third, fourth,
7            counter,realNumber):
8            herbData.myResponse= myResponse
9            herbData.myResponse= second
10           herbData.myResponse= third
11           herbData.myResponse= fourth
12           herbData.counter=counter
13   myClassStuf = herbClass(
14       'got none',      #default for myResponse
15       'second data',  # for the second data item
16       'car',       # for the third data item
17       '',          #for the fourth item, in effect nothing
18       6,           # counter assigned an integer 6 to this variable
19       4.234        # realNumber assigned a real number
20       )
21   def myCommand():
22       text1="this is my text and you leave it alone"
23       print text1
24   def myExit():
25       answer=tkMessageBox.askyesno("EXIT", "Do you really want to quit")
26       if answer==True:    # notice changed from a 1 to True
27           root.quit()
28           return
29       if answer==False:   #notice changed from a 0 to False
30           print "going to keep running the program"
31           return
32       print "something is wrong should not get here"
33       print "program at function myExit, value of answer is: ", answer
34   def myInput():
35       temp= myClassStuf.myResponse.get()
36       print temp
37       Label(root, text =temp).grid()
38   if __name__ == '__main__':
39       root = Tk()
40       root.title ('myWindow')
41       Button(root, text="myButton", command=myCommand).grid(column=0,row=1)
42       Button(root, text="EXIT",fg='red',bg='black',
43       command=myExit).grid(column=2,row=2)
44
45       myClassStuf.myResponse=StringVar()
46       myClassStuf.myResponse_entry=Entry(root,
47       textvariable=myClassStuf.myResponse).grid(column=3,row=3)
48       Button(root, text="print input",fg='red',bg='white',
49       command=myInput).grid(column=4,row=4)
50       mainloop()
```

Exhibit40

25

Exhibits41-43

C:\WINDOWS\system32\cmd.exe - python lesson02.py   _ □ x Exhibit44

```
C:\Documents and Settings\Herb Norbom\work>python lesson02.py
Hi everybody!!!!
```

I hope you spend some time going over this. Notice where the data values are assigned and the introduction of data types, more on data types later. The data values are listed in a column, separated by a comma and they have a comment on them saying what data item they belong to.

A few other changes were made to Exhibit40. Notice the handling of the response from 'myExit' function. I changed the 'True' and 'False' statements; try the options, no change to the user, either a 1 or True works. I also changed line 33. Line numbers as 'hardcode' are a problem because we tend to forget to change the reference when we add lines to our program.

Day Eight - Tkinter Displays

While we have produced a window, it is not very organized. It would be nice to adjust the size, location, and where the widgets are displayed. We will continue with the program 'lesson02.py'.

Tkinter Geometry

First let us change the size. Add the following line to your program. I like to put the line in below the root.title line. root.geometry ("220x630+250+30"):

- 220 is the width of the window or the x axis
- 630 is the height of the window or the y axis
- 250 is the position on your display screen, from the top left hand corner, going along the x axis. The top left corner of the display screen is position (0,0)
- 30 is the position on your display screen down from the top, along the y axis.

Try different values and play around with different sizes and positions. I want to display a window that is 400x200 pixels close to the center of the display screen. Try changing the geometry to root.geometry ("400x200+500+300"). To position widgets on the screen there are several options. We are going to use the 'LabelFrame' as a starting point. The 'LabelFrame' will reside in the root window. You can think of Frames much like a display case with a number of individual panels, and within each panel there are items. One nice thing about Frames is that you can move the Frame and everything in it stays in place. With the Frame you can organize widgets within the frame very easily. Also, on a window you can have multiple frames and even nested frames.

Tkinter Frames

Insert the myFrame lines below the geometry line. As the programs are starting to get larger, I will show the sections that changed. We will continue using the same program, 'lesson02.py', but save as 'lesson02_a.py'.

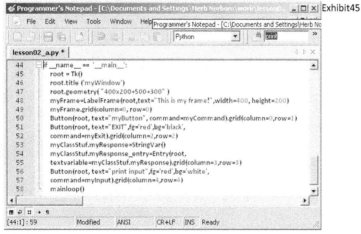

Exhibit45

```
44    if __name__ == '__main__':
45        root = Tk()
46        root.title ('myWindow')
47        root.geometry( "400x200+500+300" )
48        myFrame=LabelFrame(root,text="This is my frame!",width=400, height=200)
49        myFrame.grid(column=0,row=0)
50        Button(root, text="myButton", command=myCommand).grid(column=0,row=1)
51        Button(root, text="EXIT",fg='red',bg='black',
52        command=myExit).grid(column=2,row=2)
53        myClassStuf.myResponse=StringVar()
54        myClassStuf.myResponse_entry=Entry(root,
55        textvariable=myClassStuf.myResponse).grid(column=3,row=3)
56        Button(root, text="print input",fg='red',bg='white',
57        command=myInput).grid(column=4,row=4)
58        mainloop()
```

When you run this you may be surprised to see that while you now have a nice frame, all of your widgets are gone. This is because the frame is on top of the window and the widgets are buried under the frame and are useless at this point. What we need to do is put the widgets on the frame.

 Exhibit46

Before we change our widgets I want to explain a little about the LabelFrame. First, we did this instruction on two lines. This makes it easier to read in the program and sometimes I have found some widgets want to be defined in this manner vs. on one line. I don't like exceptions just make it a rule to break things out until you are comfortable.

myFrame = LabelFrame (root, text="This is my frame!", width=400, height=200):

- myFrame is the name of this LabelFrame
- LabelFrame is the tkinter widget name
- root is the window we want to place the LabelFrame in
- text is the title of the frame
- width and height are the size of the frame in pixels

myFrame.grid(column=0, row=0):

- myFrame.grid is the positioning feature of myFrame
- column=0 tells the program to position the LabelFrame in column 0 of the root window
- row=0 tells the program to position the LabelFrame in row 0 of the root window. Remember the column=0 and row=0 will start this LabelFrame in the top left hand corner of the root window.
- Try some different sizes and check the results.

Try myFrame=LabelFrame (root, text="This is my frame!", width=200, height=200)

 Exhibit47

Change the width back to 400 and then let's put our widgets back on the LabelFrame. On each of our three Buttons and the Entry widgets we need to change 'root' to 'myFrame'..

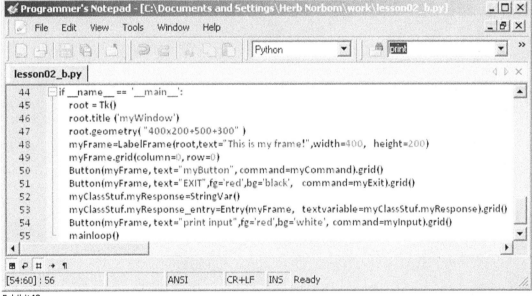

Exhibit48

When we run our program all the widgets reappear, but still not pretty and our LabelFrame shrunk.

 Exhibit49

We will fix it one item at a time. The grid function and/or the LabelFrame are trying to conserve space. The program sees that the entire myFrame window does not need to fill the entire root window. If we want the LabelFrame to fill the entire root window we will need to make changes. The grid manager is probably one of the simplest layout tools, but it needs you to understand a number of things. Grid manager thinks in terms of columns and rows within the window or frame. Columns and rows start with 0 in the top left hand corner of the frame or window. Grid manager will expand as needed based on your 'sticky' instructions. But it wants to conserve space and not take more than it needs to display your widgets. It can give you some results you probably would never expect. First, I am going to change the layout a little, assigning the widgets to different columns and rows. This gives a little better layout.

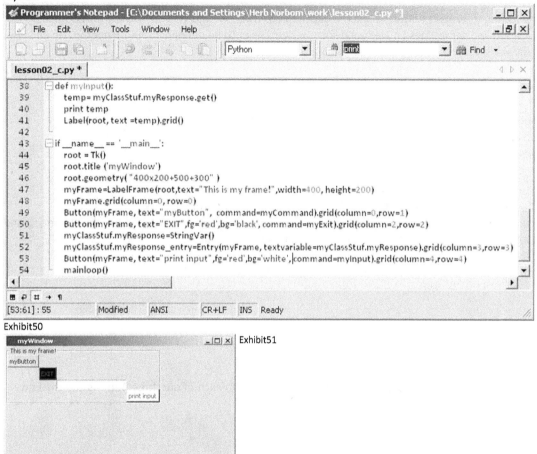

Exhibit50

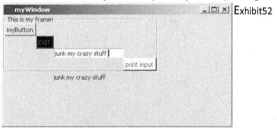
Exhibit51

Notice that the frame has been expanded.
When I enter some junk and press 'print input' I get the following, pretty much as expected.

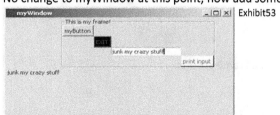
Exhibit52

Now let us make one small change to the layout. Put myFrame in column=2.
     myFrame.grid (column=2, row=0)
No change to myWindow at this point, now add some crazy junk and press print input.

Exhibit53

The grid manager says, now I have some stuff that belongs in column 0, so I better slide the LabelFrame over to the next column which is really 1, but since 1 is not used, grid manager says, 1 is available so why use what they asked for column 2. Now with grid manager trying to outguess you, unexpected results can follow. We can put a number of LabelFrame's within the same window. With additional frames we can begin to control the freethinking grid manager. Make some changes to the program and save as 'lesson03.py'.   Changes were made to the two sections shown in the following. Notice line 49 you can use either single quote (') or double quote (") just remember to match the start and end.

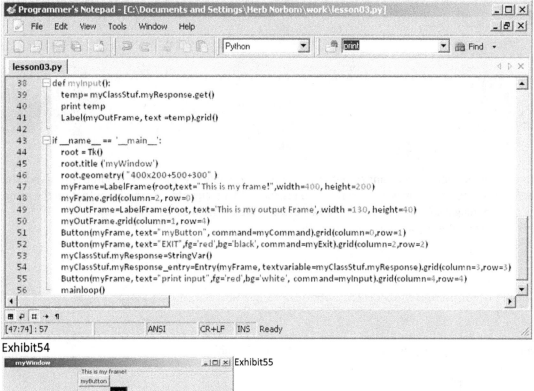

Exhibit54

Exhibit55

We now have our second LabelFrame. Try a short input like the following.

Exhibit56

Does it look like what you expected? With the program still running, press the print input button 6 times.

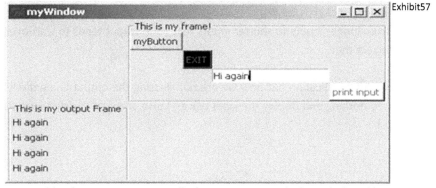
Exhibit57

We would at least expect to see all of our output. Grab the right hand bottom corner of myWindow and pull it down.

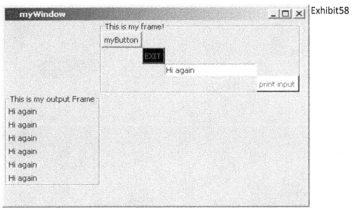 Exhibit58

There is the rest of our output. Chances are you would want something different. Probably just the current output displayed, the previous output should be cleared each time. A simple way to fix this is to instruct grid manager to display the output on the same position each time. Change line 41 by adding a column and row, as shown below. Save program as lesson03_a.py.

> Label (myOutFrame, text =temp).grid (column=0, row=0)

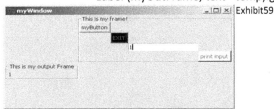 Exhibit59

Press the print output a few times, the program will just keep overwriting in the 'outFrame'.
We still have a problem; enter a short phrase "Hi I am Herb!" Press print input.

 Exhibit60

That worked fine, now with the program still running, enter 'Ralph' and press print input.

 Exhibit61

As you can see we still have a problem. Save the program as lesson03_b.py. Add the following to line 41 and try running the program again.

> Label (myOutFrame, text =temp).grid (column=0, row=0, sticky=(N,S,E,W))

If you play with the print input you may notice as you go from longer inputs to shorter inputs that your output tends to walk over from the left edge of the myOutFrame. We would like to correct that.

If we change the line above to just be sticky= (W), we solve the justification but now we are not clearing the output line entirely. One way to clean this up is to set the temp variable equal to nothing and display the label twice. I also changed the sticky values around a little.

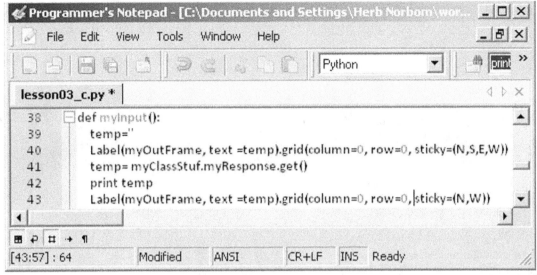

```
38   def myInput():
39       temp=''
40       Label(myOutFrame, text =temp).grid(column=0, row=0, sticky=(N,S,E,W))
41       temp= myClassStuf.myResponse.get()
42       print temp
43       Label(myOutFrame, text =temp).grid(column=0, row=0, sticky=(N,W))
```

[43:57] : 64   Modified   ANSI   CR+LF   INS   Ready

Exhibit62

There are a lot of options for tkinter's grid manager. I like the grid manager better than the other two geometry managers (pack and place). There appear to be more examples using pack than for grid. Whichever geometry manager you choose to use, do not mix them in your program, unless you are very careful. Check out the following site, there is a ton of good information, and examples.   http://effbot.org/tkinterbook/grid.htm

Now that you have the basic widget and knowledge of geometry in place, writing programs from scratch is getting easier, even if more complicated.   As we need additional widget features we will explore them. We need to add a little more functionality to our windows in the form of pull down menus.

Day Nine - Tkinter Menu System

Python has a very nice pull down menu system via tkinter. As you get into it I am sure you will see some familiarity to whatever system you currently use.   I am going to save our lesson03.py program as lesson04.py and make a few changes. The first change sets up the plain pull down menu by adding a very small amount of code to our existing program. To help us find sections, I also added some comments. When we run this the following is displayed, note the File at the top of the window.

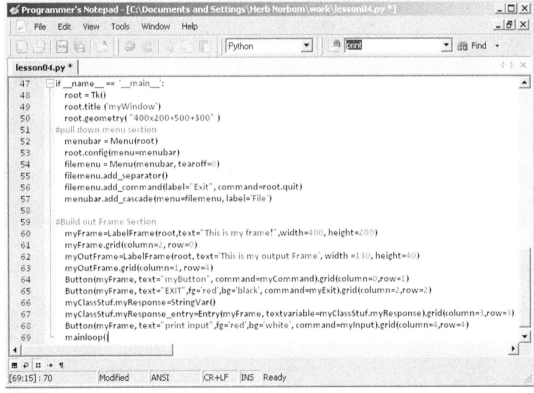

```
47   if __name__ == '__main__':
48       root = Tk()
49       root.title ('myWindow')
50       root.geometry("400x200+500+300" )
51   #pull down menu section
52       menubar = Menu(root)
53       root.config(menu=menubar)
54       filemenu = Menu(menubar, tearoff=0)
55       filemenu.add_separator()
56       filemenu.add_command(label="Exit", command=root.quit)
57       menubar.add_cascade(menu=filemenu, label='File')
58
59   #Build out Frame Section
60       myFrame=LabelFrame(root,text="This is my frame!",width=400, height=200)
61       myFrame.grid(column=2, row=0)
62       myOutFrame=LabelFrame(root, text='This is my output Frame', width =130, height=40)
63       myOutFrame.grid(column=1, row=4)
64       Button(myFrame, text="myButton", command=myCommand).grid(column=0,row=1)
65       Button(myFrame, text="EXIT",fg='red',bg='black', command=myExit).grid(column=2,row=2)
66       myClassStuf.myResponse=StringVar()
67       myClassStuf.myResponse_entry=Entry(myFrame, textvariable=myClassStuf.myResponse).grid(column=3,row=3)
68       Button(myFrame, text="print input",fg='red',bg='white', command=myInput).grid(column=4,row=4)
69       mainloop()
```

[69:15] : 70   Modified   ANSI   CR+LF   INS   Ready

Exhibit63

 Exhibit64.

When I left click on File I get the following. Notice the 'tearoff' and the Exit.

 Exhibit65

The code we just added with some explanation, line by line.

- menubar = Menu(root) – build a menu in the root window and call the Menu 'menubar'
- root.config(menu=menubar) – a continuation of the first line
- filemenu = Menu (menu=menubar, tearoff=0) –this begins the construction of our menu categories. The tearoff has do with putting a dotted tear off line, if you leave at 0 no dotted line, change to a 1 and you will see the dotted line. There are a number of options, for this purpose we are just scratching the surface.
- filemenu.add_separator() – this adds a separator line between the item, try commenting this line out and rerun the program
- filemenu.add_command (label="Exit", command=root.quit) – this is the meat of the menu structure where you actually can execute a command or call a function. In this case we are just going to call the command   root.quit   and exit the program.
- Menubar.add_cascade(menu=filemenu, label='File') – this adds the menu category File to the filemenu, and note the filemenu is part of the menubar

As we add additional items this should become a little clearer. The first change I want to make is to our 'Exit' filemenu item. The present structure calls a command and you exit the program.   I want to change that to go to our exit function, 'myExit', which we setup quite awhile ago.

Exhibit66

This is a very small change to line 54 and now from our menu when we click on Exit we get the same procedure as when we clicked on our exit button. Notice the entire program is shown, however, where there are lines like 15 where there is a + block only the heading shows. In our editor these are called 'Folds', under the View menu item you can toggle Folds, either all open or all closed.

I want to add a few other items to our menu system. These include calling Windows Notepad, our Programmer's Notepad and a number of system information commands that we will put on a different menu section. Save your program as lesson05.py and we will start a new day.

For more discussion on menus see these sites.   http://zetcode.com/gui/tkinter/menustoolbars/
http://effbot.org/tkinterbook/menu.htm , http://infohost.nmt.edu/tcc/help/pubs/tkinter/web/menu.html

Day Ten - Python Subprocess

I want to start a new day with a new program. We are going to introduce a number of new concepts and I am not going into any great discussion on them, at least not now. We will add an item to our menu that calls or starts another program. At this point my program is running on Windows XP professional version, service pack 3. While I have not tried this on other operating systems it may work and at least from a Python viewpoint you will see what is needed. We are going to need to import some functions. While you do not need all of these now, we will soon. Add or change the following highlighted items to your program.

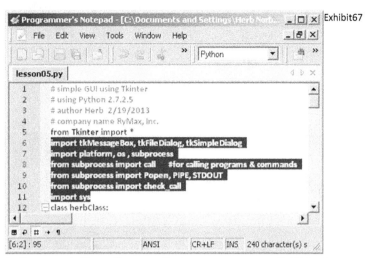

Exhibit67

Python needs these items so that our program can 'talk' to the operating system and figure some things out. I suggest you go to your web browser and do some inquiries on each of them. Next I want to add our menu item, which in this case will be for Windows Notepad.

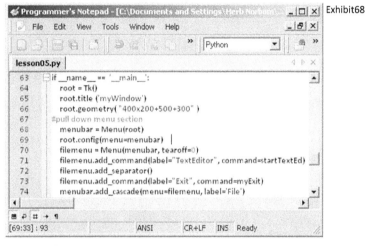

Exhibit68

Error Trapping

Then we need to define the 'startTextEd' function. There is a good chance this may not work. I would like to introduce some Python Error handling. We are going to insert what is commonly referred to as try or throw and catch or more formally as 'try' and 'except'.

Exhibit69

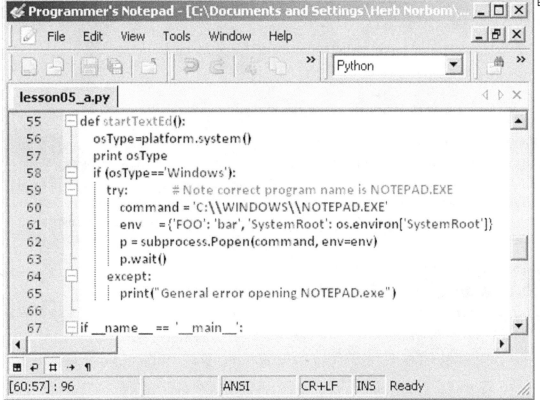

The first thing I want to do is figure out what 'platform. System()' is running so that different commands can be supported, even though only one is being used here. Then just to help figure out what is going on I print the osType to the DOS window.

Next I am using our 'if' statement and if it is Windows operating system we will 'try:' to execute the next group of commands. What Python does is let us group whatever we want in a 'try:' statement. Python will execute each line and if nothing is wrong skips over the 'except:' line. If something is wrong with any line in the 'try:' statement the items in the 'except:' group are executed.

I set a variable 'command' with the path and program name. Another key point in Python has to deal with the backslash '\'. The 'backslash' is basically a key word so to use it as I have we need to put two of them together. In effect the first 'backslash' is ignored and the second one is used.

The 'env' statement is a big one. For now go on a little faith and try it. But do research on it. A good starting point is:
http://docs.python.org/2/library/os.html

With the next line we are getting to the heart of the matter, I am assigning a 'subprocess' to 'p'. You can use any name, just be consistent. The 'subprocess' will 'Popen' our command using our previously constructed 'env'.

Both 'subprocess' and 'Popen' are complete subjects by themselves, do your research, here is a starting point. http://docs.python.org/2/library/subprocess.html. As both are closely related the documentation runs for both.

Run lesson05.py, make sure you can use the Notepad.exe to create new files, re-open them, etc. After the program is working I want to refine our error trapping to get better descriptions. To introduce an error I am going to copy (line #57) and paste it in (line # 58). Then comment out line 57.

Hint. In Microsoft Office® you are probably aware that "Ctrl c" can be used to copy selected items to memory. "Ctrl v" can then paste the selection, and of course "Ctrl x" can cut the selected item. These commands are faster for me than using the mouse or menu functions. These same Control Keys work in many programs, including our Programmer's Notepad.

Once we have made the changes, try the program just to be sure it still runs. Then we will change the command line.

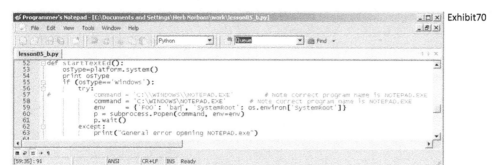
Exhibit70

When we run this you may be as surprised as I was, it worked. I was pretty sure that the absence of the second backslash would cause the error. My explanation is only a guess, that since we set the 'env' to windows our subprocess is 'smart' enough to handle the structure. Ok, let's create a real error. Change NOTEPAD.EXE to NOTEPPAD.EXE. Run the program. When you try to open the NOTEPPAD.EXE the program should detect and report an error. The error message will print on the DOS window. The message is not that great from the viewpoint of diagnosing the error. But, the program keeps running.

Exhibit71

What would happen if we did not use our error trapping abilities? With any luck you should be able to comment out the lines as shown below. Because Python is line space sensitive you may need to rework the spacing.

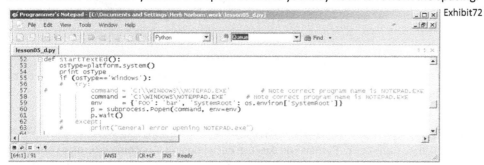
Exhibit72

Now before you run the program take a moment to think about what you expect to happen.

Exhibit73

Well, in the DOS window we got a better error message than we did before, and what maybe the most amazing thing is that the program kept running. So why bother with error handling. Several reasons come to mind. This was a non-critical area, so the program could keep going.   The message was displayed on the DOS window, and that maybe ok for us as the programmers. But what if someone was using the program and they were running the program from a desktop icon. Finally, the program could not take any action based on the error.   For the above reasons and for the reasons you came up with let's refine our error handling techniques.

Go ahead and uncomment the 'try, except, print' lines. Run the program and make sure we are back on track, catching our induced error.

Let us continue to refine our error catching and reporting. Below I have added a specific error catching line and left our general exception line.

36

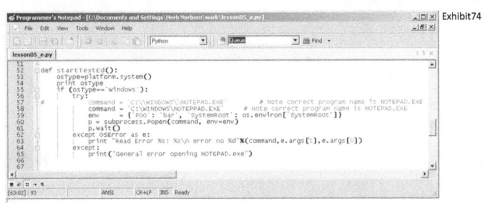
Exhibit74

In running the program our DOS window is a little more refined, notice that our system caught the error as OSError and reported as shown below. The second except line is then skipped.

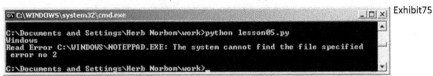
Exhibit75

As you look at the DOS window, compare the output back to our code and you will begin to see how lines can be formatted. More on the formatting subject later.

We need one more level of refinement. When we have an error it would be nice to open a window and report the error. Let's add that to our code.

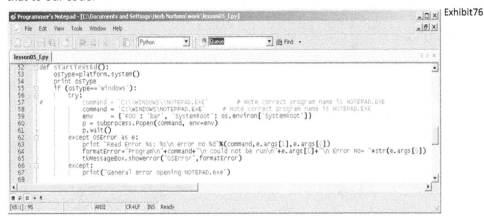
Exhibit76

We should now get the following error window.

Exhibit77

Note when you are working with tkMessageBox windows the first item "OSError" becomes the title of the window, and the second variable or string becomes the text. Here we had a rather long message, and we wanted to imbed variables in the string. That is why we defined the variable and then referenced the variable in tkMessageBox. While we spend more time on formatting later I want to point out several things now. The backslash '\' is an instruction to the Python interpreter. Whatever immediately follows it is a command. So here '\n' means make a new line. The '+' allows us to concatenate strings or to put variables into our string. The last point for now is that you may notice the part of the line '+str (e.arg[0])'. The array e.arg[0] is not a string, so to add it to a string I converted it to string with the function 'str'. The original e.arg[0] has not been changed.

Some on line sources: http://docs.python.org/2/tutorial/errors.html , http://www.tutorialspoint.com/python/tk_messagebox.htm

Day Eleven – More Tkinter Menu

I wanted to explore our menu system. Leave the error in our 'lesson05.py' and add some additional lines and save the program as 'lesson06.py'. The complete program is shown in the following two screenshots.

```python
1    # simple GUI using Tkinter
2    # using Python 2.7.2.5
3    # author Herb  2/19/2013
4    # company name RyMax, Inc.
5    from Tkinter import *
6    import tkMessageBox, tkFileDialog, tkSimpleDialog
7    import platform, os , subprocess
8    from subprocess import call     #for calling programs & commands
9    from subprocess import Popen, PIPE, STDOUT
10   from subprocess import check_call
11   import sys
12   class herbClass:
13       def __init__(herbData,myResponse, second, third, fourth,
14           counter,realNumber):
15           herbData.myResponse= myResponse
16           herbData.myResponse= second
17           herbData.myResponse= third
18           herbData.myResponse= fourth
19           herbData.counter=counter
20   myClassStuf = herbClass(
21       'got none',       #default for myResponse
22       'second data',  # for the second data item
23       'car',         # for the third data item
24       '',          #for the fourth item, in effect nothing
25       6,           # counter assigned an integer 6 to this variable
26       4.234        #realNumber assigned a real number
27       )
28   def myCommand():
29       text1="this is my text and you leave it alone"
30       print text1
31   def myExit():
32       answer=tkMessageBox.askyesno("EXIT", "Do you really want to quit")
33       if answer==True:   # notice changed from a 1 to True
34           root.quit()
35           return
36       if answer==False:    #notice changed from a 0 to False
37           print "going to keep running the program"
38           return
39       print "something is wrong should not get here"
40       print "program at function myExit, value of answer is: ", answer
41   def myInput():
42       temp=''
43       Label(myOutFrame, text =temp).grid(column=0, row=0, sticky=(N,W,E,S))
44       temp= myClassStuf.myResponse.get()
45       print temp
```

Exhibit78

38

Exhibit79

I have moved a few things around and highlighted the import code changes. What the program should do after you select File and Text Editor is generate an error; we left the Notepad file name error in, line 51. The correct name is shown in the comment on the same line (51). The program will ask if you want to use a different editor. If you say 'Yes' the program will attempt to use a subprocess.call to open our Programmer's Notepad. I set the path as 'WinAvr-20100110' your path may need to be 'WinAvr-20090313' if you did not install the latest editor. Note the change in directories also.

Call vs. Popen

There are a number of options for running external commands and programs from within your Python program. Two common parts of subprocess deal with 'call' and 'Popen'. In our first run of the program we use the 'call' function. Notice that when you run 'lesson06.py' that the Programmer's Notebook opens and our program becomes non-responsive. Once you close the Programmer's Notebook our program responds again. If Programmer's Notebook does not open make sure you have set the Tools - options for "Allow multiple instances of Programmer's Notepad to start".

Change which subprocess to run. Uncomment line 64 and comment out line 65.

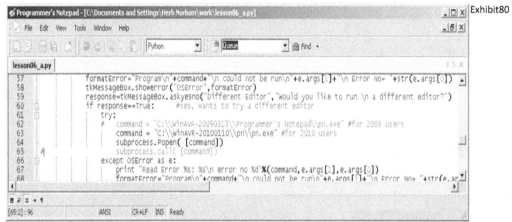

Exhibit80

Note the difference when you run the program this time. Our program lesson06.py continues to be responsive. Our new instance of Programmer's Notepad continues to run, even after you exit lesson06.py. That is a big difference. This has system security issues, be careful.

Day Twelve – System Menu Items

Save the program lesson06.py as lesson07.py. Going to 'clean it up' a bit, put the Programmer's Notepad on its own menu item and add a number of new features to the menu. A lot of little things added, I hope the concepts help you. Below I have taken screen shots of the complete program and a couple of screen shots using the new menu items.

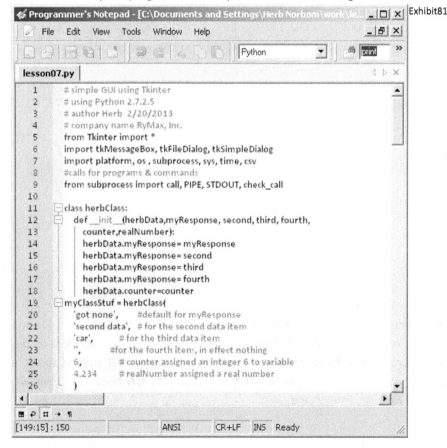

Exhibit81

```
27  def myCommand():
28      text1="this is my text and you leave it alone"
29      print text1
30  def myExit():
31      answer=tkMessageBox.askyesno("EXIT",
32      "Do you really want to quit")
33      if answer==True:    # notice changed from a 1 to True
34          root.quit()
35          return
36      if answer==False:    #notice changed from a 0 to False
37          print "going to keep running the program"
38          return
39      print "something is wrong should not get here"
40      print "program at function myExit, value of answer is: ", answer
41  def myInput():
42      temp=''
43      Label(myOutFrame, text =temp).grid(column=0, row=0, sticky=(N,W,E,S))
44      temp= myClassStuf.myResponse.get()
45      print temp
46      Label(myOutFrame, text =temp).grid(column=0, row=0, sticky=(N,W))
47  def windowsNotepad():
48      osType=platform.system()
49      print osType
50      if (osType=='Windows'):
51          try:
52              command = 'C:\WINDOWS\NOTEPAD.EXE'
53              env    ={'FOO': 'bar',
54              'SystemRoot': os.environ['SystemRoot']}
55              p = subprocess.Popen(command, env=env)
56              p.wait()
57              return
58          except OSError as e:
59              print "Read Error %s: %s\n error no %d"%(command,e.args[1], e.args[0])
60              formatError="Program\n"+command+"\n could not be run\n"
61              formatError=formatError+e.args[1]+"\n Error No= "+str(e.args[0])
62              tkMessageBox.showerror("OSError",formatError)
63          except:
64              print("General error opening NOTEPAD.exe")
65          print("Notepad appears to be unavailable on this system")
66
67  def startProNotepad():
68      try:
69          command = "C:\\WinAVR-20100110\\pn\\pn.exe" #for 2010 users
70          subprocess.call( [command])
71      except OSError as e:
72          print "Read Error %s: %s\n error no %d"%(command,e.args[1],e.args[0])
73          formatError="Program\n" +command+"\n could not be run\n"
74          formatError=formatError+e.args[1]+"\n Error No= "+str(e.args[0])
75          tkMessageBox.showerror("OSError",formatError)
76
77  def showPythonVersion():
78      pyVersion=sys.version
79      tkMessageBox.showwarning('Python Version',pyVersion)
80
81  def showSystemPlatform():
82      import platform
83      osType=platform.system()
84      osPlatform=platform.win32_ver()
85      osProcessor=platform.processor()
```

Exhibit82

41

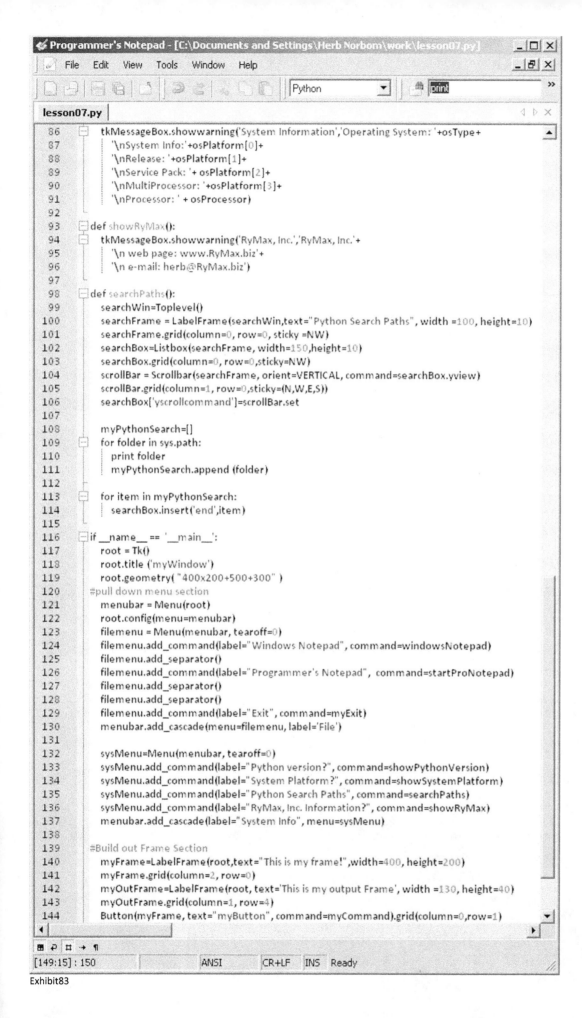

```
 86        tkMessageBox.showwarning('System Information','Operating System: '+osType+
 87           '\nSystem Info:'+osPlatform[0]+
 88           '\nRelease: '+osPlatform[1]+
 89           '\nService Pack: '+ osPlatform[2]+
 90           '\nMultiProcessor: '+osPlatform[3]+
 91           '\nProcessor: ' + osProcessor)
 92
 93   def showRyMax():
 94        tkMessageBox.showwarning('RyMax, Inc.','RyMax, Inc.'+
 95           '\n web page: www.RyMax.biz'+
 96           '\n e-mail: herb@RyMax.biz')
 97
 98   def searchPaths():
 99        searchWin=Toplevel()
100        searchFrame = LabelFrame(searchWin,text="Python Search Paths", width =100, height=10)
101        searchFrame.grid(column=0, row=0, sticky =NW)
102        searchBox=Listbox(searchFrame, width=150,height=10)
103        searchBox.grid(column=0, row=0,sticky=NW)
104        scrollBar = Scrollbar(searchFrame, orient=VERTICAL, command=searchBox.yview)
105        scrollBar.grid(column=1, row=0,sticky=(N,W,E,S))
106        searchBox['yscrollcommand']=scrollBar.set
107
108        myPythonSearch=[]
109        for folder in sys.path:
110          print folder
111          myPythonSearch.append (folder)
112
113        for item in myPythonSearch:
114          searchBox.insert('end',item)
115
116   if __name__ == '__main__':
117        root = Tk()
118        root.title ('myWindow')
119        root.geometry( "400x200+500+300" )
120     #pull down menu section
121        menubar = Menu(root)
122        root.config(menu=menubar)
123        filemenu = Menu(menubar, tearoff=0)
124        filemenu.add_command(label="Windows Notepad", command=windowsNotepad)
125        filemenu.add_separator()
126        filemenu.add_command(label="Programmer's Notepad",  command=startProNotepad)
127        filemenu.add_separator()
128        filemenu.add_separator()
129        filemenu.add_command(label="Exit", command=myExit)
130        menubar.add_cascade(menu=filemenu, label='File')
131
132        sysMenu=Menu(menubar, tearoff=0)
133        sysMenu.add_command(label="Python version?", command=showPythonVersion)
134        sysMenu.add_command(label="System Platform?", command=showSystemPlatform)
135        sysMenu.add_command(label="Python Search Paths", command=searchPaths)
136        sysMenu.add_command(label="RyMax, Inc. Information?", command=showRyMax)
137        menubar.add_cascade(label="System Info", menu=sysMenu)
138
139     #Build out Frame Section
140        myFrame=LabelFrame(root,text="This is my frame!",width=400, height=200)
141        myFrame.grid(column=2, row=0)
142        myOutFrame=LabelFrame(root, text='This is my output Frame', width =130, height=40)
143        myOutFrame.grid(column=1, row=4)
144        Button(myFrame, text="myButton", command=myCommand).grid(column=0,row=1)
```

Exhibit83

42

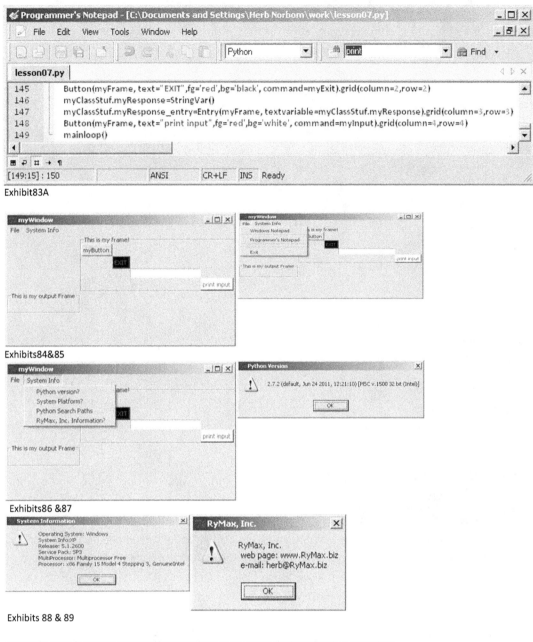

```
Programmer's Notepad - [C:\Documents and Settings\Herb Norbom\work\lesson07.py]

 File   Edit   View   Tools   Window   Help

                                    Python          print              Find

lesson07.py

145        Button(myFrame, text="EXIT",fg='red',bg='black', command=myExit).grid(column=2,row=2)
146        myClassStuf.myResponse=StringVar()
147        myClassStuf.myResponse_entry=Entry(myFrame, textvariable=myClassStuf.myResponse).grid(column=3,row=3)
148        Button(myFrame, text="print input",fg='red',bg='white', command=myInput).grid(column=4,row=4)
149        mainloop()

[149:15] : 150              ANSI      CR+LF    INS    Ready
```
Exhibit83A

Exhibits84&85

Exhibits86 &87

Exhibits 88 & 89

Exhibit90

Try adding your own menu items and playing with various different options. In the next step we are going to look at reading from and writing to data files.

Day Thirteen - Python Read and Write Files

I want to start with a bare bones Python program. We will only add what we need to work with files. First, using our Programmer's Notepad creates a <u>text file</u> containing a few lines. Click on File, New, Plain Text and save as 'test1.txt' in your work directory (same as the programs). Now create the Python program lesson08.py.

43

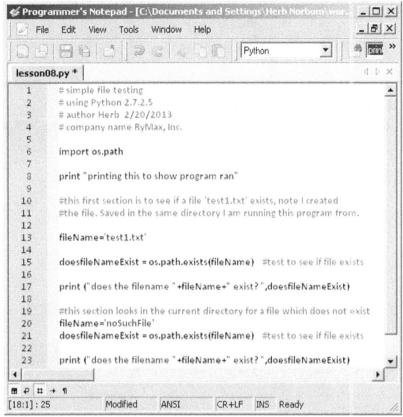

```
1   # simple file testing
2   # using Python 2.7.2.5
3   # author Herb 2/20/2013
4   # company name RyMax, Inc.
5
6   import os.path
7
8   print "printing this to show program ran"
9
10  #this first section is to see if a file 'test1.txt' exists, note I created
11  #the file. Saved in the same directory I am running this program from.
12
13  fileName='test1.txt'
14
15  doesfileNameExist = os.path.exists(fileName)   #test to see if file exists
16
17  print ("does the filename "+fileName+" exist? ",doesfileNameExist)
18
19  #this section looks in the current directory for a file which does not exist
20  fileName='noSuchFile'
21  doesfileNameExist = os.path.exists(fileName)   #test to see if file exists
22
23  print ("does the filename "+fileName+" exist? ",doesfileNameExist)
```

Exhibit91

Our output is shown in the trusty DOS window.

Exhibit92

I am going to save the program as lesson09.py and change it around. We will add just enough code to read and print our test1.txt file to the DOS window. The simple file I created had two lines of text. Below we show the complete program code and the output. At some point that occurs very quickly you will find the need to work with data files. Python has great file utilities. There are Python add on modules that will be of use as you advance, but for now we will stick to standard Python modules.

There are a number of ways to work with files. In the following we will use the 'with open' which is a great tool, when finished reading the file, the file is closed automatically.   If you do not want to close automatically try some of the other methods. A good starting point is section 7.2 Reading and Writing Files at:

http://docs.python.org/2/tutorial/inputoutput.html

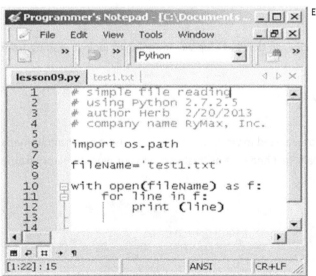

Exhibit93

```
1   # simple file reading
2   # using Python 2.7.2.5
3   # author Herb  2/20/2013
4   # company name RyMax, Inc.
5
6   import os.path
7
8   fileName='test1.txt'
9
10  with open(fileName) as f:
11      for line in f:
12          print (line)
13
14
```

44

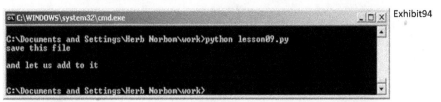
Exhibit94

Now we will add some text, save the file and display the entire text file. Save the program as 'lesson10.py'. We are going to do this several ways. The first way will erase the test1.txt and write a new line to it. Use your Programmer's Notepad to look at the file test1.txt. Go ahead and open that file prior to running the program.

Exhibit95

Exhibit96

Exhibit97

The program in effect deleted or erased the test1.txt file and created a new test1.txt file. You can run the program a number of times and the result will be the same. The file 'modes' are a critical part of understanding the actions Python will take on files:

- 'r'   for reading file only, starts at beginning of file
- 'r+'   for reading and writing, starts at beginning of file
- 'w'   for writing only, starts at beginning of file, cleans or removes data from file
- 'w+'   opens file for reading and writing. Will create file if it doesn't exist
- 'a'   opens file for writing. Will append to end of file
- 'a+'   opens file for reading and writing. File created if it doesn't exist. If file exists appends to end of file.

Save our program as lesson11.py and make the changes to it. We will first read the file test1.txt, then we will open if for writing and finally we will do two appends to the data file. In between each step we will read the file and write the output to the DOS window.

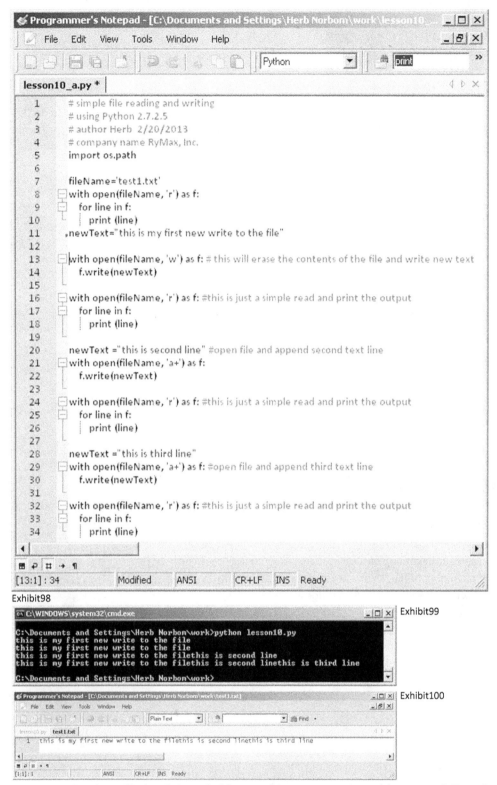

Exhibit98

Exhibit99

Exhibit100

As you can see it works, but it is probably not what you want. I would want each line of output on a separate line. So let's add what we need to the program to get that format. What we add is that great backslash we have been talking about and an 'n'. Add to the end of each line '\n' when we are writing to the file.

```
1    # simple file reading and writing
2    # using Python 2.7.2.5
3    # author Herb  2/20/2013
4    # company name RyMax, Inc.
5    import os.path
6
7    fileName='test1.txt'
8    with open(fileName, 'r') as f:
9        for line in f:
10           print (line)
11   newText="this is my first new write to the file\n"     #NOTE the \n added
12
13   with open(fileName, 'w') as f: # this will erase the contents of the file and write new text
14       f.write(newText)
15
16   with open(fileName, 'r') as f: #this is just a simple read and print the output
17       for line in f:
18           print (line)
19
20   newText ="this is second line\n"        #open file and append second text line
21   with open(fileName, 'a+') as f:
22       f.write(newText)
23
24   with open(fileName, 'r') as f: #this is just a simple read and print the output
25       for line in f:
26           print (line)
27
28   newText ="this is third line\n"
29   with open(fileName, 'a+') as f: #open file and append third text line
30       f.write(newText)
31
32   with open(fileName, 'r') as f: #this is just a simple read and print the output
33       for line in f:
34           print (line)
```

```
C:\Documents and Settings\Herb Norbom\work>python lesson10.py
this is my first new write to the filethis is second linethis is third line
this is my first new write to the file

this is my first new write to the file

this is second line

this is my first new write to the file

this is second line

this is third line

C:\Documents and Settings\Herb Norbom\work>
```

```
1    this is my first new write to the file
2    this is second line
3    this is third line
4
```

Day Fourteen – Python File Testing

In this section I want to go over some simple tests. We will see if the file exists, if we can delete the file and if we can create the file. Because functions are so important to organizing programs we are going to use them. A new concept of passing variables to and from functions is introduced. We are also going to expand on the use of 'if statements', nested ones and the use of the 'else' portion of the 'if statement'. We will also include error handling because in working with files, errors should be anticipated.

I am going to start with a new program lesson11.py; you can make the changes to lesson10.py and save as lesson11.py if you like. The changes are extensive, remember you can highlight an area and press the delete key.

Another useful concept is interfacing with your program from the DOS window. For this we will use 'raw_input'. While there are other commands that work this one is safer. The web site listed below gives a good discussion on input.

http://www.daniweb.com/software-development/python/threads/12326/how-to-do-input-in-python

The full code for lesson11.py is shown below in two screen shots. The program looks convoluted and it is. Image it without functions. Analyze the program and try to anticipate the flow before running it.

The program lines above if__name__ == '__main__': are processed before the program starts with the lines below the if__name__ == '__main__': line being executed when the program 'really starts'. In a simplistic sense when you give the command to run the program, the interpreter checks for all the import items, syntax, definitions and references. The program sets up what memory it needs. The program is now ready to process your instructions and it will start with our line "fileName='test2.txt'", and proceed line by line.

The first function we call is to see if the file exists. Note we set that call equal to where we want to store the value returned from running the function. Also when we call the function we put a variable in the (). After the function runs it returns the variable we placed in return ().

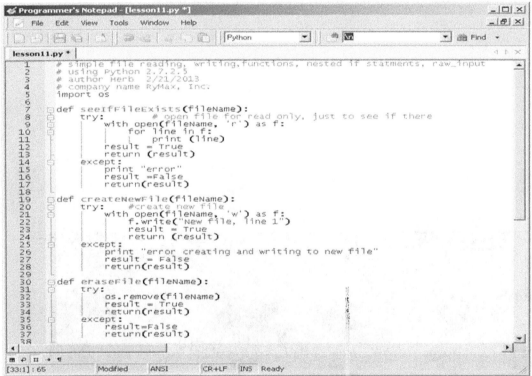

Exhibit104

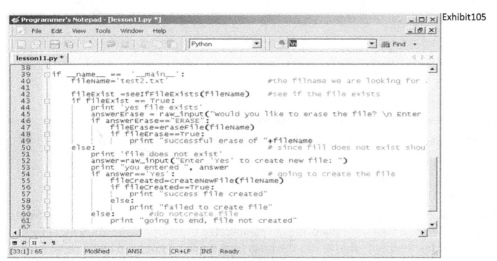
Exhibit105

```
38      if __name__ == '__main__':
39          fileName='test2.txt'                    #the filename we are looking for
40
41          fileExist =seeIfFileExists(fileName)    #see if the file exists
42          if fileExist == True:
43              print 'yes file exists'
44              answerErase = raw_input("would you like to erase the file? \n Enter
45              if answerErase=="ERASE":
46                  fileErase=eraseFile(fileName)
47                  if fileErase==True:
48                      print "successful erase of "+fileName
49          else:                                   # since fill does not exist shou
50              print 'file does not exist'
51              answer=raw_input("Enter 'Yes' to create new file: ")
52              print "you entered ", answer
53              if answer=='Yes':                   # going to create the file
54                  fileCreated=createNewFile(fileName)
55                  if fileCreated==True:
56                      print "success file created"
57                  else:
58                      print "failed to create file"
59              else:                               #do notcreate file
60                  print "going to end, file not created"
```

Notice in the above screen shots along the left hand side the little blocks with a '–'. Click on the block to condense the lines shown, click again to expand. Below I have set all the blocks to +. These are called Folds. Look at the menu under view, Folding and toggle Folds.

Exhibit106

Various screen shots while running the program. Run when file test2.txt does not exist.

Exhibit107

```
C:\Documents and Settings\Herb Norbom\work>python lesson11.py
error
file does not exist
Enter 'Yes' to create new file:
```

Enter 'Yes'

Exhibit108

```
C:\Documents and Settings\Herb Norbom\work>python lesson11.py
error
file does not exist
Enter 'Yes' to create new file: Yes
you entered  Yes
success file created
C:\Documents and Settings\Herb Norbom\work>
```

Note program ended. Take a look at the file.

Exhibit109

Let's run again, you can leave Programmer's Notepad open.

Exhibit110

```
C:\Documents and Settings\Herb Norbom\work>python lesson11.py
New file, line 1
yes file exists
Would you like to erase the file?
Enter 'ERASE' to erase: _
```

Enter 'ERASE'

Exhibit111

```
C:\Documents and Settings\Herb Norbom\work>python lesson11.py
New file, line 1
yes file exists
Would you like to erase the file?
Enter 'ERASE' to erase: ERASE
successful erase of test2.txt
C:\Documents and Settings\Herb Norbom\work>
```

In Programmer' Notepad close the test2.txt file. You will get a prompt like below, BE **SURE to click No.**

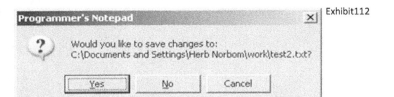

Exhibit112

If you clicked 'No' the Notepad will not recreate the file, if you said yes it will put the file back. Sort of seems reversed to me. Now try to open the file, it should be gone. Run the program a few times and try to follow the flow while looking at the program code.

Day Fifteen – Python Data Types

We have been dancing around data types, Boolean Operations and Comparisons until now. I want to get into these items from a Python viewpoint, for manipulation and saving them in a file. This subject can get complicated in a hurry. As you may recall Python dynamically assigns the data type based on what the assigned value is. As the programmer you do not need to define an integer. For example, x=5. Python does the assignment of type for you, x is an integer type. Most of what we will be using is pretty straight forward, but you need to be aware of the terms and the diversity. Some excellent references are:

http://docs.python.org/2/library/stdtypes.html, http://zetcode.com/lang/python/datatypes/,http://www.ibm.com/developerworks/library/os-python1/. The Data Types that are built in or standard that we will look at are: Bool, Number, Strings and Tuples.

Bool variables have only two possible values, True and False. Many of the built in functions that do some sort of testing return a yes/no response. Meaning there is a True or False type response. We saw earlier that 'True' could be a '1' and 'False' could be a '0'. There are other values as well. Let us start with 'False' first. False can be represented by None, False, 0, 0.0, '', (), [], {}, (basically any value that starts with a '0' or an empty value).

True is practically anything else, for example: 'True' is any non-zero value. Examples: Yes, 1, 11111111, myname, (23), etc.

Operator	Meaning
<	less than
<=	less than or equal
>	greater than
>=	greater than or equal
==	equal
!=	not equal

Exhibit112A

Your algebra days have caught up with you. These are the main Operator's that we will be concerned with. You may see others that do the same thing, some of those are from prior versions of Python, even though they may work. I recommend you use these. In the Python documentation you will find items referred to as 'depreciated'. For Python 'depreciated' means you are being warned of future non-support. You can use it, but it is on the way out. There is a newer item that you should start using in your code.

Number Types are int, long, float, and complex, and are basically the same in most computer languages. One of the most frustrating things in technical descriptions is that they always seem to refer to another technical description. For example the difference between 'int' and 'long' is the precision. I am glad we cleared that up for you. In Python, unless you are well into developing big numbers you do not care, Python is handling it for you. So I am going to skip over 'precision' until we need it. Float deals with the decimal point and the precision (positions to the right of the point). A complex number, we will not use other than maybe in as example is a number that has real and imaginary components. If you need more information there is a bunch on the web.

Python Strings are just about any character or number contained within quotation marks.

Tuples are an extremely useful data type because you can mix data types within a tuple. We will do examples on this. Once the data type is assigned within the tuple you cannot change the data type.

In working with numbers you need to consider the order of operations. Python uses the standard order of operations that you may have learned in algebra. Do you remember the mnemonic PEMDAS?

Please Excuse My Dear Aunt Sally.

	Order of Operations	Python Syntax
P	Parentheses	(...)
E	Exponents	**
M	Multiplication	*
D	Division	/
A	Addition	+
S	Subtraction	-

Remember with Parentheses you work from the inside out.

Start a new program as lesson12.py; I suggest using a new empty Python file. The complete code and the DOS window results are shown. This set of examples deals with number manipulation and Boolean comparisons. I suggest you play with this a bit until you are comfortable.

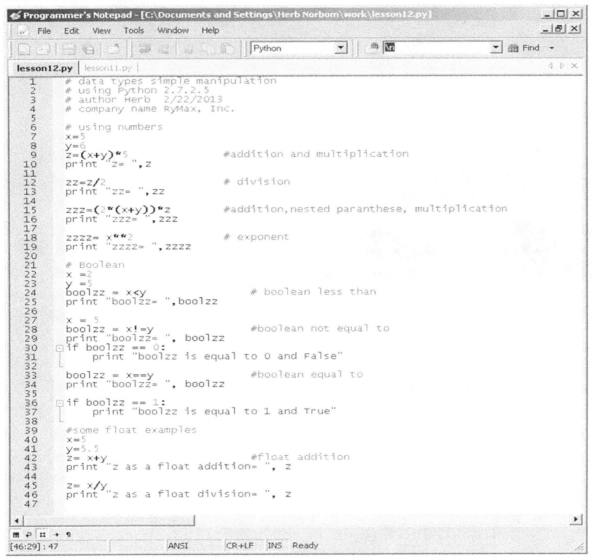

Exhibit113

Exhibit114

I am starting a new file lesson13.py for working with strings. The file includes some simple examples of assignment to variables and combining string variables. A good reference site is: http://pguides.net/python-tutorial/python-string-methods/

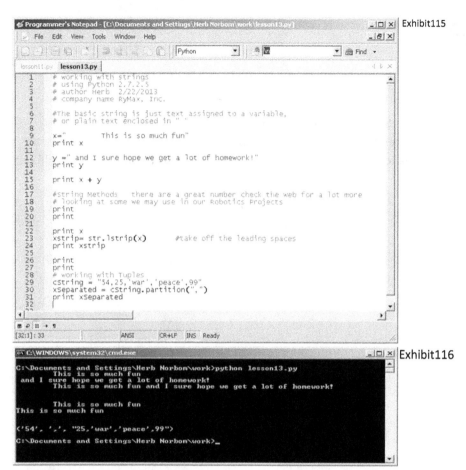

Exhibit115

Exhibit116

Remember the integer 1 and the string "1" are very different. With Python we can covert the integer type to text and back again with ease, the hard part is remembering what you are working with. Sometimes we need to use methods to determine what our variable type is and then decide how to proceed. Our next program lesson14.py works with some of the issues. Note in the program that the same variable changes from 'int' to 'str' type.

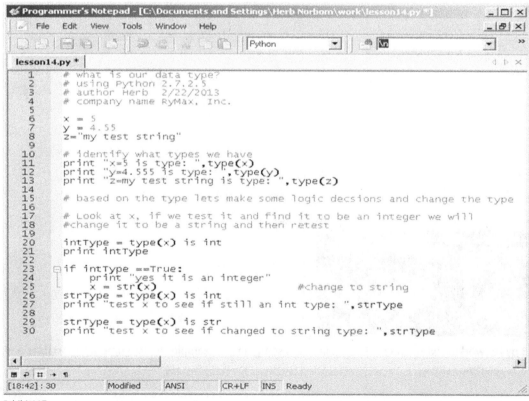

Exhibit117

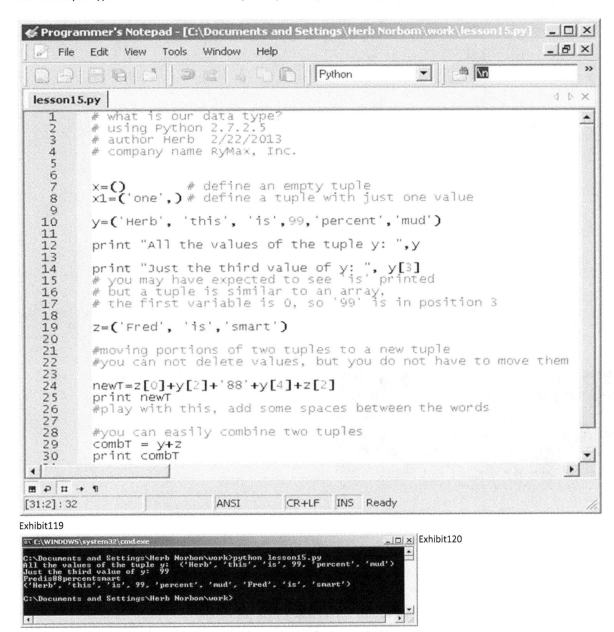

Exhibit118

If you are going from string to integer you should use the error catching techniques we discussed earlier. For that matter anytime you can have an uncertain result it is good technique to use error catching, within reasonable limits of course.

Tuples are extremely useful; once you have mastered them you will wish all programming languages had the capability. Tuples are similar to lists and arrays. In a tuple you can change the individual values but not the individual types in the list. Yes a tuple can have multiple types within it. The best way to explain tuples is through an example. Start a new file, lesson15.py.

Exhibit119

Exhibit120

For additional information try: http://www.tutorialspoint.com/python/python_tuples.htm

Day Sixteen – Python Output Formatting

As our skills have grown our ability to produce 'nice' formatted output has not grown to any extent. We are going to spend a little time formatting output. This gets a little cryptic, but Python is logical, once you get the hang of what it is trying to do. We are just going to produce output to the DOS window, but printing is really the same. For this lesson we will use the older '%' string formatter. Start another new program, lesson16.py.

Some other good sites are: http://mkaz.com/solog/python-string-format ,

http://infohost.nmt.edu/tcc/help/pubs/python/web/old-str-format.html, http://www.tutorialspoint.com/python/python_strings.htm

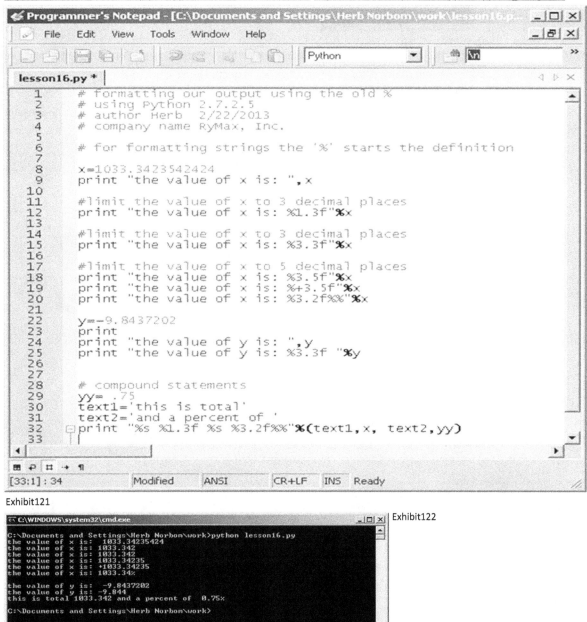

Exhibit121

Exhibit122

Day Seventeen – Format Method

To continue with formatting our output we need to look at the newer format class. This was introduced or became standard in Python 2.6, and I would expect it to be the dominant format option in the future. Start another new program lesson17.py. Many of the web references cited in Day Sixteen apply here. As you work through the example think how to enhance it, add a tuple, and work on formatting that output. With the format class you can also format dates, right justify, and many more features.

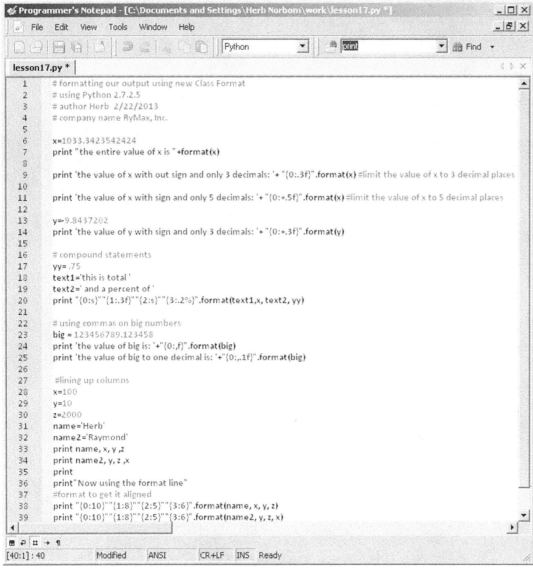

Exhibit123

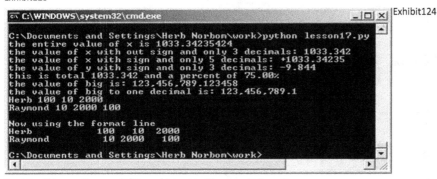

Exhibit124

See http://docs.python.org/2/library/string.html for more information.

Day Eighteen - While Loop

We have all these great tools, but to get to the real power of computing we need to be able to loop through events. As you may recall with 'tkinter' our program did keep looping or running. With the programs we have been running lately they simply run the commands and terminate. We are going to look at several loop options. Of course let's start a new program, lesson18.py.

Exhibit125

Exhibit126

Day Nineteen – Robot Control Center

I think you have been patient, and it is time to give you a little more input to our overall plan. In building our robot we are going to need a control point. From our control point we want to send commands to the robot, normal stuff like forward, back, turn and speed. We are also going to add a simple arm, a bumper, speakers, a microphone, and a camera. Back at Command we want to monitor all systems and of course we want our robot to speak. Our robot is going to use batteries. We will also want to measure the voltage levels back at Command. We are going to need communications between the Command Center and "Max" the robot. For communications I have used infrared, toy radio controls, a serial USB cable from NerdKit and a Serial Communication Module I purchased from Sure Electronics. For our initial tests of the robot and software we will use the Serial USB Cable. At this point we have the basic knowledge to use Python. We need to add a few more pieces to our puzzle before we can bring it all together. We need to be able to play sounds and gain the ability to speak. We will need to use the tkinter canvas widget to control robot movement. We will also need to use queue and the threading capabilities of Python for performance issues.

In the succeeding chapters we will begin our electronics journey and then our actual build of the robot.   While we are still a bit away from building the robot it is not too early to start looking for parts.   If your computer does not have speakers you can find some at Goodwill®, The Salvation Army®, Habitat for Humanity®, other such stores. Even if your computer has speakers your robot will want them. While you are there look for toys that have wheels and motors. Sometimes you even find remote control vehicles with the controller.   I suggest you not pay much, study them, take them apart, put them back together and as necessary swap parts from other toys and try to get them working.   Some of your finds will work with a fresh set of batteries. Many times you can use a solution of water and baking soda to clean battery terminals. Try cleaning the terminal with the solution on a q-tip. In any event you are going to need wheels, motors, etc. Another item to look for is the AC to DC power converter 3 to 12 volts. They will come in handy when developing the hardware of the robot.

Day Twenty - Sounds for your Robot

We are going to need to add two Python modules to our Python library in order to have text to speech and serial communications.

Adding Python Modules using PyPM

The easiest way to download additional modules is using the ActiveState® PyPM Index (Python Package Manager). Here is the direct link to the site.   http://code.activestate.com/pypm/ I recommend you look through the site before continuing. The PyPM software is included with the ActiveState Community Addition. Now the package we are after is available on Source Forge, but PyPM is not used there. This discussion is going to focus on the installation with PyPM.

I like to use the web site to see what modules are available, note we are using Python 2.7, so make sure what you are looking for is available. Also there are various operating system versions available. In the Search PyPM Packages enter "serial". Select the 'pyserial (2.6)' module.

Exhibit127

I see at this point that pyserial is now available for Python 3.2, but our program is in Python 2.7 so that will be the version we want. In the future I will help you convert your programs to the 3.x version.

When you click on the Install> button some general install instructions are displayed.

Exhibit128

Now to actually install you need to get back to our Command Prompt. We want to use our batch file, 'mypython27' because we set up some paths for python. Let us try some simple PyPM commands. A good one is list. At the command prompt type 'PyPM list' this will show you the additional modules installed. This can take a few minutes to run. In the following screen shot I show my results which will be different from yours as I have installed a number of extra modules for various experiments. Some were good.

Exhibit129

I expect your display to show no modules. If you have problems with the list command the install will probably not work. Could be a firewall problem as the internet is accessed, or you might not have the ActiveState version.

Let us go ahead and install the pyserial module. Enter PyPM install pyserial. Because we set the paths in our batch file the PyPM figures out that you have version 2.7.x and where to actually install the module. After this finishes try our simple test for the module again. At the command prompt type Python and then import serial. It is worth while trying the 'PyPM list' command again to see the results.

Some other good commands are: PyPM help, PyPM info --full, PyPM show 'package name', PyPM upgrade, PyPM uninstall 'package name'.

We also need to install the pyttsx module, the current version is 1.0. You do this in a manner similar to the pyserial module. This module is for text to speech.

My robot wants to talk, how about yours? Let's add that software capability next. Of course you are going to need working speakers on your PC. We will start with a fresh program, lesson20.py. We are going to play some system sounds, just to get things going. In this program we will open a tkinter window and an input box, enter whatever you like and it should be spoken for you.

There are many sound file definitions to consider, we are sticking with the wav file format. You can play files from memory or from a file to mention two options. In our program we will play from a file and from our text input.
Some good sites for information are: http://svn.python.org/projects/python/trunk/PC/winsound.c http://docs.python.org/2/library/winsound.html and http://www.villagegeek.com/html/wavfiles1.htm .

Some possible sources for sound bites are: http://dir.yahoo.com/computers_and_internet/multimedia/audio/archives/wav/, http://www.dailywav.com/ .

You will want to either make your wav files or download them. For downloading I suggest you type 'free wav files' into your search browser. Lots of sites, I suggest you be careful that malware does not get included. Be aware that you are not violating any copyrights. Some of the sites will permit you to play, but not download. For our purpose we need to get the wav file on our computer. Download it to your 'work' directory. For some sites you need to play the sound bite, then right click and save as into appropriate directory.

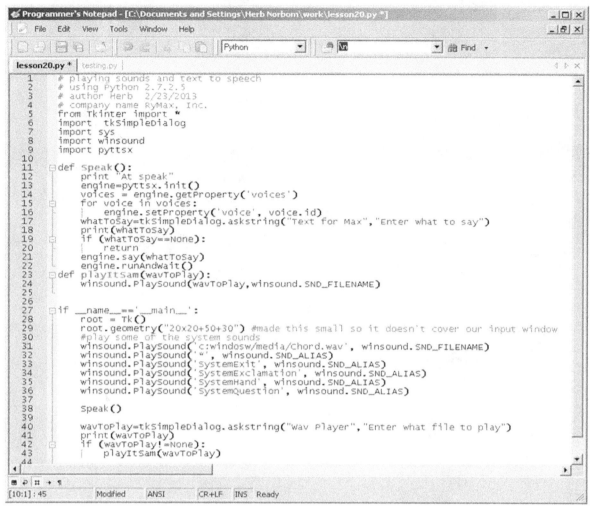
Exhibit130

When you are entering the programs from scratch you may want to think about entering them in sections. For example here if you enter lines 1 – 9 and 27-31 you can get a basic program running. Go back and add in the rest as you like. On lines 31-36 various system sounds are played. Some of the lines will produce the same sounds, just trying to show some different methods of calling them. As you continue working with sound you will find that Python has many tools for working with sound files, and for reading and changing their formats. There are also extensive add on modules.

List Box Widget

I have found sound to be a fun item on robots. You may find you want a number of sound bites. In our next program we will add a list box widget to enable you to pick and play. Save the program as lesson21.py and we will add a new widget that lets us do just that. While we are at it we will begin to build our Max Control Center. We are going to build this out so that it keeps running until you close the program, added the 'mainloop()' line. Also we want our list box widget to display txt and wav files. We are also going to bring a number of features to our program that we have previously worked with.

The main new feature is the list box widget. You will note we have included a scroll bar. In line 15 you will need to set your path as appropriate. Remember Python thinks that '\' is a special command, so either use '/' or a double '\\'.

You may wonder if there are other voices, the answer is yes there are. I am not going to go into that area at this point, please research it for your own information. I suggest you go through the program line by line and get a good understanding of what is occurring. We are going to use this as the base for building our control center.

```python
1   # playing sounds and text to speech
2   # using Python 2.7.2.5
3   # author Herb 2/23/2013
4   # company name RyMax, Inc.
5   from Tkinter import *
6   import tkSimpleDialog
7   import sys, os
8   import winsound
9   import pyttsx
10
11  class DataFileClass:
12      def __init__(Data,defPath):
13          Data.defPath= defPath
14  SELF = DataFileClass(
15      'C:\\Documents and Settings\\Herb Norbom\\work\\'   #my default dir for this program
16      )
17
18
19  def on_click_listbox(event):
20      index = soundBox.curselection()       # get selected line index
21      soundFile = soundBox.get(index)       # get the line's text
22      label1.configure(text=soundFile)      # show selected text in label
23      path=SELF.defPath                     # use our Class defined path
24      if soundFile != None:
25          extension = os.path.splitext(soundFile)[1][1:]
26          print (extension)
27          if ((extension=='wav') | (extension=='WAV')):   # this is the or |
28              winsound.PlaySound(str(path)+soundFile,0)
29          if(extension=='txt'):
30              engine=pyttsx.init()
31              voices = engine.getProperty('voices')
32              for voice in voices:
33                  engine.setProperty('voice', voice.id)
34              with open(str(path)+soundFile) as f:
35                  for line in f:
36                      engine.say(line)
37                      engine.runAndwait()
38
39  if __name__=='__main__':
40      root = Tk()
41      root.title( "Max Control Center" )
42      root.geometry( "550x450+50+30" ) #width, height, placement y  x
43
44      #setup a list box to list our wav and txt files
45      soundFrame = LabelFrame(root, text="Max Sounds",width=20, height=10,cursor="arrow")
46      soundFrame.grid(column=0, row =2, sticky=(N,W,S))
47      soundBox=Listbox(soundFrame, width=20, height=18)
48      soundBox.grid(column=0,row=1,sticky=(N,W,S))
49      scrollBar = Scrollbar(soundFrame, orient=VERTICAL, command=soundBox.yview)
50      scrollBar.grid(column=1,row=1, sticky=(N,E,S))
51      soundBox['yscrollcommand']=scrollBar.set
52      path=SELF.defPath
53      print path
54      soundlist = os.listdir(path)
55  # load the listbox
56      for sound in soundlist:
57          extension = os.path.splitext(sound)[1][1:]
58          if ((extension=='wav') | (extension=='WAV') |(extension=='txt')):
59              soundBox.insert('end', sound)
60      label1 = Label(soundFrame, text='click to play', width=20, bg='white')
61      label1.grid(column=0, row=0)
62      soundBox.bind('<ButtonRelease-1>', on_click_listbox)
63
64      mainloop()
```

Exhibit131

Day Twenty One - Tkinter Canvas

There are many ways to control our robot. I have found that I like a screen graphic. Some people may prefer a joy stick or other device. For this first control program I will stick with the screen graphic. In order to do this I need to introduce another widget. The canvas widget can be a lot of fun for your drawings and developing games. For now we will just focus on what we need. We need a little display and while the mouse is on that display we need to know where it is and what mouse clicks are occurring. We will build this out in steps. Save your lesson21.py as lesson22.py. I am going to show the complete program in two screen shots in the following. As our program is going to grow I will be using the minimize program blocks or Folds in the future.

```python
1   # Max Control Program
2   # using Python 2.7.2.5
3   # author Herb  2/23/2013
4   # company name RyMax, Inc.
5   from Tkinter import *
6   import  tkSimpleDialog
7   import sys, os
8   import winsound
9   import pyttsx
10
11  class DataFileClass:
12      def __init__(Data,defPath):
13          Data.defPath= defPath
14  SELF = DataFileClass(
15      'C:\\Documents and Settings\\Herb Norbom\\work\\'    #my default dir for this program
16      )
17
18  def on_click_listbox(event):
19      index = soundBox.curselection()      # get selected line index
20      soundFile = soundBox.get(index)      # get the line's text
21      label1.configure(text=soundFile)     # show selected text in label
22      path=SELF.defPath                    # use our Class defined path
23      if soundFile != None:
24          extension = os.path.splitext(soundFile)[1][1:]
25          print (extension)
26          if ((extension=='wav') | (extension=='WAV')):    # this is the or  |
27              winsound.PlaySound(str(path)+soundFile,0)
28          if(extension=='txt'):
29              engine=pyttsx.init()
30              voices = engine.getProperty('voices')
31              for voice in voices:
32                  engine.setProperty('voice', voice.id)
33              with open(str(path)+soundFile) as f:
34                  for line in f:
35                      engine.say(line)
36                      engine.runAndWait()
37
38  def paint( event ):
39      try:
40          cx=(event.x-200)    #center x value  and scale for max
41          cy=(event.y-150)       #center y value  and scale for max
42      except:
43          cx=0
44          cy=0
45      print "x coord = ",cx, " y coord= ",cy
46
47  def stop ( event):
48      pass
49
50  def setupCanvas():
51      myCanvas = Canvas( root, width =400, height=300 )
52      myCanvas.grid(column=1,columnspan=3, row=2)
53      myCanvas.configure(cursor="crosshair")
54      myCanvas.bind( "<B1-Motion>", paint )
55      myCanvas.bind("<ButtonRelease-1>",stop)
56      myCanvas.create_line(125, 150, 175, 150, width=1)
57      myCanvas.create_line(225, 150, 275, 150, width=1)
58      myCanvas.create_line(200, 85, 200, 135,  width=1)
59      myCanvas.create_line(200, 165, 200, 215, width=1)
60
```

Exhibit132

61

File   Edit   View   Tools   Window   Help

Python   Find

<new>   lesson22.py

```
60
61   if __name__=='__main__':
62       root = Tk()
63       root.title( "Max Control Center" )
64       root.geometry( "550x450+50+30" ) #width, height, placement y  x
65
66       setupCanvas()
67
68   #setup a list box to list our wav and txt files
69       soundFrame = LabelFrame(root, text="Max Sounds",width=20, height=10,cursor="arrow")
70       soundFrame.grid(column=0, row =2, sticky=(N,W,S))
71       soundBox=Listbox(soundFrame, width=20, height=18)
72       soundBox.grid(column=0,row=1,sticky=(N,W,S))
73       scrollBar = Scrollbar(soundFrame, orient=VERTICAL, command=soundBox.yview)
74       scrollBar.grid(column=1,row=1, sticky=(N,E,S))
75       soundBox['yscrollcommand']=scrollBar.set
76       path=SELF.defPath
77       print path
78       soundlist = os.listdir(path)
79   # load the listbox
80       for sound in soundlist:
81           extension = os.path.splitext(sound)[1][1:]
82           if ((extension=='wav') | (extension=='WAV') |(extension=='txt')):
83               soundBox.insert('end', sound)
84       label1 = Label(soundFrame, text='click to play', width=20, bg='white')
85       label1.grid(column=0, row=0)
86       soundBox.bind('<ButtonRelease-1>', on_click_listbox)
87
88       mainloop()
89
```

[1:1] : 90   ANSI   CR+LF   INS   Ready

Exhibit133

When you run the program you should see the following, I shrank it a little to fit here.

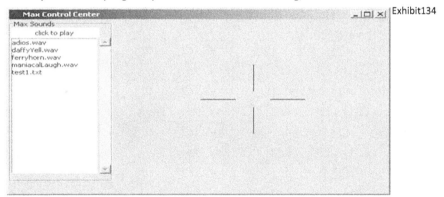Exhibit134

I have added a few sounds bites, note the text file also shows, give it a play. With the cursor over the canvas note the cross hairs. The canvas widget has many features; you can set foreground, background, width, etc. This just touches the surface. What is very important is the 'events', notice how we are beginning to use mouse events to trigger actions. There are of course excellent on line sources of information on the canvas widget. Here are some web sites.

http://effbot.org/tkinterbook/canvas.htm,   http://www.tutorialspoint.com/python/tk_canvas.htm

Mouse Events

Back to our mouse events as that is our focus here. We want to know where the mouse is when an event occurs. We will eventually use that position to control the direction and speed of Max.

Run the program shown in Exhibit136; notice the locations printing on the DOS window when you left click the mouse. Also notice that unless you see cross hairs for the mouse position no coordinates are printed in the DOS window. To somewhat simply the control of the robot we want to make the center position of the canvas, where the cross hairs are displayed to give mouse coordinates of x=0, and y =0. Notice what the coordinates are at that position when you drag the mouse over the cross hairs with the left button pressed.

Exhibit135

Try changing the code by subtracting 200 from the x and 150 from the y coordinates.

Exhibit136

Now run again and when over the cross hairs on the canvas with the left mouse button pressed you should see x and y coordinates pretty close to 0. We will fine tune this later.

Exhibit137

Let's think of the canvas in terms of quarters and how we want our Max to move. The top half will be forward, the bottom half will be backwards. The right side will be for right turns and the left side for left turns. The closer we are to the center cross hairs the slower the robot will move. Conversely, the further away from the cross hairs the faster Max will move. At this point it is a good idea to get an idea of the wheels of our robot. Max has two drive wheels, left and right, and a third wheel that is a swivel caster mainly for balance. Since we have not built our robot at this point I want to setup a test drive canvas to practice and refine our movements. This will give you a general idea of how it works. Once we hook up to the physical robot we will be using Pulse Width Modulation (PWM) to control the speed. So we will put some of that logic in as well. For the first pass we are not going to try to control the speed, just the direction.

Day Twenty Two – Virtual Robot and Driving Range

The first item we need is our driving range. We will create another canvas for that purpose. Save lesson22.py as lesson23.py. We are adding the global concept so that data can be shared by functions. There are several methods of sharing the data including putting the variables into the call of the function, or putting it in our Class definition. I went with this as it is a new concept and one that is very simple but confusing if you read some of the descriptions on it. You have to remember to declare the variable as global prior to using it. In any function that may change the variable you must declare it as global. In the program listed below I just define it as global in the paint function, when I use it in the "setUpDriveCanvas" function it is available. When you run the program nothing new will happen until you click the left mouse button and drag while in the setupCanvas. When you do the setupDriveCanvas will display. You can grab the bottom of the MaxControl window and pull down to enlarge. You will also notice that the black box moves as you left click and drag the mouse around the setupCanvas.

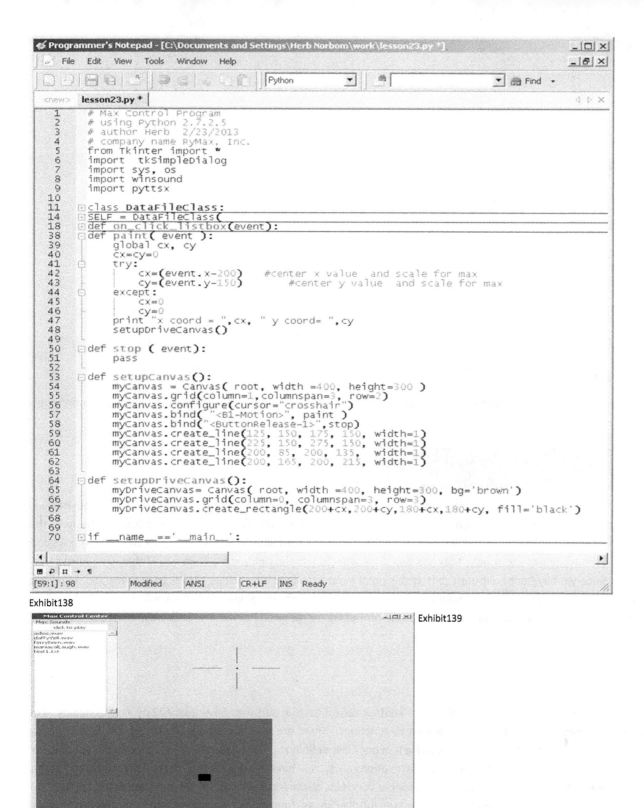

Exhibit138

Exhibit139

This gives you the general idea, but not what we want. We want the box to move when we left click on the canvas and in the direction we specify, for as long as we hold down the left mouse button. We are going to add a fair amount of code, so save as lesson24.py. For what we are going to do now, visualize your algebra graphic pad.

I have made a number of changes to our program. First of all I took out the global variables and put those data variables into our Class, you could really go either way. Just thought the Class approach was the cleaner method or should I say classier.

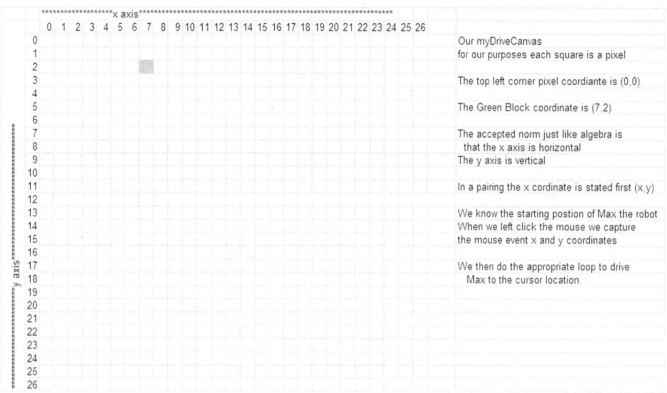

```
********************x axis**********************************************************
      0 1 2 3 4 5 6 7 8 9 10 11 12 13 14 15 16 17 18 19 20 21 22 23 24 25 26
   0
   1
   2
   3
   4
   5
   6
   7
   8
   9
  10
  11
  12
  13
  14
  15
  16
  17
  18
  19
  20
  21
  22
  23
  24
  25
  26
```

Our myDriveCanvas
for our purposes each square is a pixel

The top left corner pixel coordiante is (0,0)

The Green Block coordinate is (7,2)

The accepted norm just like algebra is
  that the x axis is horizontal
The y axis is vertical

In a pairing the x cordinate is stated first (x,y)

We know the starting postion of Max the robot
When we left click the mouse we capture
the mouse event x and y coordinates

We then do the appropriate loop to drive
  Max to the cursor location.

Exhibit139A

Think of the grid above. I am going to adjust the window size at this point and begin the direction coding process. The complete code is shown in the following screen shots. I suggest you run the program and observe it in action. I am sure you noticed all the redundant code as you were writing the program. Hopefully you used the cut and paste technique. The code can be improved; one suggestion would be to put the redundant code into functions. At this point we are running a simulation on a limited canvas. Once we are controlling our robot our field of operation will be as big as our communications. When we connect to our robot the coding for controlling the robot will totally change. Remember we need to control speed as well as direction. That is why I am not concerned with having the 'best' code at this point.

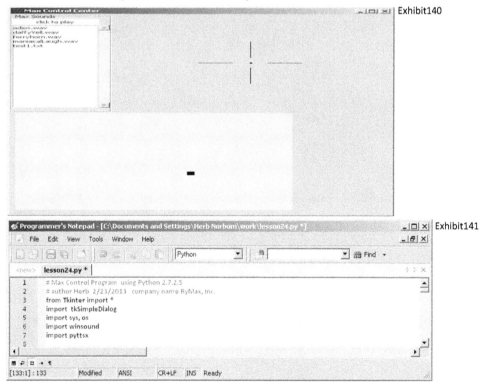

Exhibit140

Exhibit141

```
1  # Max Control Program  using Python 2.7.2.5
2  # author Herb  2/23/2013   company name RyMax, Inc.
3  from Tkinter import *
4  import tkSimpleDialog
5  import sys, os
6  import winsound
7  import pyttsx
8
```

```python
 9   class DataFileClass:
10       def __init__(Data,defPath,xMaxLoc, yMaxLoc):
11          Data.defPath= defPath
12          Data.xMaxLoc=xMaxLoc
13          Data.yMaxLoc=yMaxLoc
14   SELF = DataFileClass(#my default dir for this program
15       'C:\\Documents and Settings\\Herb Norbom\\work\\',
16       xMaxLoc = 200,
17       yMaxLoc = 205
18       )
19   def on_click_listbox(event):
20       index = soundBox.curselection()   #get selected line index
21       soundFile = soundBox.get(index)   #get the line's text
22       label1.configure(text=soundFile) #show selected text in label
23       path=SELF.defPath          #use our Class defined path
24       if soundFile != None:
25          extension = os.path.splitext(soundFile)[1][1:]
26          print (extension)
27          if ((extension=='wav') | (extension=='WAV')):#the or | connector
28             winsound.PlaySound(str(path)+soundFile,0)
29          if(extension=='txt'):
30             engine=pyttsx.init()
31             voices = engine.getProperty('voices')
32             for voice in voices:
33                engine.setProperty('voice', voice.id)
34             with open(str(path)+soundFile) as f:
35                for line in f:
36                   engine.say(line)
37                   engine.runAndWait()
38
39   def paint( event ):
40       cx=cy=0
41       try:
42          cx=(event.x)
43          cy=(event.y)
44       except:
45          cx=0          # if something not working want to
46          cy=0          # set mouse event location to (0,0)
47       setupDriveCanvas(cx, cy)
48
49   def stop ( event):
50       # will use this with the actual robot control to issue a stop command
51       pass
52
53   def setupCanvas():
54       myCanvas = Canvas( root, width =400, height=300 )
55       myCanvas.grid(column=1,columnspan=3, row=2)
56       myCanvas.configure(cursor="crosshair")
57       myCanvas.bind( "<B1-Motion>", paint )
58       myCanvas.bind("<ButtonRelease-1>",stop)
59       myCanvas.create_line(125, 150, 175, 150, width=1)
60       myCanvas.create_line(225, 150, 275, 150, width=1)
61       myCanvas.create_line(200,  85, 200, 135, width=1)
62       myCanvas.create_line(200, 165, 200, 215, width=1)
63
64   def setupDriveCanvas(cx, cy):
65       print 'Goto coord cx = ',cx,' cy = ', cy
66       myDriveCanvas= Canvas( root, width =400, height=300, bg='yellow')
67       myDriveCanvas.grid(column=0, columnspan=3, row=3)
68       myDriveCanvas.create_rectangle(SELF.xMaxLoc, SELF.yMaxLoc, SELF.xMaxLoc -10, SELF.yMaxLoc -10, fill='black')
69       if (cx > SELF.xMaxLoc):
70          while cx != SELF.xMaxLoc:
```

Exhibit142

66

```python
71        SELF.xMaxLoc = SELF.xMaxLoc+1
72        myDriveCanvas= Canvas( root, width =400, height=300, bg='yellow')
73        myDriveCanvas.grid(column=0, columnspan=3, row=3)
74        myDriveCanvas.create_rectangle(SELF.xMaxLoc, SELF.yMaxLoc, SELF.xMaxLoc-10, SELF.yMaxLoc-10, fill='black')
75     if (cy > SELF.yMaxLoc):
76        while cy != SELF.yMaxLoc:
77           SELF.yMaxLoc = SELF.yMaxLoc+1
78           myDriveCanvas= Canvas( root, width =400, height=300, bg='yellow')
79           myDriveCanvas.grid(column=0, columnspan=3, row=3)
80           myDriveCanvas.create_rectangle(SELF.xMaxLoc, SELF.yMaxLoc, SELF.xMaxLoc-10, SELF.yMaxLoc-10, fill='black')
81     if (cy < SELF.yMaxLoc):
82        while cy != SELF.yMaxLoc:
83           SELF.yMaxLoc = SELF.yMaxLoc-1
84           myDriveCanvas= Canvas( root, width =400, height=300, bg='yellow')
85           myDriveCanvas.grid(column=0, columnspan=3, row=3)
86           myDriveCanvas.create_rectangle(SELF.xMaxLoc, SELF.yMaxLoc, SELF.xMaxLoc-10, SELF.yMaxLoc-10, fill='black')
87  if (cx < SELF.xMaxLoc):
88     while cx != SELF.xMaxLoc:
89        SELF.xMaxLoc = SELF.xMaxLoc-1
90        myDriveCanvas= Canvas( root, width =400, height=300, bg='yellow')
91        myDriveCanvas.grid(column=0, columnspan=3, row=3)
92        myDriveCanvas.create_rectangle(SELF.xMaxLoc, SELF.yMaxLoc, SELF.xMaxLoc-10, SELF.yMaxLoc-10, fill='black')
93     if (cy > SELF.yMaxLoc):
94        while cy != SELF.yMaxLoc:
95           SELF.yMaxLoc = SELF.yMaxLoc+1
96           myDriveCanvas= Canvas( root, width =400, height=300, bg='yellow')
97           myDriveCanvas.grid(column=0, columnspan=3, row=3)
98           myDriveCanvas.create_rectangle(SELF.xMaxLoc, SELF.yMaxLoc, SELF.xMaxLoc-10, SELF.yMaxLoc-10, fill='black')
99     if (cy < SELF.yMaxLoc):
100       while cy != SELF.yMaxLoc:
101          SELF.yMaxLoc = SELF.yMaxLoc-1
102          myDriveCanvas= Canvas( root, width =400, height=300, bg='yellow')
103          myDriveCanvas.grid(column=0, columnspan=3, row=3)
104          myDriveCanvas.create_rectangle(SELF.xMaxLoc, SELF.yMaxLoc, SELF.xMaxLoc-10, SELF.yMaxLoc-10, fill='black')
105 if __name__=='__main__':
106    root = Tk()
107    root.title("Max Control Center" )
108    root.geometry( "550x620+50+30" ) #width, height, placement y  x
109    setupCanvas()
110 #setup a list box to list our wav and txt files
111    soundFrame = LabelFrame(root, text="Max Sounds",width=20,
112       height=10,cursor="arrow")
113    soundFrame.grid(column=0, row =2, sticky=(N,W,S))
114    soundBox=Listbox(soundFrame, width=20, height=18)
115    soundBox.grid(column=0,row=1,sticky=(N,W,S))
116    scrollBar = Scrollbar(soundFrame, orient=VERTICAL, command=soundBox.yview)
117    scrollBar.grid(column=1,row=1, sticky=(N,E,S))
118    soundBox['yscrollcommand']=scrollBar.set
119    path=SELF.defPath
120    print path
121    soundlist = os.listdir(path)
122    # load the listbox
123    for sound in soundlist:
124       extension = os.path.splitext(sound)[1][1:]
125       if ((extension=='wav') | (extension=='WAV') | (extension=='txt')):
126          soundBox.insert('end', sound)
127    label1 = Label(soundFrame, text='click to play', width=20, bg='white')
128    label1.grid(column=0, row=0)
129    soundBox.bind('<ButtonRelease-1>', on_click_listbox)
130    mainloop()
```

Exhibit142A

Day Twenty Three – Queues

When we actually go 'live' with our robot there is the real potential for system conflicts. While the computer is waiting for something to happen something else is happening. We are going to be sending our robot a stream of instructions and the robot is going to send back a stream of data. It would be very easy for one function to be in a 'wait' period while important data is coming in, or needs to be processed, and sent out. Two important methods are available to help us get around this problem. The first is the queue. In Python this is a standard module that has a number of different options. We are going to go just deep enough to put our send instructions into the queue, and have them extracted from the queue, and processed.

Save your program as lesson25.py and let us get a queue working. Of course there is a lot of information on the web. http://docs.python.org/2/library/queue.html ,
http://www.blog.pythonlibrary.org/2012/08/01/python-concurrency-an-example-of-a-queue/

Python likes to communicate in strings and our future serial or WiFi communication will be easier using strings. That is why we went to the effort of converting integers to string and converting the string back to integers when pulled from the queue. As you look at the code you will see a number of print statements. These are just there to help us debug as we are developing the application.

We need to import the queue module and then define which queue we are using. For now we will use the Lifo.Queue. When using the queues you need to 'put' items in the queue and 'get' or retrieve them. There are various classes and objects that are referred to. I also added some data elements to our 'DataFileClass', they will be used as we develop our communications. The following 3 screen shots show the entire program.

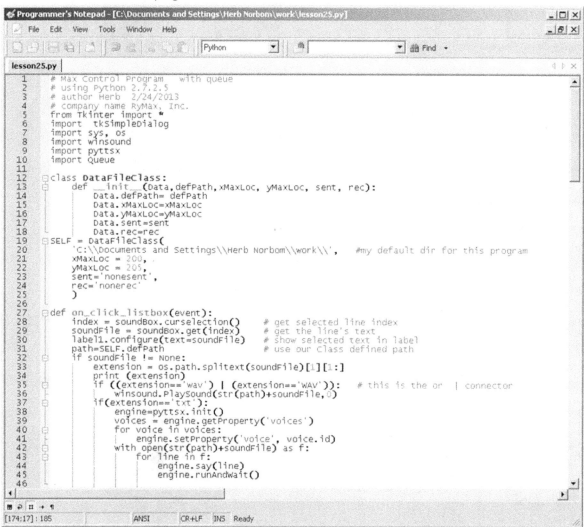

```python
# Max Control Program   with queue
# using Python 2.7.2.5
# author Herb  2/24/2013
# company name RyMax, Inc.
from Tkinter import *
import  tkSimpleDialog
import sys, os
import winsound
import pyttsx
import Queue

class DataFileClass:
    def __init__(Data,defPath,xMaxLoc, yMaxLoc, sent, rec):
        Data.defPath= defPath
        Data.xMaxLoc=xMaxLoc
        Data.yMaxLoc=yMaxLoc
        Data.sent=sent
        Data.rec=rec
SELF = DataFileClass(
    'C:\\Documents and Settings\\Herb Norbom\\work\\',   #my default dir for this program
    xMaxLoc = 200,
    yMaxLoc = 205,
    sent='nonesent',
    rec='nonerec'
    )

def on_click_listbox(event):
    index = soundBox.curselection()     # get selected line index
    soundFile = soundBox.get(index)     # get the line's text
    label1.configure(text=soundFile)    # show selected text in label
    path=SELF.defPath                   # use our Class defined path
    if soundFile != None:
        extension = os.path.splitext(soundFile)[1][1:]
        print (extension)
        if ((extension=='wav') | (extension=='WAV')):   # this is the or | connector
            winsound.PlaySound(str(path)+soundFile,0)
        if(extension=='txt'):
            engine=pyttsx.init()
            voices = engine.getProperty('voices')
            for voice in voices:
                engine.setProperty('voice', voice.id)
            with open(str(path)+soundFile) as f:
                for line in f:
                    engine.say(line)
                    engine.runAndwait()
```

Exhibit143

68

```python
47  def paint( event ):
48      cx=cy=0
49      try:
50          cx=(event.x)
51          cy=(event.y)
52      except:
53          cx=0                                # if something not working want to
54          cy=0                                # set mouse event location to (0,0)
55      SELF.sent=(str(cx) +','+ str(cy))       # Python likes to communicate in strings
56                                              # converting our coordinates to strings, insert
57                                              # a comma to make it easier to separate later
58      try:
59          SendQueue.put(SELF.sent)            # writing to our queue
60      except:
61          print'Quene error on write'         # we want to know about an error, but
62          pass                                #    keep running
63
64      setupDriveCanvas()
65
66  def stop ( event):      # will use this with the actual robot control to issue a stop command
67      pass
68
69  def setupCanvas():
70      myCanvas = Canvas( root, width =400, height=300 )
71      myCanvas.grid(column=1,columnspan=3, row=2)
72      myCanvas.configure(cursor="crosshair")
73      myCanvas.bind( "<B1-Motion>", paint )
74      myCanvas.bind("<ButtonRelease-1>",stop)
75      myCanvas.create_line(125, 150, 175, 150, width=1)
76      myCanvas.create_line(225, 150, 275, 150, width=1)
77      myCanvas.create_line(200,  85, 200, 135, width=1)
78      myCanvas.create_line(200, 165, 200, 215, width=1)
79
80  def setupDriveCanvas():
81      try:
82          qaction = SendQueue.qsize()                 #see if a message in queue
83      except:
84          print('error on get queue size')
85          qaction=0
86      if (qaction >0):
87          msgLen=0
88          msgRec =''
89          msgRec = SendQueue.get()                    #retrieve string from queue
90
91          try:
92              msgLen = msgRec.__len__()
93              print msgLen                            # while not needed it may help in debugging
94          except:
95              print 'error getting queue msg'
96              pass
97          if (msgLen > 2):
98              myTup=msgRec.partition(',')
99              print 'myTup = ', myTup                  # while not needed it may help in debugging
100             print 'myTup[0] = ', myTup[0]            # while not needed it may help in debugging
101             print 'myTup[2] = ', myTup[2]            # while not needed it may help in debugging
102             try:
103                 cx = int(myTup[0])
104                 cy = int(myTup[2])
105             except:
106                 print 'Error on conversion to integer'
107                 pass
108
109         print 'Goto coord cx = ',cx,'  cy = ', cy     # while not needed it may help in debugging
110
111         myDriveCanvas= Canvas( root, width =400, height=300, bg='yellow')
112         myDriveCanvas.grid(column=0, columnspan=3, row=3)
113         myDriveCanvas.create_rectangle(SELF.xMaxLoc, SELF.yMaxLoc, SELF.xMaxLoc -10,
114         SELF.yMaxLoc -10, fill='black')
115         if (cx > SELF.xMaxLoc):
116             while cx != SELF.xMaxLoc:
117                 SELF.xMaxLoc = SELF.xMaxLoc+1
118                 myDriveCanvas= Canvas( root, width =400, height=300, bg='yellow')
```

Exhibit144

69

```
119             myDriveCanvas.grid(column=0, columnspan=3, row=3)
120             myDriveCanvas.create_rectangle(SELF.xMaxLoc, SELF.yMaxLoc, SELF.xMaxLoc -10,
121             SELF.yMaxLoc -10, fill='black')
122         if (cy > SELF.yMaxLoc):
123             while cy != SELF.yMaxLoc:
124                 SELF.yMaxLoc = SELF.yMaxLoc+1
125                 myDriveCanvas= Canvas( root, width =400, height=300, bg='yellow')
126                 myDriveCanvas.grid(column=0, columnspan=3, row=3)
127                 myDriveCanvas.create_rectangle(SELF.xMaxLoc, SELF.yMaxLoc, SELF.xMaxLoc -10,
128                 SELF.yMaxLoc -10, fill='black')
129         if (cy < SELF.yMaxLoc):
130             while cy != SELF.yMaxLoc:
131                 SELF.yMaxLoc = SELF.yMaxLoc-1
132                 myDriveCanvas= Canvas( root, width =400, height=300, bg='yellow')
133                 myDriveCanvas.grid(column=0, columnspan=3, row=3)
134                 myDriveCanvas.create_rectangle(SELF.xMaxLoc, SELF.yMaxLoc, SELF.xMaxLoc -10,
135                 SELF.yMaxLoc -10, fill='black')
136     if (cx < SELF.xMaxLoc):
137         while cx != SELF.xMaxLoc:
138             SELF.xMaxLoc = SELF.xMaxLoc-1
139             myDriveCanvas= Canvas( root, width =400, height=300, bg='yellow')
140             myDriveCanvas.grid(column=0, columnspan=3, row=3)
141             myDriveCanvas.create_rectangle(SELF.xMaxLoc, SELF.yMaxLoc, SELF.xMaxLoc -10,
142             SELF.yMaxLoc -10, fill='black')
143         if (cy > SELF.yMaxLoc):
144             while cy != SELF.yMaxLoc:
145                 SELF.yMaxLoc = SELF.yMaxLoc+1
146                 myDriveCanvas= Canvas( root, width =400, height=300, bg='yellow')
147                 myDriveCanvas.grid(column=0, columnspan=3, row=3)
148                 myDriveCanvas.create_rectangle(SELF.xMaxLoc, SELF.yMaxLoc, SELF.xMaxLoc -10,
149                 SELF.yMaxLoc -10, fill='black')
150         if (cy < SELF.yMaxLoc):
151             while cy != SELF.yMaxLoc:
152                 SELF.yMaxLoc = SELF.yMaxLoc-1
153                 myDriveCanvas= Canvas( root, width =400, height=300, bg='yellow')
154                 myDriveCanvas.grid(column=0, columnspan=3, row=3)
155                 myDriveCanvas.create_rectangle(SELF.xMaxLoc, SELF.yMaxLoc, SELF.xMaxLoc -10,
156                 SELF.yMaxLoc -10, fill='black')
157 if __name__=='__main__':
158     root = Tk()
159     root.title( "Max Control Center" )
160     root.geometry( "550x620+50+30" ) #width, height, placement y  x
161     setupCanvas()
162
163     #setup a list box to list our wav and txt files
164     soundFrame = LabelFrame(root, text="Max Sounds",width=20, height=10,cursor="arrow")
165     soundFrame.grid(column=0, row =2, sticky=(N,W,S))
166     soundBox=Listbox(soundFrame, width=20, height=18)
167     soundBox.grid(column=0,row=1,sticky=(N,W,S))
168     scrollBar = Scrollbar(soundFrame, orient=VERTICAL, command=soundBox.yview)
169     scrollBar.grid(column=1,row=1, sticky=(N,E,S))
170     soundBox['yscrollcommand']=scrollBar.set
171     path=SELF.defPath
172     print path
173     soundlist = os.listdir(path)
174     # load the listbox
175     for sound in soundlist:
176         extension = os.path.splitext(sound)[1][1:]
177         if ((extension=='wav') | (extension=='WAV') |(extension=='txt')):
178             soundBox.insert('end', sound)
179     label1 = Label(soundFrame, text='click to play', width=20, bg='white')
180     label1.grid(column=0, row=0)
181     soundBox.bind('<ButtonRelease-1>', on_click_listbox)
182     SendQueue = Queue.LifoQueue()
183     mainloop()
```

Exhibit145

Day Twenty Four - Threading

We are also going to introduce threading. Unless you are setup with multiple processors you may not think this does anything for you, but it does. What threading does is let a program's branch run while a different program branch is waiting. While not needed at this point, the concept will be needed to keep the program running smoothly once we introduce the communication with Max. Save the program as lesson26.py.

We need to import threading and Thread. We also need to start two child threads. The original program is really a thread and it is the parent in our case. The two new threads will be send and receive. Some good sites are:

http://stackoverflow.com/questions/2846653/python-multithreading-for-dummies , http://www.tutorialspoint.com/python/python_multithreading.htm .

For a thread to keep running it needs to be active. That is why in our two new functions we put the while True statement in.   We just want to get the threads running before we do anything with them. Here is the code you need to add. An important note, we want our child threads to stop when the parent thread stops. To do this set the thread daemon to 'True'.

Exhibit146

Exhibit147

Exhibit148

When you run the program you will see the number of threads and their names displayed in the DOS window.

Exhibit149

If you would like to see what happens if the functions called are not active. Comment out the 'while True' statements in our sending and receiving functions. You may have to adjust the spacing for the 'pass' statement. Did all the threads display? Change it back and we will proceed. There are some other items with threads that you need to be aware of. Before starting the thread you need to setup all the child threads. When you stop the parent thread the child's are also stopped.

The next steps are somewhat of a step backward, but we need to move the queue reading from the setupDriveCanvas function to our new sending function. We are also going to pass the variables 'cx' and 'cy' as arguments between the functions. We also changed where setupDriveCanvas is called from, rather than call from the paint function; we now call from our send thread function.

We are using our queue function, last in first out, LIFO. Our last command is really the one we care about in this design. After each send we are emptying the queue.

One of the problems with high speed signal devices, mouse, joysticks, etc. is that they send a stream of data very quickly. This flood of instructions happens many times too quickly for our program to process. There are various ways to handle them, including writing to our queue and just extracting the last instructions. What I did here was just add a wait time, approx .2 seconds. In

71

human time not slow at all, but in computer time, like towing a boulder. While we are slowing down the main thread our other two threads continue unfazed. As you run the program notice the steady stream of messages regarding queue size, and the slight jumpy movement of our virtual Max. You can try adjusting the time delay and watching the movements. If you eliminate the time delay and move the mouse with the left click pressed fairly rapidly around the canvas you will probably get an error.

Our main concern here is getting the communication running. The virtual display is just to help us visualize Max in action. Even though the movement is not at all smooth it serves our current purpose. After all, we want to drive a real robot and we will be deleting the visual canvas drive sections later on. Not to mention, our real robot will take some time to get somewhere. We have made a number of changes to the program. The following 4 screen shots list the entire program.

Exhibit150

```python
22  SELF = DataFileClass(
23      'C:\\Documents and Settings\\Herb Norbom\\work\\',   #my default dir for this program
24      xMaxLoc = 200,
25      yMaxLoc = 205,
26      sent='nonesent',
27      rec='nonerec'
28      )
29
30  def on_click_listbox(event):
31      index = soundBox.curselection()      # get selected line index
32      soundFile = soundBox.get(index)      # get the line's text
33      label1.configure(text=soundFile)     # show selected text in label
34      path=SELF.defPath                    # use our Class defined path
35      if soundFile != None:
36          extension = os.path.splitext(soundFile)[1][1:]
37          print (extension)
38          if ((extension=='wav') | (extension=='WAV')):   # this is the or  | connector
39              winsound.PlaySound(str(path)+soundFile,0)
40          if(extension=='txt'):
41              engine=pyttsx.init()
42              voices = engine.getProperty('voices')
43              for voice in voices:
44                  engine.setProperty('voice', voice.id)
45              with open(str(path)+soundFile) as f:
46                  for line in f:
47                      engine.say(line)
48                      engine.runAndwait()
49
50  def paint( event ):
51      cx=cy=0
52      try:
53          cx=(event.x)
54          cy=(event.y)
55      except:
56          cx=0                             # if something not working want to
57          cy=0                             # set mouse event location to (0,0)
58      SELF.sent=(str(cx) +','+ str(cy))    # Python likes to communicate in strings
59                                           # converting our coordinates to strings, insert
60                                           # a comma to make it easier to separate later
61      try:
62          SendQueue.put(SELF.sent)         # writing to our queue
63      except:
64          print'Quene error on write'      # we want to know about an error, but
65
66      time.sleep(.2)          # need to slow down the works, when you are left clicking  the mouse
67                             # the stream of signals is too fast for the program to keep up with
68
69
70  def stop ( event):          # will use this with the actual robot control to issue a stop command
71      pass
72
73  def setupCanvas():
74      myCanvas = Canvas( root, width =400, height=300 )
75      myCanvas.grid(column=1,columnspan=3, row=2)
76      myCanvas.configure(cursor="crosshair")
77      myCanvas.bind( "<B1-Motion>", paint )
78      myCanvas.bind("<ButtonRelease-1>",stop)
79      myCanvas.create_line(125, 150, 175, 150, width=1)
80      myCanvas.create_line(225, 150, 275, 150, width=1)
81      myCanvas.create_line(200,  85, 200, 135, width=1)
82      myCanvas.create_line(200, 165, 200, 215, width=1)
83
84  def setupDriveCanvas(cx, cy):
85      print 'Goto coord cx = ',cx,'  cy = ', cy      # while not needed it may help in debugging
86      try:
87          cx+=1              #add 1 to make sure cx and cy are integers
88          cy+=1
89          cx-=1              #return to correct values
90          cy-=1
91      except:
92          print "cx or cy was not an integer"
```

Exhibit151

73

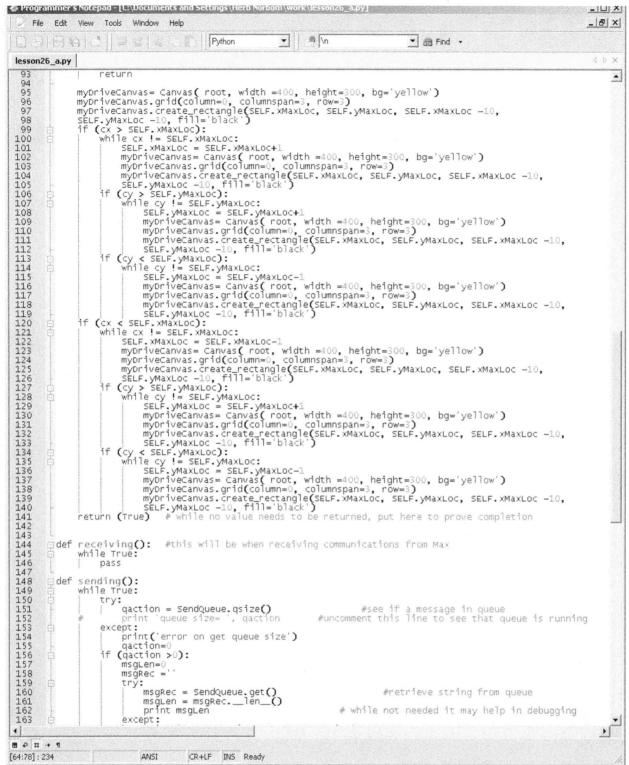

```python
 93          return
 94
 95      myDriveCanvas= Canvas( root, width =400, height=300, bg='yellow')
 96      myDriveCanvas.grid(column=0, columnspan=3, row=3)
 97      myDriveCanvas.create_rectangle(SELF.xMaxLoc, SELF.yMaxLoc, SELF.xMaxLoc -10,
 98      SELF.yMaxLoc -10, fill='black')
 99      if (cx > SELF.xMaxLoc):
100          while cx != SELF.xMaxLoc:
101              SELF.xMaxLoc = SELF.xMaxLoc+1
102              myDriveCanvas= Canvas( root, width =400, height=300, bg='yellow')
103              myDriveCanvas.grid(column=0, columnspan=3, row=3)
104              myDriveCanvas.create_rectangle(SELF.xMaxLoc, SELF.yMaxLoc, SELF.xMaxLoc -10,
105              SELF.yMaxLoc -10, fill='black')
106          if (cy > SELF.yMaxLoc):
107              while cy != SELF.yMaxLoc:
108                  SELF.yMaxLoc = SELF.yMaxLoc+1
109                  myDriveCanvas= Canvas( root, width =400, height=300, bg='yellow')
110                  myDriveCanvas.grid(column=0, columnspan=3, row=3)
111                  myDriveCanvas.create_rectangle(SELF.xMaxLoc, SELF.yMaxLoc, SELF.xMaxLoc -10,
112                  SELF.yMaxLoc -10, fill='black')
113          if (cy < SELF.yMaxLoc):
114              while cy != SELF.yMaxLoc:
115                  SELF.yMaxLoc = SELF.yMaxLoc-1
116                  myDriveCanvas= Canvas( root, width =400, height=300, bg='yellow')
117                  myDriveCanvas.grid(column=0, columnspan=3, row=3)
118                  myDriveCanvas.create_rectangle(SELF.xMaxLoc, SELF.yMaxLoc, SELF.xMaxLoc -10,
119                  SELF.yMaxLoc -10, fill='black')
120      if (cx < SELF.xMaxLoc):
121          while cx != SELF.xMaxLoc:
122              SELF.xMaxLoc = SELF.xMaxLoc-1
123              myDriveCanvas= Canvas( root, width =400, height=300, bg='yellow')
124              myDriveCanvas.grid(column=0, columnspan=3, row=3)
125              myDriveCanvas.create_rectangle(SELF.xMaxLoc, SELF.yMaxLoc, SELF.xMaxLoc -10,
126              SELF.yMaxLoc -10, fill='black')
127          if (cy > SELF.yMaxLoc):
128              while cy != SELF.yMaxLoc:
129                  SELF.yMaxLoc = SELF.yMaxLoc+1
130                  myDriveCanvas= Canvas( root, width =400, height=300, bg='yellow')
131                  myDriveCanvas.grid(column=0, columnspan=3, row=3)
132                  myDriveCanvas.create_rectangle(SELF.xMaxLoc, SELF.yMaxLoc, SELF.xMaxLoc -10,
133                  SELF.yMaxLoc -10, fill='black')
134          if (cy < SELF.yMaxLoc):
135              while cy != SELF.yMaxLoc:
136                  SELF.yMaxLoc = SELF.yMaxLoc-1
137                  myDriveCanvas= Canvas( root, width =400, height=300, bg='yellow')
138                  myDriveCanvas.grid(column=0, columnspan=3, row=3)
139                  myDriveCanvas.create_rectangle(SELF.xMaxLoc, SELF.yMaxLoc, SELF.xMaxLoc -10,
140                  SELF.yMaxLoc -10, fill='black')
141      return (True)   # while no value needs to be returned, put here to prove completion
142
143
144  def receiving():   #this will be when receiving communications from Max
145      while True:
146          pass
147
148  def sending():
149      while True:
150          try:
151              qaction = SendQueue.qsize()               #see if a message in queue
152  #           print 'queue size= ', qaction       #uncomment this line to see that queue is running
153          except:
154              print('error on get queue size')
155              qaction=0
156          if (qaction >0):
157              msgLen=0
158              msgRec =''
159              try:
160                  msgRec = SendQueue.get()                 #retrieve string from queue
161                  msgLen = msgRec.__len__()
162                  print msgLen                     # while not needed it may help in debugging
163              except:
```

Exhibit152

File   Edit   View   Tools   Window   Help

Python   \n   Find

lesson26_a.py

```
164              print 'error getting queue msg or size'
165          if (msgLen > 2):
166              myTup=msgRec.partition(',')
167              print 'myTup = ', myTup          # while not needed it may help in debugging
168              print 'myTup[0] = ', myTup[0]    # while not needed it may help in debugging
169              print 'myTup[2] = ', myTup[2]    # while not needed it may help in debugging
170              try:
171                  cx = int(myTup[0])
172                  cy = int(myTup[2])
173              except:
174                  print 'Error on conversion to integer'
175              print 'sending cx ,cy', cx, ' ',cy
176              finished=setupDriveCanvas(cx, cy)
177              print finished                        #simple verifation from the function
178              while 1:                              #throw away eveything in queue, when we get
179                  try:                              #error queue is empty.  with the delay built
180                      trash = SendQueue.get_nowait()  #in, this is probbly not needed, but we will
181                  except:                           #need to empty the queue in later programs
182                      break                         # break just means stop this function and continue,
183                                                    # pass will probably lock up the program
184
185  def threadStart():          #starting child threads
186      recTh=Thread(target=receiving, name='recThread',args=())
187      recTh.setDaemon(True)          # must set all child threads before starting
188      senTh=Thread(target=sending,name='sendThread', args=())
189      senTh.setDaemon(True)
190      try:
191          print'staring recTh'
192          recTh.start()
193      except:
194          print('CRITICAL ERROR starting recThread')
195      try:
196          print 'starting senTh'
197          senTh.start()
198      except:
199          print('CRITICAL ERROR starting sendThread')
200      thCount= threading.active_count()
201      print('# of threads = ',thCount)
202      thNames= threading.enumerate()
203      print (thNames)
204
205  if __name__=='__main__':
206      root = Tk()
207      root.title( "Max Control Center" )
208      root.geometry( "550x620+50+30" ) #width, height, placement y  x
209      setupCanvas()
210
211  #setup a list box to list our wav and txt files
212      soundFrame = LabelFrame(root, text="Max Sounds",width=20, height=10,cursor="arrow")
213      soundFrame.grid(column=0, row =2, sticky=(N,W,S))
214      soundBox=Listbox(soundFrame, width=20, height=18)
215      soundBox.grid(column=0,row=1,sticky=(N,W,S))
216      scrollBar = Scrollbar(soundFrame, orient=VERTICAL, command=soundBox.yview)
217      scrollBar.grid(column=1,row=1, sticky=(N,E,S))
218      soundBox['yscrollcommand']=scrollBar.set
219      path=SELF.defPath
220      print path
221      soundlist = os.listdir(path)
222  # load the listbox
223      for sound in soundlist:
224          extension = os.path.splitext(sound)[1][1:]
225          if ((extension=='wav') | (extension=='WAV') |(extension=='txt')):
226              soundBox.insert('end', sound)
227      label1 = Label(soundFrame, text='click to play', width=20, bg='white')
228      label1.grid(column=0, row=0)
229      soundBox.bind('<ButtonRelease-1>', on_click_listbox)
230      SendQueue = Queue.LifoQueue()
231      threadStart()
232      mainloop()
```

[64:78] : 234   ANSI   CR+LF   INS   Ready

Exhibit153

In the following screen shot of the DOS window you get a flavor for the print statements. In the program you may want to comment some of them out, and turn some others on by removing or inserting the '#'.

Exhibit154

```
C:\WINDOWS\system32\cmd.exe - python lesson26.py

C:\Documents and Settings\Herb Norbom\work>python lesson26.py
C:\Documents and Settings\Herb Norbom\work\
staring recTh
starting senTh
('# of threads = ', 3)
[<_MainThread(MainThread, started 7656)>, <Thread(recThread, started daemon 9040
>>, <Thread(sendThread, started daemon 8804)>]
?
myTup =  ('194', ',', '119')
myTup[0] =  194
myTup[2] =  119
sending cx .cy 194    119
Goto coord cx =  194    cy =  119
True
?
myTup =  ('204', ',', '138')
myTup[0] =  204
myTup[2] =  138
sending cx .cy 204    138
Goto coord cx =  204    cy =  138
True
_
```

Day Twenty Five – Enhancing our Control Program

Save our program as lesson27.py. We need to add some additional frames, setup some buttons, and add back in our menu system. First add back the menu system, see program lesson07.py, you might want to look back at Day Twelve. I suggest you open two Programmer's Notepads, one with lesson07.py and the other with lesson27.py. Use the cut and paste functions of the editor to move code from lesson07.py to lesson27.py.

Create the menu system. Copy the lines 114 – 131 and paste after the 'setupCanvas ()' line 209. We also need all the functions called by the menu program. Copy lines 28-109 and paste after the 'def threadStart ():' function line 203. Copy line 7 and paste it over line 6. Copy line 7 and paste it over line 7. Copy line 8 and paste it after 'import time'. Save the program as lesson27_a.py and run it. Try all the menu items and the other functions of the program. Once everything is running save as lesson27_b.py. We will move on to adding additional frames and setting up some buttons. Our goal is to define our control panel completely, except for the actual communication to the robot over the serial port. We will print out the commands that would be sent to the DOS window and display them in a status window.

There will be a lot of changes to our existing program. We are going to write our commands to move the virtual robot to look just like what we would send to the physical robot, except for speed. When we communicate with the actual robot we need to send commands to the left and right motor. For now our virtual robot will work much as it did. A few changes have been made which you will see as you go through the code. I found the queue processing to be simpler if we use a string vs. a tuple. The split method is used in breaking the queue items into a 'list'. We begin writing our commands for Max to the queue also. For now we will just ignore them.

When developing the code I have tried to keep in mind that the memory on Max is limited, also the processor speed is many times slower than on the PC. With that in mind, I have tried to do as much data preparation on the PC as possible before transmitting to Max. There is the possibility or reality for partial signals to be received by Max. To help Max identify 'real and complete' signals, each transmission begins with an 'X' for the motors and a ']' for the arm. The drive motors are of course controlled by the on-board chip, and the chip is using 8 bit PWM. That is why the top speed is 255.

Note for the menu item EXIT I have changed the function called to shutdown. Note in the shutdown function how I combined portions of the EXIT function. I then deleted the old EXIT function you will see this when you look at the complete code that is included in several screen shots. Before making the MANY additional changes save your program as lesson27_c.py. I have taken the 'font' lines out of the button widget functions, you can put back in if you like. Also starting some of the much needed program cleanup. Like any construction site there is debris around and the trim work needs to be cleaned up. A CLASS 'UpdateDisplay' for displaying messages from the system, to and from Max has been added. This use of a Class makes the repeated displays of rapidly changing data a lot easier. I have not shown a complete program in awhile, so before doing some more cleaning here it is.

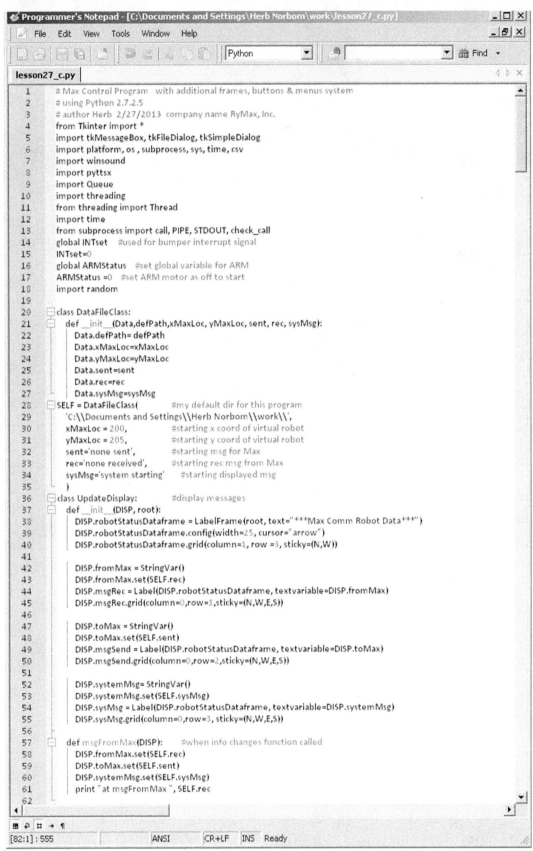

```python
1    # Max Control Program   with additional frames, buttons & menus system
2    # using Python 2.7.2.5
3    # author Herb 2/27/2013  company name RyMax, Inc.
4    from Tkinter import *
5    import tkMessageBox, tkFileDialog, tkSimpleDialog
6    import platform, os , subprocess, sys, time, csv
7    import winsound
8    import pyttsx
9    import Queue
10   import threading
11   from threading import Thread
12   import time
13   from subprocess import call, PIPE, STDOUT, check_call
14   global INTset   #used for bumper interrupt signal
15   INTset=0
16   global ARMStatus   #set global variable for ARM
17   ARMStatus =0   #set ARM motor as off to start
18   import random
19
20   class DataFileClass:
21       def __init__(Data,defPath,xMaxLoc, yMaxLoc, sent, rec, sysMsg):
22           Data.defPath= defPath
23           Data.xMaxLoc=xMaxLoc
24           Data.yMaxLoc=yMaxLoc
25           Data.sent=sent
26           Data.rec=rec
27           Data.sysMsg=sysMsg
28   SELF = DataFileClass(           #my default dir for this program
29       'C:\\Documents and Settings\\Herb Norbom\\work\\',
30       xMaxLoc = 200,              #starting x coord of virtual robot
31       yMaxLoc = 205,              #starting y coord of virtual robot
32       sent='none sent',          #starting msg for Max
33       rec='none received',       #starting rec msg from Max
34       sysMsg='system starting'   #starting displayed msg
35       )
36   class UpdateDisplay:          #display messages
37       def __init__(DISP, root):
38           DISP.robotStatusDataframe = LabelFrame(root, text="***Max Comm Robot Data***")
39           DISP.robotStatusDataframe.config(width=25, cursor="arrow")
40           DISP.robotStatusDataframe.grid(column=1, row =3, sticky=(N,W))
41
42           DISP.fromMax = StringVar()
43           DISP.fromMax.set(SELF.rec)
44           DISP.msgRec = Label(DISP.robotStatusDataframe, textvariable=DISP.fromMax)
45           DISP.msgRec.grid(column=0,row=1,sticky=(N,W,E,S))
46
47           DISP.toMax = StringVar()
48           DISP.toMax.set(SELF.sent)
49           DISP.msgSend = Label(DISP.robotStatusDataframe, textvariable=DISP.toMax)
50           DISP.msgSend.grid(column=0,row=2,sticky=(N,W,E,S))
51
52           DISP.systemMsg= StringVar()
53           DISP.systemMsg.set(SELF.sysMsg)
54           DISP.sysMsg = Label(DISP.robotStatusDataframe, textvariable=DISP.systemMsg)
55           DISP.sysMsg.grid(column=0,row=3, sticky=(N,W,E,S))
56
57       def msgFromMax(DISP):    #when info changes function called
58           DISP.fromMax.set(SELF.rec)
59           DISP.toMax.set(SELF.sent)
60           DISP.systemMsg.set(SELF.sysMsg)
61           print "at msgFromMax ", SELF.rec
62
```

[82:1] : 555   ANSI   CR+LF   INS   Ready

Exhibit155

77

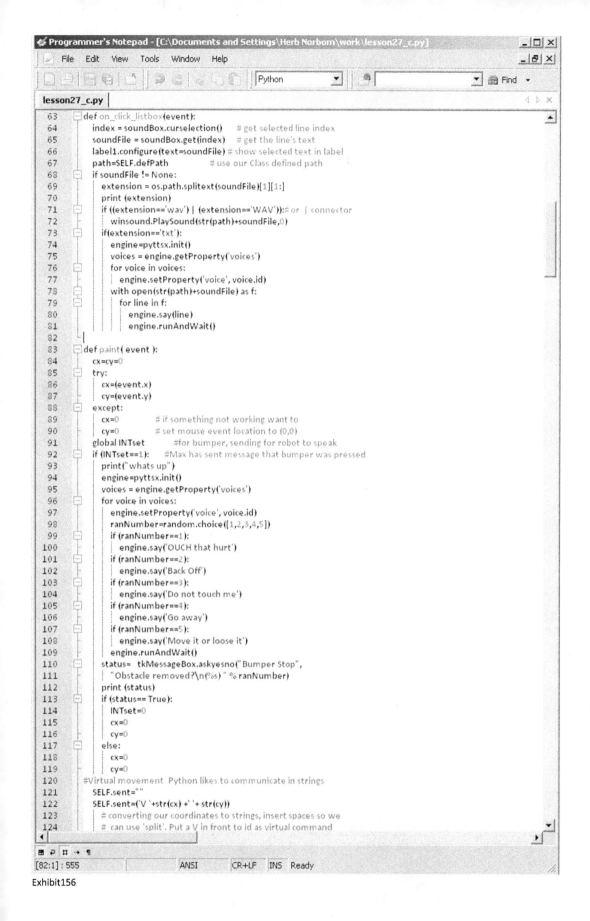

```
63   def on_click_listbox(event):
64       index = soundBox.curselection()      # get selected line index
65       soundFile = soundBox.get(index)      # get the line's text
66       label1.configure(text=soundFile)  # show selected text in label
67       path=SELF.defPath            # use our Class defined path
68       if soundFile != None:
69           extension = os.path.splitext(soundFile)[1][1:]
70           print (extension)
71           if ((extension=='wav') | (extension=='WAV')):# or | connector
72               winsound.PlaySound(str(path)+soundFile,0)
73           if(extension=='txt'):
74               engine=pyttsx.init()
75               voices = engine.getProperty('voices')
76               for voice in voices:
77                   engine.setProperty('voice', voice.id)
78               with open(str(path)+soundFile) as f:
79                   for line in f:
80                       engine.say(line)
81                       engine.runAndWait()
82
83   def paint( event ):
84       cx=cy=0
85       try:
86           cx=(event.x)
87           cy=(event.y)
88       except:
89           cx=0            # if something not working want to
90           cy=0            # set mouse event location to (0,0)
91       global INTset        #for bumper, sending for robot to speak
92       if (INTset==1):      #Max has sent message that bumper was pressed
93           print("whats up")
94           engine=pyttsx.init()
95           voices = engine.getProperty('voices')
96           for voice in voices:
97               engine.setProperty('voice', voice.id)
98               ranNumber=random.choice([1,2,3,4,5])
99               if (ranNumber==1):
100                  engine.say('OUCH that hurt')
101              if (ranNumber==2):
102                  engine.say('Back Off')
103              if (ranNumber==3):
104                  engine.say('Do not touch me')
105              if (ranNumber==4):
106                  engine.say('Go away')
107              if (ranNumber==5):
108                  engine.say('Move it or loose it')
109              engine.runAndWait()
110          status=  tkMessageBox.askyesno("Bumper Stop",
111              "Obstacle removed?\n(%s) " % ranNumber)
112          print (status)
113          if (status== True):
114              INTset=0
115              cx=0
116              cy=0
117          else:
118              cx=0
119              cy=0
120      #Virtual movement  Python likes to communicate in strings
121          SELF.sent=""
122          SELF.sent=('V '+str(cx) +' ' + str(cy))
123              # converting our coordinates to strings, insert spaces so we
124              # can use 'split'. Put a V in front to id as virtual command
```

Exhibit156

```python
125    try:
126        SendQueue.put(SELF.sent)        # writing to our queue
127    except:
128        print'Queue error on write' # we want to know about an error,
129    time.sleep(.2)   # keep running, slow down the works, mouse data
130        # stream of signals is too fast for the program to keep up
131        # with.
132    #Max physical movement
133    try:
134        calLeft=leftWheel(cx, cy)   #cal power & direction left wheel
135        calRight=rightWheel(cy,cx)   #cal power & direction right wheel
136    except:
137        print 'error on Max speed calLeft= ',calLeft,'calRight= ',calRight
138        calLeft='X+000'            #if error want to set power to 0
139        calRight='Y+000'
140    SELF.sent=(str(calLeft) + str(calRight)) #put into string format
141    try:
142        SendQueue.put(SELF.sent)            #write to queue
143    except:
144        print'Queue error on write' # we want to know about an error,
145    SELF.sysMsg='Robot movement'    # keep running, display on message
146    updatedisplay.msgFromMax()    # pannel refresh the display
147
148    def leftWheel(cx, cy):       #Physical Max, compute left wheel power
149        calLeft=0
150        try:
151            calLeft=(-cy+cx)
152        except:
153            calLeft=0
154        if (calLeft==0):
155            calLeft="X+000"
156            return calLeft
157        if (calLeft >0):
158            if (calLeft > 255):
159                calLeft = "X+255"
160                return calLeft
161            if (calLeft>99):
162                calLeft ="X+" +str(calLeft)
163                return calLeft
164            if (calLeft>9):
165                calLeft ="X+0" +str(calLeft)
166                return calLeft
167            else:
168                calLeft ="X+00" +str(calLeft)
169                return calLeft
170        if (calLeft < 0):
171            calLeft = abs(calLeft)
172            if (calLeft > 255):
173                calLeft = "X-255"
174                return calLeft
175            if (calLeft>99):
176                calLeft ="X-" +str(calLeft)
177                return calLeft
178            if (calLeft>9):
179                calLeft ="X-0" +str(calLeft)
180                return calLeft
181            else:
182                calLeft ="X-00" +str(calLeft)
183                return calLeft
184        else:
185            calLeft="X+000"
186            return calLeft
```

Exhibit157

79

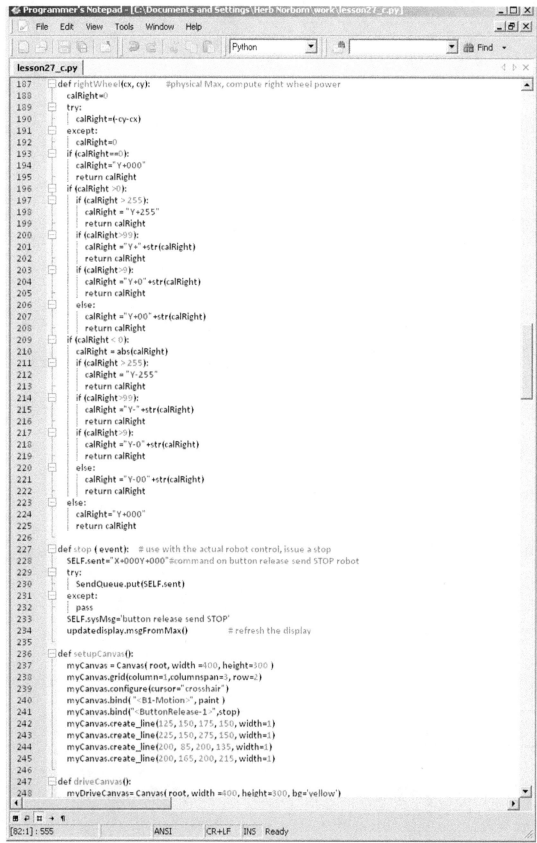

```python
187    def rightWheel(cx, cy):      #physical Max, compute right wheel power
188        calRight=0
189        try:
190            calRight=(-cy-cx)
191        except:
192            calRight=0
193        if (calRight==0):
194            calRight="Y+000"
195            return calRight
196        if (calRight >0):
197            if (calRight > 255):
198                calRight = "Y+255"
199                return calRight
200            if (calRight>99):
201                calRight ="Y+"+str(calRight)
202                return calRight
203            if (calRight>9):
204                calRight ="Y+0"+str(calRight)
205                return calRight
206            else:
207                calRight ="Y+00"+str(calRight)
208                return calRight
209        if (calRight < 0):
210            calRight = abs(calRight)
211            if (calRight > 255):
212                calRight = "Y-255"
213                return calRight
214            if (calRight>99):
215                calRight ="Y-"+str(calRight)
216                return calRight
217            if (calRight>9):
218                calRight ="Y-0"+str(calRight)
219                return calRight
220            else:
221                calRight ="Y-00"+str(calRight)
222                return calRight
223        else:
224            calRight="Y+000"
225            return calRight
226
227    def stop (event):    # use with the actual robot control, issue a stop
228        SELF.sent="X+000Y+000"#command on button release send STOP robot
229        try:
230            SendQueue.put(SELF.sent)
231        except:
232            pass
233        SELF.sysMsg='button release send STOP'
234        updatedisplay.msgFromMax()            # refresh the display
235
236    def setupCanvas():
237        myCanvas = Canvas( root, width =400, height=300 )
238        myCanvas.grid(column=1,columnspan=3, row=2)
239        myCanvas.configure(cursor="crosshair")
240        myCanvas.bind( "<B1-Motion>", paint )
241        myCanvas.bind("<ButtonRelease-1>",stop)
242        myCanvas.create_line(125, 150, 175, 150, width=1)
243        myCanvas.create_line(225, 150, 275, 150, width=1)
244        myCanvas.create_line(200,  85, 200, 135, width=1)
245        myCanvas.create_line(200, 165, 200, 215, width=1)
246
247    def driveCanvas():
248        myDriveCanvas= Canvas( root, width =400, height=300, bg='yellow')
```

Exhibit158

80

Programmer's Notepad - [C:\Documents and Settings\Herb Norbom\work\lesson27_c.py]
File   Edit   View   Tools   Window   Help
Python   Find ▾

lesson27_c.py

```python
249        myDriveCanvas.grid(column=0, columnspan=3, row=4)
250        myDriveCanvas.create_rectangle(SELF.xMaxLoc, SELF.yMaxLoc, SELF.xMaxLoc -10, SELF.yMaxLoc -10, fill='black')
251        return
252
253    def setupDriveCanvas(cx,cy):
254        try:
255            cx+=1        #add 1 to make sure cx and cy are integers
256            cy+=1
257            cx-=1        #return to correct values
258            cy-=1
259        except:
260            return("ERROR not integer")
261
262        driveCanvas()
263        if (cx > SELF.xMaxLoc):
264            while cx != SELF.xMaxLoc:
265                SELF.xMaxLoc = SELF.xMaxLoc+1
266                driveCanvas()
267            if (cy > SELF.yMaxLoc):
268                while cy != SELF.yMaxLoc:
269                    SELF.yMaxLoc = SELF.yMaxLoc+1
270                    driveCanvas()
271            if (cy < SELF.yMaxLoc):
272                while cy != SELF.yMaxLoc:
273                    SELF.yMaxLoc = SELF.yMaxLoc-1
274                    driveCanvas()
275        if (cx < SELF.xMaxLoc):
276            while cx != SELF.xMaxLoc:
277                SELF.xMaxLoc = SELF.xMaxLoc-1
278                driveCanvas()
279            if (cy > SELF.yMaxLoc):
280                while cy != SELF.yMaxLoc:
281                    SELF.yMaxLoc = SELF.yMaxLoc+1
282                    driveCanvas()
283            if (cy < SELF.yMaxLoc):
284                while cy != SELF.yMaxLoc:
285                    SELF.yMaxLoc = SELF.yMaxLoc-1
286                    driveCanvas()
287        return (True)        # no value needs to be returned, put here to prove completion
288
289    def receiving():
290        #this will be when receiving communications from Max
291        while True:
292            pass
293
294    def sending():
295        while True:
296            try:
297                qaction = SendQueue.qsize()        #see if a message in queue
298            except:
299                print('error on get queue size')
300                qaction=0
301            if (qaction >0):
302                msgLen=0
303                msgRec =''
304                try:
305                    msgRec = SendQueue.get()  #retrieve string from queue
306                    msgLen = msgRec.__len__()
307                    newMsg= msgRec.split()        #works like a tuple
308                except:
309                    print 'error getting queue msg or size'
310                if (msgLen > 2):
```

Exhibit159

81

```python
311        #for virtual robot
312            if newMsg[0] =='V':        # virtual robot command
313                try:
314                    cx = int(newMsg[1])
315                    cy = int(newMsg[2])
316                    finished=setupDriveCanvas(cx, cy)
317                    print finished   #simple verifation for debugging
318                except:
319                    print 'Error on conversion to integer'
320
321            while 1:#throw away eveything in queue, when we get error
322                try:# With the delay built in, probably not needed,
323                    trash = SendQueue.get_nowait() #but we will need
324                except:    #to empty the queue in later programs
325                    break # break just means stop this function and
326                    # continue, using pass would lock up the program
327
328    def threadStart():      #starting child threads
329        recTh=Thread(target=receiving, name='recThread',args=())
330        recTh.setDaemon(True) # must set all child threads before starting
331        senTh=Thread(target=sending,name='sendThread', args=())
332        senTh.setDaemon(True)
333        try:
334            print'staring recTh'
335            recTh.start()
336        except:
337            print('CRITICAL ERROR starting recThread')
338        try:
339            print 'starting senTh'
340            senTh.start()
341        except:
342            print('CRITICAL ERROR starting sendThread')
343        thCount= threading.active_count()
344        print('# of threads = ',thCount)
345        thNames= threading.enumerate()
346        print (thNames)
347
348    def shutdown():
349        print("called shutdown")
350        answer=tkMessageBox.askyesno("EXIT", "Do you really want to quit")
351        if answer==True:
352            thCount= threading.active_count()
353            print('# of threads to stop = ',thCount)
354            thNames= threading.enumerate()
355            print (thNames)
356            while 1:        #try to send any messages in the queue
357                try:
358                    sending = SendQueue.get_nowait()
359                except:
360                    break
361            try:
362                root.quit() #with daemon set 'True' kills child threads also
363            except:
364                print(" ERROR   could not be terminated")
365
366    def windowsNotepad():
367        osType=platform.system()
368        print osType
369        if (osType=='Windows'):
370            try:
371                command = 'C:\WINDOWS\NOTEPAD.EXE'
372                env    ={'FOO': 'bar', 'SystemRoot': os.environ['SystemRoot']}
```

Exhibit160

```
373            p = subprocess.Popen(command, env=env)
374            p.wait()
375            return
376         except OSError as e:
377            print "Read Error %s: %s\n error no %d"%(command,e.args[1], e.args[0])
378            formatError="Program\n"+command+"\n could not be run\n"+e.args[1]
379            formatError=formatError+"\n Error No= "+str(e.args[0])
380            tkMessageBox.showerror("OSError",formatError)
381         except:
382            print("General error opening NOTEPAD.exe")
383      print("Notepad appears to be unavailable on this system")
384
385   def startProNotepad():
386      try:
387         command = "C:\\WinAVR-20100110\\pn\\pn.exe" #for 2010 users
388         subprocess.call( [command])
389      except OSError as e:
390         print "Read Error %s: %s\n error no %d"%(command,e.args[1], e.args[0])
391         formatError="Program\n"+command+"\n could not be run\n"+e.args[1]
392         formatError=formatError+"\n Error No= "+str(e.args[0])
393         tkMessageBox.showerror("OSError",formatError)
394
395   def showPythonVersion():
396      pyVersion=sys.version
397      tkMessageBox.showwarning('Python Version',pyVersion)
398
399   def showSystemPlatform():
400      import platform
401      osType=platform.system()
402      osPlatform=platform.win32_ver()
403      osProcessor=platform.processor()
404      tkMessageBox.showwarning('System Information', 'Operating System: '+ osType +
405         '\nSystem Info:'+osPlatform[0]+'\nRelease: '+osPlatform[1]+'\nService Pack: '+
406         osPlatform[2]+'\nMultiProcessor: '+osPlatform[3]+'\nProcessor: ' + osProcessor)
407
408   def showRyMax():
409      tkMessageBox.showwarning('RyMax, Inc.','RyMax, Inc.'+
410         '\n web page: www.RyMax.biz'+
411         '\n e-mail: herb@RyMax.biz')
412
413   def searchPaths():
414      searchWin=Toplevel()
415      searchFrame = LabelFrame(searchWin,text="Python Search Paths", width =100,   height=10)
416      searchFrame.grid(column=0, row=0, sticky =NW)
417      searchBox=Listbox(searchFrame, width=150,height=10)
418      searchBox.grid(column=0, row=0,sticky=NW)
419      scrollBar = Scrollbar(searchFrame, orient=VERTICAL, command=searchBox.yview)
420      scrollBar.grid(column=1, row=0,sticky=(N,W,E,S))
421      searchBox['yscrollcommand']=scrollBar.set
422
423      myPythonSearch=[]
424      for folder in sys.path:
425         print folder
426         myPythonSearch.append (folder)
427
428      for item in myPythonSearch:
429         searchBox.insert('end',item)
430
431   def ARMOnOff():
432      global ARMStatus
433      if (ARMStatus==0):           #ARM is off
434         SELF.sent="]134567890"     #turn ARM on
```

Exhibit161

83

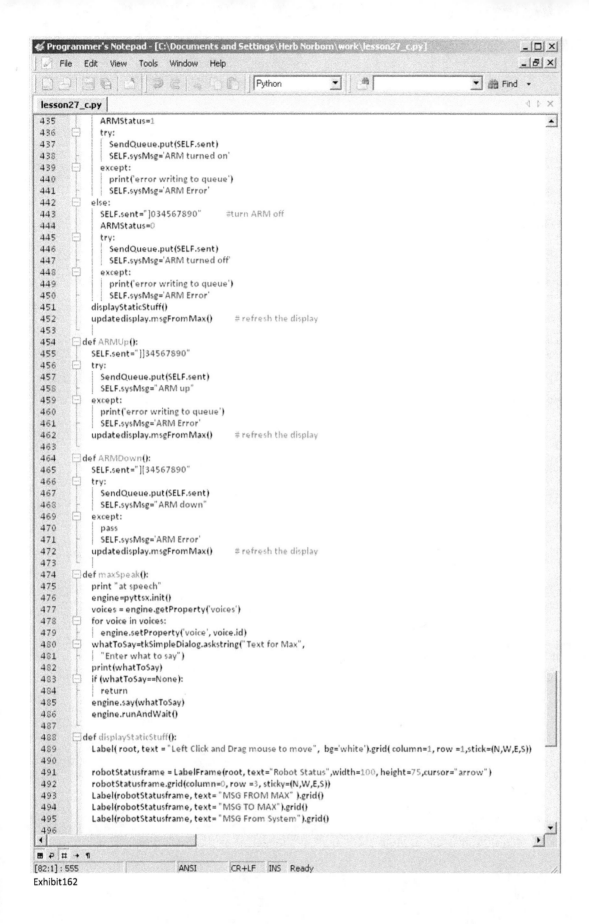

```
435        ARMStatus=1
436        try:
437            SendQueue.put(SELF.sent)
438            SELF.sysMsg='ARM turned on'
439        except:
440            print('error writing to queue')
441            SELF.sysMsg='ARM Error'
442        else:
443            SELF.sent="]034567890"        #turn ARM off
444        ARMStatus=0
445        try:
446            SendQueue.put(SELF.sent)
447            SELF.sysMsg='ARM turned off'
448        except:
449            print('error writing to queue')
450            SELF.sysMsg='ARM Error'
451        displayStaticStuff()
452        updatedisplay.msgFromMax()        # refresh the display
453
454    def ARMUp():
455        SELF.sent="]]34567890"
456        try:
457            SendQueue.put(SELF.sent)
458            SELF.sysMsg="ARM up"
459        except:
460            print('error writing to queue')
461            SELF.sysMsg='ARM Error'
462        updatedisplay.msgFromMax()        # refresh the display
463
464    def ARMDown():
465        SELF.sent="][34567890"
466        try:
467            SendQueue.put(SELF.sent)
468            SELF.sysMsg="ARM down"
469        except:
470            pass
471            SELF.sysMsg='ARM Error'
472        updatedisplay.msgFromMax()        # refresh the display
473
474    def maxSpeak():
475        print "at speech"
476        engine=pyttsx.init()
477        voices = engine.getProperty('voices')
478        for voice in voices:
479            engine.setProperty('voice', voice.id)
480        whatToSay=tkSimpleDialog.askstring("Text for Max",
481            "Enter what to say")
482        print(whatToSay)
483        if (whatToSay==None):
484            return
485        engine.say(whatToSay)
486        engine.runAndWait()
487
488    def displayStaticStuff():
489        Label( root, text = "Left Click and Drag mouse to move",  bg='white').grid( column=1, row =1,stick=(N,W,E,S))
490
491        robotStatusframe = LabelFrame(root, text="Robot Status",width=100, height=75,cursor="arrow")
492        robotStatusframe.grid(column=0, row =3, sticky=(N,W,E,S))
493        Label(robotStatusframe, text= "MSG FROM MAX" ).grid()
494        Label(robotStatusframe, text= "MSG TO MAX").grid()
495        Label(robotStatusframe, text= "MSG From System").grid()
496
```

Exhibit162

```
497        bFrame = LabelFrame(root,width=100, height=15)
498        bFrame.grid(column=0,columnspan=4, row=0, sticky=(N,W,S))
499        Button(bFrame, text = "MAXSPEAK", fg="white", command = maxSpeak).grid(column=0, row=0)
500        print 'armstatus= ',ARMStatus
501        if (ARMStatus==0):
502            Button(bFrame, text = "ARM OFF", fg="yellow", command=ARMOnOff).grid(column=2, row=0)
503        if (ARMStatus==1):
504            Button(bFrame, text = "ARM ON", fg="green", command=ARMOnOff).grid(column=2, row=0)
505        Button(bFrame, text = "ARMUp", fg="green", command = ARMUp).grid(column=3, row=0)
506        Button(bFrame, text = "ARMDown", fg="green", command = ARMDown).grid(column=4,row=0)
507        Button(bFrame, text = "SHUTDOWN", fg="red", command = shutdown).grid(column=5, row=0)
508
509    if __name__=='__main__':
510        root = Tk()
511        root.title( "Max Control Center" )
512        root.geometry( "550x620+50+30" ) #width, height, place on y & x axis
513        setupCanvas()
514    #pull down menu section
515        menubar = Menu(root)
516        root.config(menu=menubar)
517        filemenu = Menu(menubar, tearoff=0)
518        filemenu.add_command(label="Windows Notepad", command=windowsNotepad)
519        filemenu.add_separator()
520        filemenu.add_command(label="Programmer's Notepad", command=startProNotepad)
521        filemenu.add_separator()
522        filemenu.add_separator()
523        filemenu.add_command(label="Exit", command=shutdown)#note function chg
524        menubar.add_cascade(menu=filemenu, label='File')
525        sysMenu=Menu(menubar, tearoff=0)
526        sysMenu.add_command(label="Python version?", command=showPythonVersion)
527        sysMenu.add_command(label="System Platform?", command=showSystemPlatform)
528        sysMenu.add_command(label="Python Search Paths", command=searchPaths)
529        sysMenu.add_command(label="RyMax, Inc. Information?", command=showRyMax)
530        menubar.add_cascade(label="System Info", menu=sysMenu)
531    #setup a list box to list our wav and txt files
532        soundFrame = LabelFrame(root, text="Max Sounds",width=20, height=10,cursor="arrow")
533        soundFrame.grid(column=0, row =2, sticky=(N,W,S))
534        soundBox=Listbox(soundFrame, width=20, height=18)
535        soundBox.grid(column=0,row=1,sticky=(N,W,S))
536        scrollBar = Scrollbar(soundFrame, orient=VERTICAL, command=soundBox.yview)
537        scrollBar.grid(column=1,row=1, sticky=(N,E,S))
538        soundBox['yscrollcommand']=scrollBar.set
539        path=SELF.defPath
540        print path
541        soundlist = os.listdir(path)
542    # load the listbox
543        for sound in soundlist:
544            extension = os.path.splitext(sound)[1][1:]
545            if ((extension=='wav') | (extension=='WAV') | (extension=='txt')):
546                soundBox.insert('end', sound)
547        label1 = Label(soundFrame, text='click to play', width=20, bg='white')
548        label1.grid(column=0, row=0)
549        soundBox.bind('<ButtonRelease-1>', on_click_listbox)
550        SendQueue = Queue.LifoQueue()
551        threadStart()
552        displayStaticStuff()
553        updatedisplay=UpdateDisplay(root)#get the initial display filled in
554        mainloop()
```

[82:1] : 555   ANSI   CR+LF   INS Ready

Exhibit162A

We are getting very close, but before we add our serial communications, I want to add something that our virtual robot can bump into and set off the bumper interrupt. On Max the bumper will only be on the front bumper, but for our virtual robot it will be on all sides. Why? This method is easier.

Save your file as lesson28.py and move on to the next day.

Day Twenty Six - Virtual Bumper

As you saw with our previous code screen shots, our program is getting a little large. While we can break it into modules, for now I will leave as is. I will just be showing the new code and code changes for now. I added some code that our virtual robot executes if it drives off the canvas. Put in your own wise guy remarks. Once we begin communicating with Max we need to remember to change this around.

Exhibit163

I changed some of the remarks around, notice line 109 with the use of an apostrophe inside of the quotation marks. At this point while we have covered many of the basic features of Python, we have only scratched the surface. To continue we are going to import a module. As I said earlier I like ActiveState because of their easy access to updates and importing of new modules.

Day Twenty Seven - Serial Communications

We are ready to develop our serial communications, but first we need to see if you have the module installed. The easiest way to see if the serial module is installed on your computer is to use our command prompt the usual way. At the command prompt type python, and when Python starts type import serial, if you get error messages you will need to obtain the module, if no errors you already have it. In case you forgot how to exit, it is Ctrl z. If it is not installed go back to Day Twenty - Sounds for your Robot.

Day Twenty Eight - Getting Ready to Build

This is where the robot meets the road. This is arguably the most difficult section. It becomes difficult for a number of reasons that include: new concepts in Python, communication between a PC and a microchip, uses serial communication, uses C programming language with bit manipulation, understanding Data Sheets and registers, and wiring a board. We are going to try somewhat easy steps with suggestions for outside projects that if completed will help you master the basics. Each step of the process has the potential to make success of the project difficult.

You are going to need some components to complete this section. If you already have good knowledge you can choose your own path. For those of you just getting started I suggest you look at some of the learning kits and instructions available. I went down the NerdKit path as this was priced very well and their web site offers great tutorials. Their forum has good advice also. You can even email and get some help. Their site is http://www.nerdkits.com/. While my examples will use the ATMEGA328p, the standard ATMEGA168 is adequate for your startup needs. The chips are very similar from a programming view, and you will not waste time learning how to use the 168 chip.   You are also going to need a fairly good digital MultiMeter. As you get into buying chips and other parts, you may notice that you can buy micro processing chips for less at some distributors. Be aware that the chips need to have a bootloader, or bootstrap on them before you can load your program on to them. You need special hardware to load the bootloader. For now get chips that have the bootloader on them.

As you query the internet you will find many references to the Arduino®. Their basic info site is: http://www.arduino.cc/ . There are a lot of places to buy the boards from. Generally you can get a manufactured board that you can buy preassembled or that you can build out. There are a lot of products, you will need to research which one is best for you. If you go this route and want to follow the lessons you will want one with the ATmega328 chip.   There is a lot of information available on the web for these products.

At some point you are going to want to solder. There are a number of tutorials on the web, just do a search. A soldering iron that has variable temperature setting is worth the investment. While you can get by without one for now, keep your eyes open for a fairly good one.

Day Twenty Nine - The Microchip

Hardware

For this section to work you need to have established communication with your microchip. I will be using hardware purchased from NerdKit. I have the LCD wired and referenced in the program. If you do not want to use the LCD comment out the reference lines. I will be using the ATMega328p with the NerdKit crystal, a serial usb connection cable also from NerdKit. As you can see from the picture I am just using wires plugged into the breadboard. For development purposes breadboards are great, they come in different sizes. I also like to use connection wires with alligator clips. Instead of a battery I am using a 9v DC power supply. The voltage regulator brings the voltage down to 5v.   The hardware setup is pretty much from the NerdKit Guide. You may notice the component that the chip is set in.   It is called a ZIF Socket. While you can plug the chip directly into the breadboard I like the ease of using the ZIF Socket. The other change is that I added a LED with a resistor that flashes when the program starts.

Exhibit164

Additional information on pySerial: http://pyserial.sourceforge.net/. Before we get to the new program I hope you have completed the NerdKit Guide and have an understanding of C programming. Your knowledge needs to include how to upload your program to the microchip.

Hint. Static electricity is not your friend. If you fry a part or two you will be a believer. Get used to grounding yourself prior to touching parts or setup a grounded work space environment.

The LCD used is part of the NerdKit. Note this component uses the NerdKit software library.   See www.nerdkits.com for the LCD wiring diagram.

Bread Board Diagram

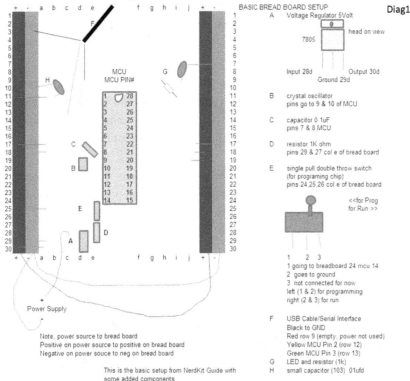

Make Command

The NerdKit Guide gives an excellent introduction to C programming. I hope you have tried some of their tutorials also. With C programming the programs must be compiled and linked prior to uploading them to the microcomputer. This is accomplished via the 'make' command. As you have noticed each program that you upload needs specific instructions in the 'make' file. For each C program you will want a separate directory. If you have a working program, make a new directory, and copy the contents over to that new directory. Assuming you are using the NerdKit examples you will need to have your new directory at the same level as the other NerdKit directories, so that your program can access the NerdKit libraries. I made a new directory ATMEGA328TEST. Once you have copied over the files. Start your new program add some comments for now. Save as AT328serial.c. Make the appropriate changes to the make file. I like to use the search and replace feature of the Programmer's Notepad.

You are going to be in and out of this directory a lot, I suggest you set up a bat file. Very similar to what we set up earlier. Save the bat file in the directory where your command prompt opens, just as before. As I tend to have multiple versions of many items I like to name the bat files with identifiers in the name.

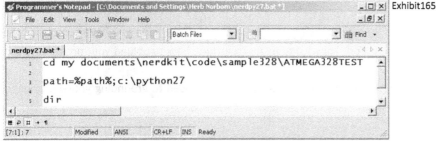

Exhibit165

Setup your bat file as appropriate for your directory structure. If you haven't already done it, you need to change your 'make' file to something similar to the following which is from the NerdKit examples.

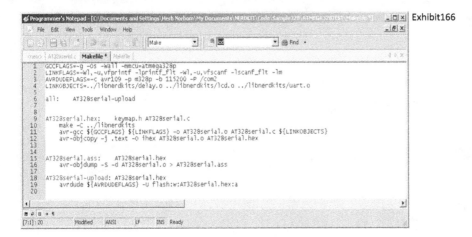
Exhibit166

PuTTY

For our communications you will need HyperTerminal® or PuTTY© or some other terminal interface program. If you do not have HyperTerminal I suggest you try PuTTY. The following describes how to obtain the PuTTY executable. Go to the main PuTTY Download Page.   http://www.chiark.greenend.org.uk/~sgtatham/putty/download.html.   From this page you can select the appropriate file. I suggest you get the Windows installer for everything except PuTTYel. At this point the latest release is version .62.   Installer: putty-062-installer.exe. After you download run the 'putty-0.62-installer.exe'.   As I said before I use the default installations.

Exhibits 167 - 169

Exhibits 170- 172

Exhibits 173 & 174

Open PuTTY and click on Serial, make appropriate changes.   I am setting up for baud of 9600, as this speed is what I plan to use in our communication to the Robot. Also I have set Flow control to 'None'. The PuTTY help files should be included if things are not working. Saving your session is just a little tricky. Step by step. Open PuTTY, I have saved a number of sessions as shown in the following.   Name your session putty_9600. Enter 'putty_9600' in the Saves Sessions label. Notice the default values have been loaded, in my case they are COM2 and Speed 155500.

Exhibit175

Click on Serial and make the appropriate changes. Click 'Session', the starting window will reopen.

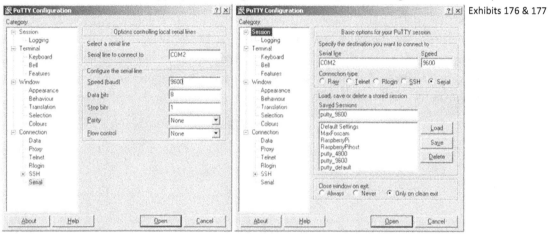
Exhibits 176 & 177

Click the Save button. You can go ahead and open and close. Check that your settings have been saved.

HyperTerminal

With HyperTerminal you will go through something similar but of course very different. On the NerdKit web site under the 'servo squirter' tutorial, there is a good discussion on HyperTerminal. If you have HyperTerminal it can generally be found from the Start window, All Programs, Accessories, and Communications. Suggest you create a shortcut and paste to your desktop. Open HyperTerminal and click on the Cancel button of the Connection Description.

Exhibit178

You will then click on File, New Connection and below I show what my setup is.

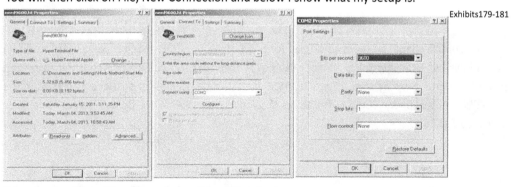
Exhibits179-181

Save your configuration file and close HyperTerminal.

Now when you reopen HyperTerminal, cancel as before, click on File and Open and you should see your configuration file. If you need to adjust the configuration highlight the file and right click and open Properties. You can setup multiple configuration files, just like with PuTTY.

Day Thirty - C program with Serial Communication

We are now ready to get back to our AT328serial.c program. One item of key importance is for you to get familiar with product Data Sheets. In the code for this project I will be referencing the Atmega328P Data Sheet. We are going to be setting up registers in our code that turn on and off various features for USART, our serial protocol. I have selected 9600 as our desired BAUD rate. I selected it because of the very low error rate for the crystal oscillator we are using, and it is fast enough for our purposes. Our crystal frequency is 14.7456 MHz's. Based on the table below, we want to set the UBRRn register at 95. (We are using U2Xn =0, of the UCSRnA register and has an Initial Value of 0. See page 195 of Data Sheet. We are not going to bother with setup, just know we are using it.)

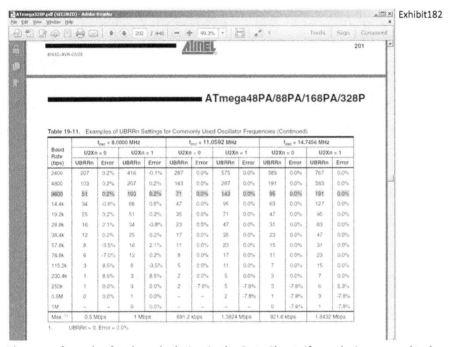 Exhibit182

There are formulas for the calculation in the Data Sheet, if you desire or need to because your frequency is not shown.

Bit Manipulation

In order to program or set the registers on a microchip you have to understand bit manipulation. There are excellent sources on the web, including the NerdKit site and their Guide. Some other sites are: http://www.cprogramming.com/tutorial/bitwise_operators.html, http://en.wikipedia.org/wiki/Bitwise_operations_in_C. There are many examples. As you look at examples on the web you will quickly become aware that there are many programming languages that can do bit manipulation. In the following, I briefly touched on the subject. Just like other programming commands you will find there are different ways to skin the cat.

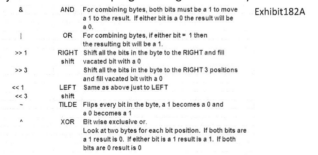 Exhibit182A

A small sample of decimal numbers and their 8 bit binary representation are shown in Exhibit182B.

Ref Code	Decimal Value	7 6 5 4 3 2 1 0 BIT POSITION
A	0	0 0 0 0 0 0 0 0
B	1	0 0 0 0 0 0 0 1
C	2	0 0 0 0 0 0 1 0
D	3	0 0 0 0 0 0 1 1
E	4	0 0 0 0 0 1 0 0
F	5	0 0 0 0 0 1 0 1
G	6	0 0 0 0 0 1 1 0
H	7	0 0 0 0 0 1 1 1
I	8	0 0 0 0 1 0 0 0
J	9	0 0 0 0 1 0 0 1
K	10	0 0 0 0 1 0 1 0

SIMPLE EXAMPES USING ABOVE AS REFERENCE POINTS

	Bits	Decimal Value
A & B =	0 0 0 0 0 0 0 0	0
A | B =	0 0 0 0 0 0 0 1	1
G & H =	0 0 0 0 0 1 1 0	6
G | H =	0 0 0 0 0 1 1 1	7
K >>1 =	0 0 0 0 0 1 0 1	5
K<<1 =	0 0 0 1 0 1 0 0	20

In the following, we will set up actual C code for setting ATmega328P registers. As for now, we are working with the USART we will look at those registers. Hopefully, you have followed the various NerdKit tutorials as this register is more complicated than most because it splits into a High and Low register. For now, think of two individual registers. The register is split because a low baud rate UBRRn value would exceed 255, which is beyond the capacity of an 8 bit register. While we are really only concerned with the UBRRnL register we will also look at setting the UBRRnH register. From page 199 in the Data Sheet the register settings and definitions can be found.

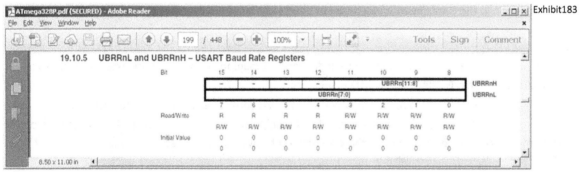

Exhibit183

Note that both registers have Initial Values of 0 for all bits. For a baud rate of 9600 we need to set the register at 95. Since 95 is less than 255 it will fit in the lower register. The simplest way to set both registers is the following C code. UBRROH=0; UBRROL=95; As you progress you are going to have to understand bit manipulation, so another way to think of it is to convert the decimal value of 95 to an 8 bit binary number, "01011111 ". One way to set it would be. UBRROL=(1<<6 | 1<<4 | 1<<3 | 1<<2 | 1<<1 |1<<0); The best way to explain this is in the first step, move over to bit #6 of UBRROL and insert 1, continue with each of the rest. There are many ways to set the bits, while above may not be the best way, I have found it easier to understand than many of the other methods.

To help visualize this remember how this will look in the register.

7	6	5	4	3	2	1	0	BIT POSITION
0	1	0	1	1	1	1	1	

This is an area that requires practice, also keep in mind you are going to see samples where programs use hex values to set the registers. While you need to know the various methods, pick what works for you and stick with it. Remember to comment your code.

In the following, I am posting the complete source code for AT328serial.c. If this is your first look at C you are going to have your hands full. I am not going to go into depth on items that I believe you may know.   I highly recommend the tutorials at NerdKit or for the Arduino.   You should be aware that C compliers can have differences and be aware of what libraries are being referenced. In particular there are differences in running the programs on the microcomputer vs. a PC. I am going to comment on a few general items that took some time to understand.

- Where we saw in Python that strings are pretty easy to work with, in C strings really do not exist as a data type. Strings are stored as arrays in C.
- A variable defined as 'Volatile' declares that the variable is to be available throughout the program.
- The order functions are listed in the program is critical from the view point that you need to define the function before referencing it as a call.
- The LCD display is neat but there are a number of sticky items. The display of variable data types that are integer or float or double are easy. The display of a variable array such as a string is cumbersome.
- Your PC is many times faster than our microchip. This creates timing problems when the two are communicating.
- The microchip has different memory types, vs. what you commonly use on your PC. The better your understanding of the microchip memory types the easier the code is to understand.

After you have keyed in the program, compiled, linked and uploaded to the microchip you are ready to run the program. As I mentioned before I am using the USB serial connector wire from NerdKit. I have found that I can let the make file use the 115200 speed of the com port. Even though I have the com port set at 9600. Serial and USB communications can be flaky. The buffers on the PC can fill up and bring on the blue screen of death, not to mention whatever else can crash your PC. Keep your files backed up and try not to have too much open on your PC when testing.

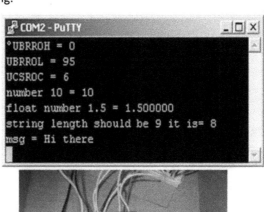

Exhibits 184-186

For these examples I left the USB serial cable in place. Open either PuTTY or HyperTerminal with the 9600 baud and other settings mentioned earlier and set the microchip to 'run' and turn on the power. You should get the above displayed. If you put the LED on the board you should also get a brief flash as the program loads and begins to run. Notice your LCD message also.

On the PuTTY screen type without spaces a short message, 10 characters max. As soon as you press a key a light on the breadboard will flash. When you press enter the program knows you are finished and displays in on the LCD and transmits it back to the PuTTY interface.

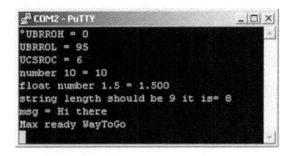

```
COM2 - PuTTY
°UBRROH = 0
UBRROL = 95
UCSROC = 6
number 10 = 10
float number 1.5 = 1.500
string length should be 9 it is= 8
msg = Hi there
Max ready WayToGo
```

The LCD clears the screen and displays the message on line 1. LCD should also display message. If you played with this you have noticed that a space is treated just like a return. I leave you to solve that issue if you like. For our communications with Max it will not matter. We are going to send a structured code to Max that is 10 characters long with no spaces. In this program I have put a number of extras that we will not need, but I thought it was worthwhile to demo them.

Programmer's Notepad - [C:\Documents and Settings\Herb Norbom\My Documents\NERDKIT\Code\Sample328\ATMEGA328TEST\AT328serial.c]

File   Edit   View   Tools   Window   Help

C/C++   tcsize   Find ▾

<new> | maxRobotControl83.py   **AT328serial.c**

```c
1    //for ATMega328 Herb Norbom, RyMax, Inc.3/3/2013
2    //for communications using serial port at 9600 BAUD via Hyper Termianal or Putty
3    //program will also work with our Python program
4    //to microchip with various displays on LCD
5    #define F_CPU 14745600
6    #include <stdio.h>
7    #include <stdlib.h>
8    #include <avr/io.h>
9    #include <avr/interrupt.h>
10   #include <avr/pgmspace.h>
11   #include <inttypes.h>
12   #include <string.h>
13   #include "../libnerdkits/io_328p.h"
14   #include "../libnerdkits/delay.h"
15   #include "../libnerdkits/lcd.h"
16   #include "../libnerdkits/uart.h"
17
18   volatile int i=0;                   //use as counter/incrementer
19   volatile unsigned char tcread[13];  //variable that receives from PC
20   volatile char aa;                   //a temp variable for LCD display of variable
21
22   void flash_led()
23       {
24       PORTC |= (1<<PC5);              // turn on LED signal ready and received
25       delay_ms(20);                   //delay  20 milliseconds light on
26       PORTC &= ~(1<<PC5);             // turn off LED
27       }
28
29   void myDisplay()
30       {
31       lcd_clear_and_home();
32       aa ='0';
33       if (tcread[0] !='\0'){aa=tcread[0];lcd_write_data(aa);}    // if not a space, display it
34       if (tcread[1] !='\0'){aa=tcread[1];lcd_write_data(aa);}
35       if (tcread[2] !='\0'){aa=tcread[2];lcd_write_data(aa);}
36       if (tcread[3] !='\0'){aa=tcread[3];lcd_write_data(aa);}
37       if (tcread[4] !='\0'){aa=tcread[4];lcd_write_data(aa);}
38       if (tcread[5] !='\0'){aa=tcread[5];lcd_write_data(aa);}
39       if (tcread[6] !='\0'){aa=tcread[6];lcd_write_data(aa);}
40       if (tcread[7] !='\0'){aa=tcread[7];lcd_write_data(aa);}
41       if (tcread[8] !='\0'){aa=tcread[8];lcd_write_data(aa);}
42       if (tcread[9] !='\0'){aa=tcread[9];lcd_write_data(aa);}
43       }
44
45   ISR(USART_RX_vect)
46       {
47           flash_led();                        //flash as interrupt fired have msg
48           lcd_clear_and_home();
49           for (i=0;i<13;i++)                        //clear variable
50               {
51               tcread[i]= ' ';
52               }
53
54           scanf_P(PSTR("%12s"),&tcread);      // read from uart receiver
55           printf_P(PSTR("Max ready %s\r\n"),tcread);   //send to uart
56           myDisplay();                        //display on LCD
57       }
58
59
```

Exhibit189

95

Programmer's Notepad - [C:\Documents and Settings\Herb Norbom\My Documents\NERDKIT\Code\Sample328\ATMEGA328TEST\AT328serial.c]

File   Edit   View   Tools   Window   Help

C/C++   ▼   tcsize   ▼   Find ·

<new>   maxRobotControl83.py   AT328serial.c

```c
60   int main() {
61       cli();                                      //stop the interupt detection while loading
62       uart_init();                                // start serial port
63       FILE uart_stream = FDEV_SETUP_STREAM(uart_putchar, uart_getchar, _FDEV_SETUP_RW);//uart stream
64       stdin = stdout = &uart_stream;
65       |       // SEE DATA SHEET PAGES 195 - 203 for setting on usart
66   //   UBRR0L = 95;            //WORKS  TRY uncommenting this line and comment out the next line
67       UBRR0L = (1<<6 | 1<<4 | 1<<3 | 1<<2 | 1<<1 | 1<<0);   //set BAUD at 9600
68       UBRR0H = 0;
69       UCSR0B |= (1<<RXCIE0); // enable uart RX RECEIVE Interrupt page 196
70
71       DDRC |= (1<<PC5);        // ready port LED signal-for valid receive and startup
72       delay_ms(500);           // pause to let you watch a little better
73       flash_led();             // flash ready signal
74
75       lcd_init();
76       FILE lcd_stream = FDEV_SETUP_STREAM(lcd_putchar, 0, _FDEV_SETUP_WRITE);  //LCD stream
77       printf_P(PSTR("UBRR0H = %d\r\n"),UBRR0H);      //sent to uart our register
78       printf_P(PSTR("UBRR0L = %d\r\n"),UBRR0L);      //sent to uart our register
79       printf_P(PSTR("UCSR0C = %d\r\n"),UCSR0C);      //sent to uart our register
80       lcd_home();              //ready LCD for display on line one
81       sei();                   //turn interrupt handler on
82
83       lcd_line_one();          // a little redundant but set LCD for line one
84       lcd_write_string(PSTR(" Congratulations! "));  //writes to LCD line one
85
86       lcd_line_two();
87       i=10;                    // set i = 10, defined as volatile
88       fprintf_P(&lcd_stream, PSTR(" Number 10 = %d"),i);   //write to LCD
89       printf_P(PSTR("number 10 = %d\r\n"),i);        //sent to uart
90
91       lcd_line_three();
92       double fp =1.5;
93       fprintf_P(&lcd_stream, PSTR("Number 1.5 = %.3f"),fp);  //write to LCD
94       printf_P(PSTR("float number 1.5 = %.3f\r\n"),fp);      //sent to uart
95
96       lcd_line_four();
97       const char *text1= PSTR("Hi there");
98       int lineLength =strlen_P(text1);             //computes lenth of variable text1 whic is in PSTR
99       printf_P(PSTR("string length should be 8 it is= %d\r\n"),lineLength);     //sent to uart
100      printf_P(PSTR("msg = "));        //sent to uart
101      printf_P(PSTR("%c"),text1[0]); //sent to uart
102      printf_P(PSTR("%c"),text1[1]); //sent to uart
103      printf_P(PSTR("%c"),text1[2]); //sent to uart
104      printf_P(PSTR("%c"),text1[3]); //sent to uart
105      printf_P(PSTR("%c"),text1[4]); //sent to uart
106      printf_P(PSTR("%c"),text1[5]); //sent to uart
107      printf_P(PSTR("%c"),text1[6]); //sent to uart
108      printf_P(PSTR("%c"),text1[7]); //sent to uart
109      printf_P(PSTR("%c"),text1[8]); //sent to uart
110      printf_P(PSTR("%c\r\n"));         //sent to uart END of message
111
112      while(1) {
113          delay_ms(50);
114
115      }
116      return 0;
117  }
```

Exhibit190

In developing a program like the one above I go through hundreds of failures. Just getting the program to compile is sometimes a major victory. You may have noticed in some of your compiles that you get warning messages. The program loads and appears to run fine, so you may be tempted to ignore the warnings. If you really understand what the warning means and are sure your program will never encounter those events you may be ok leaving them. But, let's face it we probably do not understand the cryptic compiler message. At some point your program will blow up, it may be due to the warning message; it may be low battery power, or any number of other events. It would be nice to know you at least had a clean compile. Some of the program lines key points are shown in the following:

- Line 18 – volatile sets the variable to be available to all functions, similar to global in Python
- Line 19 – tcread [13] sets the variable to a maximum size of 13, remember to allow for the termination character. Space is not too critical, give yourself some extra room.
- Line 20—Set the 'aa' for the LCD, writing a string to the LCD is tricky. The function myDisplay uses it. Feel free to come up with a better way of handling.
- Line 45 – This is the interrupt for USART. When a signal is detected this function executes.
- Line 54 – While you have certainly seen the scan functions, note that you can set the length of the string output. Without this limit if your input is greater than the size of the variable your program will crash. Try setting to just %s and running

96

with input from PuTTY or HyperTerminal and entering 15 characters. It may take a line or two of input but you will crash. In some cases your microchip will simply reboot. If you were running the microchip with a battery and just gave the motor a startup command a voltage drop would look just like this error.

- Lines 67-69 –Set the Baud rate and enable the UART interrupt for receive.
- Lines 77 -79 – Just wanted to show that you can print out registers. Certainly not needed in the program, but good to know.
- Lines 83-110 – Are just to show various LCD types of display.

Before we put the code into our control panel I want to get a simple version running. HINT. While we are developing our transmission to Max you can just type the message into HyperTerminal or PuTTY. This is the same as sending from our soon to be working Python program. A simple way of testing communication and seeing if the motors work as planned.

Day Thirty One – Python to C communication

Now that we have some communications going on between the PC and microchip via HyperTerminal or PuTTY you may be thinking 'hey piece of cake'. Maybe, but we still need to have our Python program which runs many times faster than our microchip transmit to the microchip over a 'touchy' serial port. Then have the microchip respond back thought the 'touchy' serial port to our Python program. Then have our Python program display the results of the communication. Below I will list the complete Python code, remember you should type in the code and save in your "Work" directory. Execute from the DOS prompt after running our Python bat file, 'mypython27.bat'.

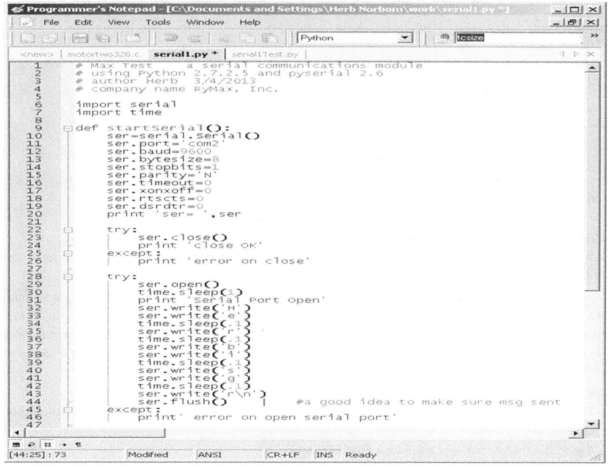

Exhibit191

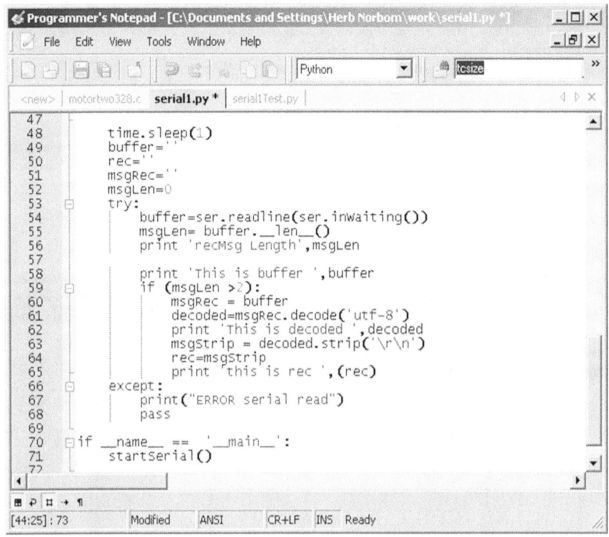

```
47
48          time.sleep(1)
49          buffer=''
50          rec=''
51          msgRec=''
52          msgLen=0
53          try:
54              buffer=ser.readline(ser.inwaiting())
55              msgLen= buffer.__len__()
56              print 'recMsg Length',msgLen
57
58              print 'This is buffer ',buffer
59              if (msgLen >2):
60                  msgRec = buffer
61                  decoded=msgRec.decode('utf-8')
62                  print 'This is decoded ',decoded
63                  msgStrip = decoded.strip('\r\n')
64                  rec=msgStrip
65                  print 'this is rec ',(rec)
66          except:
67              print("ERROR serial read")
68              pass
69
70  if __name__ == '__main__':
71      startSerial()
72
```

Exhibit192

Some comments on the reason for a few of the code lines:

- Lines 6-7 – Modules that we need to import. Serial is how we load the pySerial module.

- Lines 9-20 – Setup a function to define 'ser' and to define our port settings.

- Line 22 – Anytime there is a good potential for error put the statements in an error trap. We are opening our serial port and there is a lot of potential for error.

- Line 28 – We are writing a message to the serial port, once again big potential for error. Because the PC runs so much faster than the microchip there is a good chance that your entire message may not be received by the microchip. That is why I choose to write a character at a time with delay built in. Please experiment with this, note I did not need to delay every character. I found that two characters was the maximum without a delay. Within pySerial there is a command interCharTimeout which I thought would be great to use. I was not successful in getting it to work.
  - A reference site is http://pyserial.sourceforge.net/

- Line 43 – Transmitting the character 'r' and the '\n' which is the end of line. The end of line indicated end of transmission for the microchip.

- Line 44 – A good idea to make sure your transmission had been sent.

- Line 53 – Another try group as want to read from our serial port. Notice we loaded into buffer and printing buffer length. I also showed several ways of handling the message.

Day Thirty Two – Adding Communication to our Control Program

With our communications working we will continue developing our Python Control program. Save program lesson28.py as lesson29.py. Our goal is to get the serial communications working in this program. On line 20 insert 'import serial' press return to keep a line space. We are not going to start our serial port unless the threads start correctly. So we are going to copy def startSerial

(): procedure from serial1.py and paste it below the threadstart function. For now copy the lines 9 though 68. Paste to lesson29.py at approximately line 332. We copied the entire function to test our program. On approximately line 331 at the end of the threadStart function add the following:

If (thCount ==3):
        startSerial ()

Turn on your microcomputer and run this program. You should see displays like we had when running serial1.py. I am going to save the program as lesson29a.py. With that step successfully completed we will set the queue for using the serial connections. As you are aware our program has grown considerably. Before we add the physical robot communications to the queue I am going to remove all the visual robot code. If you want to keep that code I highly recommend that you start another thread and if possible use a 'pipe'. Be aware that a 'pipe' can only have one in and one out. When I am making radical changes, as in removing a lot of code, I like to just comment out the lines and then test the program. If I am happy with that then I actually delete them. Lines I am commenting out are: 91-95, 127-137, and 253-294. In the DataFile Class I have taken out the references to xMaxLoc and yMaxLoc. Save your program and run it, have the microchip connected and running. I think you will notice quite an improvement in the performance. Try the various buttons; make sure everything is still working.

I am going to make a number of changes to the sending function. The code changes are shown in the following. Note, a little bit of renaming also going on and deleting the code for the virtual robot. First we need to make our variable 'ser' global. Insert at approximately line 355 'global ser' as the first line of our startSerial function. I also adjusted the tab position of the queue 'trash'. When you run the program you will notice that what is printed on the DOS window is not the same as on the LCD, or on the tkinter window under the 'Max Comm Robot Data' frame. If you look back at the paint function you will see where we adjusted the values and also computed the power and direction for the left and right wheels. We need to move the queue empty routine to the stop function. We want a stop command executed as quickly as possible. After empting the queue, send the stop command again.

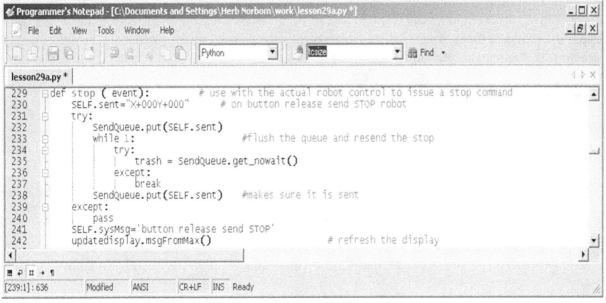

Exhibit193

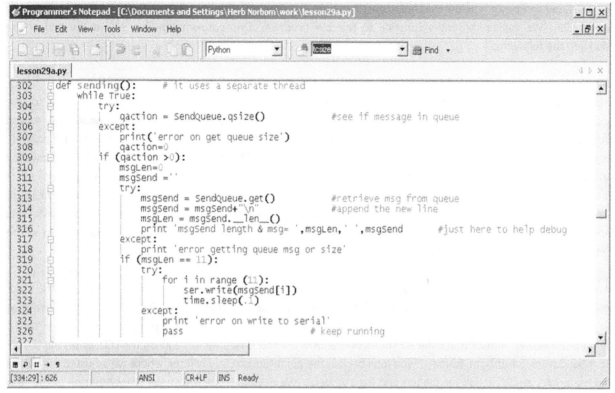

Exhibit194

Let us get our receiving function working. I added some code for our bumper message and for a test com button that we will add shortly. As you run this you will notice not all messages sent to Max are being sent back and displayed. We still have code to work on for the microchip and some timing issues to address. As you are running the program try the arm buttons, note the message window displays and the LCD. Code for the receiving function follows.

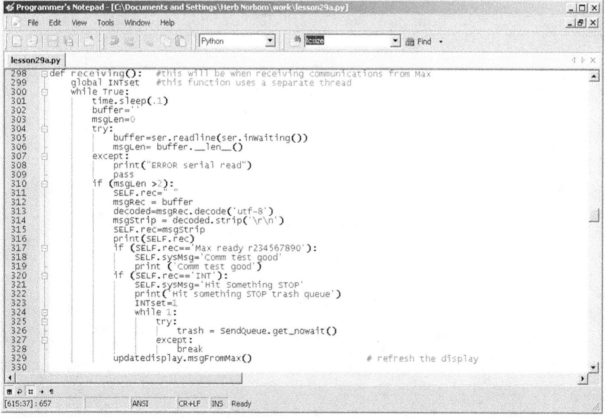

Exhibit195

The order of calling some start up functions was changed, as shown in the following.

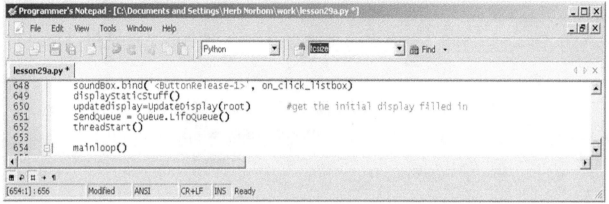

Exhibit196

As we have made a lot of changes save your program as lesson29b.py. Note I also set our root.geometry back to a smaller size of (550x450).

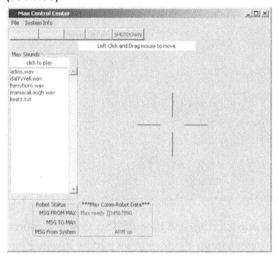
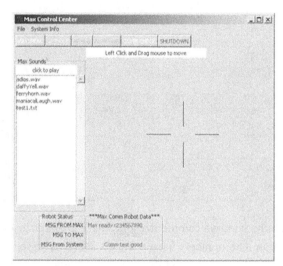

Exhibits 197 & 198

The function code for the 'COMM CHECK' button has been added as shown in the right hand screen shot. A few changes have been made to the function displayStaticStuff as shown in the following.

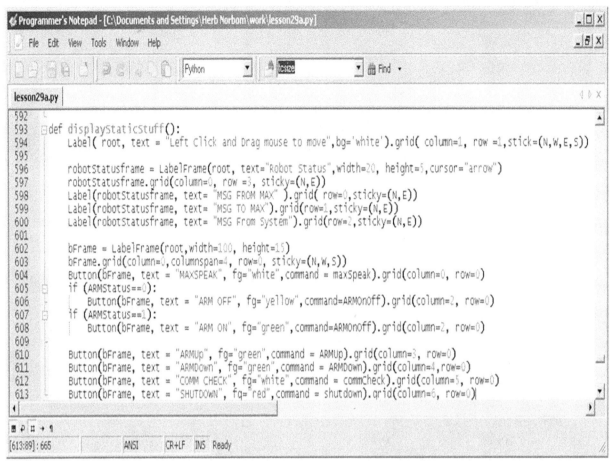

Exhibit199

I am going to delete all the lines we commented out, make changes to the serial port startup, and then list the complete source code again as the program line numbers have changed. Save as lesson29b.py. I cleaned up the format by putting in some line wraps so the lines are not too long. Moved the ARMStatus variable to the DataFileClass and deleted the global references to it. I did the same with the INTset for the bumper. Note the adjustment for mouse position, lines 122-123.

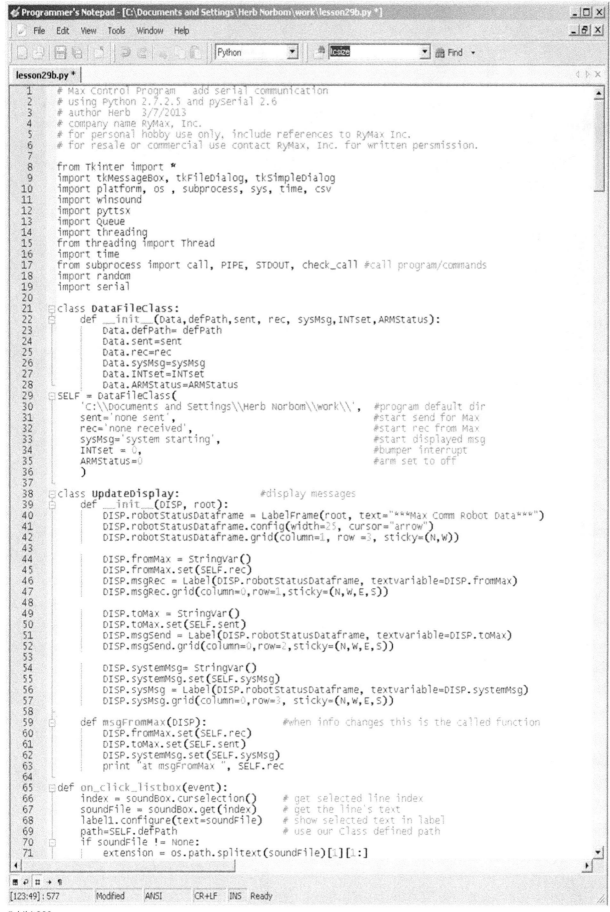

lesson29b.py *

```python
1    # Max Control Program    add serial communication
2    # using Python 2.7.2.5 and pySerial 2.6
3    # author Herb  3/7/2013
4    # company name RyMax, Inc.
5    # for personal hobby use only, include references to RyMax Inc.
6    # for resale or commercial use contact RyMax, Inc. for written persmission.
7
8    from Tkinter import *
9    import tkMessageBox, tkFileDialog, tkSimpleDialog
10   import platform, os , subprocess, sys, time, csv
11   import winsound
12   import pyttsx
13   import Queue
14   import threading
15   from threading import Thread
16   import time
17   from subprocess import call, PIPE, STDOUT, check_call #call program/commands
18   import random
19   import serial
20
21   class DataFileClass:
22       def __init__(Data,defPath,sent, rec, sysMsg,INTset,ARMStatus):
23           Data.defPath= defPath
24           Data.sent=sent
25           Data.rec=rec
26           Data.sysMsg=sysMsg
27           Data.INTset=INTset
28           Data.ARMStatus=ARMStatus
29   SELF = DataFileClass(
30       'C:\\Documents and Settings\\Herb Norbom\\work\\',   #program default dir
31       sent='none sent',                                    #start send for Max
32       rec='none received',                                 #start rec from Max
33       sysMsg='system starting',                            #start displayed msg
34       INTset = 0,                                          #bumper interrupt
35       ARMStatus=0                                          #arm set to off
36       )
37
38   class UpdateDisplay:              #display messages
39       def __init__(DISP, root):
40           DISP.robotStatusDataframe = LabelFrame(root, text="***Max Comm Robot Data***")
41           DISP.robotStatusDataframe.config(width=25, cursor="arrow")
42           DISP.robotStatusDataframe.grid(column=1, row =3, sticky=(N,W))
43
44           DISP.fromMax = StringVar()
45           DISP.fromMax.set(SELF.rec)
46           DISP.msgRec = Label(DISP.robotStatusDataframe, textvariable=DISP.fromMax)
47           DISP.msgRec.grid(column=0,row=1,sticky=(N,W,E,S))
48
49           DISP.toMax = StringVar()
50           DISP.toMax.set(SELF.sent)
51           DISP.msgSend = Label(DISP.robotStatusDataframe, textvariable=DISP.toMax)
52           DISP.msgSend.grid(column=0,row=2,sticky=(N,W,E,S))
53
54           DISP.systemMsg= StringVar()
55           DISP.systemMsg.set(SELF.sysMsg)
56           DISP.sysMsg = Label(DISP.robotStatusDataframe, textvariable=DISP.systemMsg)
57           DISP.sysMsg.grid(column=0,row=3, sticky=(N,W,E,S))
58
59       def msgFromMax(DISP):              #when info changes this is the called function
60           DISP.fromMax.set(SELF.rec)
61           DISP.toMax.set(SELF.sent)
62           DISP.systemMsg.set(SELF.sysMsg)
63           print "at msgFromMax ", SELF.rec
64
65   def on_click_listbox(event):
66       index = soundBox.curselection()      # get selected line index
67       soundFile = soundBox.get(index)      # get the line's text
68       label1.configure(text=soundFile)     # show selected text in label
69       path=SELF.defPath                    # use our class defined path
70       if soundFile != None:
71           extension = os.path.splitext(soundFile)[1][1:]
```

Exhibit200

103

```python
72              print (extension)
73              if ((extension=='wav') | (extension=='WAV')):    # this is the or  | connector
74                  winsound.PlaySound(str(path)+soundFile,0)
75              if(extension=='txt'):
76                  engine=pyttsx.init()
77                  voices = engine.getProperty('voices')
78                  for voice in voices:
79                      engine.setProperty('voice', voice.id)
80                  with open(str(path)+soundFile) as f:
81                      for line in f:
82                          engine.say(line)
83                          engine.runAndWait()
84
85      def paint( event ):
86          cx=cy=0
87          try:
88              cx=(event.x)
89              cy=(event.y)
90          except:
91              cx=0                              # if something not working want to
92              cy=0                              # set mouse event location to (0,0)
93          if (SELF.INTset==1):                  #Max's bumper was pressed
94              print("whats up")
95              engine=pyttsx.init()
96              voices = engine.getProperty('voices')
97              for voice in voices:
98                  engine.setProperty('voice', voice.id)
99                  ranNumber=random.choice([1,2,3,4,5])
100                 if (ranNumber==1):
101                     engine.say('OUCH that hurt')
102                 if (ranNumber==2):
103                     engine.say("Who's driving this bus?")
104                 if (ranNumber==3):
105                     engine.say('Do not touch me')
106                 if (ranNumber==4):
107                     engine.say('Go away')
108                 if (ranNumber==5):
109                     engine.say('Move it or loose it')
110                 engine.runAndWait()
111             status= tkMessageBox.askyesno("Bumper","Obstacle removed?\n(%s) " % ranNumber)
112             print (status)
113             if (status== True):
114                 INTset=0
115                 cx=0
116                 cy=0
117             else:
118                 cx=0
119                 cy=0
120
121         try:
122             calLeft=leftwheel(cx-200, cy-155)       #power and direction of left wheel
123             calRight=rightwheel(cy-200,cx-155)      #power and direction of right wheel
124         except:
125             print 'error on Max speed calLeft= ', calLeft, 'calRight= ',calRight
126             calLeft='X+000'                         #if error want to set power to 0
127             calRight='Y+000'
128         SELF.sent=(str(calLeft) + str(calRight))    #put into string format
129         try:
130             SendQueue.put(SELF.sent)                #write to queue
131         except:
132             print'Queue error on write'      # print error, but keep running
133         SELF.sysMsg='Robot movement'         # display on message pannel
134         updatedisplay.msgFromMax()                  # refresh the display
135
136     def leftwheel(cx, cy):                   #compute left wheel pwr/dir and format for
137         calLeft=0                            #sending to Max
138         try:
139             calLeft=(-cy+cx)
140         except:
141             calLeft=0
142         if (calLeft==0):
```

Exhibit201

File   Edit   View   Tools   Window   Help

lesson29b.py *

```python
143             calLeft="X+000"
144             return calLeft
145     if (calLeft >0):
146         if (calLeft > 255):
147             calLeft = "X+255"
148             return calLeft
149         if (calLeft>99):
150             calLeft ="X+"+str(calLeft)
151             return calLeft
152         if (calLeft>9):
153             calLeft ="X+0"+str(calLeft)
154             return calLeft
155         else:
156             calLeft ="X+00"+str(calLeft)
157             return calLeft
158     if (calLeft < 0):
159         calLeft = abs(calLeft)
160         if (calLeft > 255):
161             calLeft = "X-255"
162             return calLeft
163         if (calLeft>99):
164             calLeft ="X-"+str(calLeft)
165             return calLeft
166         if (calLeft>9):
167             calLeft ="X-0"+str(calLeft)
168             return calLeft
169         else:
170             calLeft ="X-00"+str(calLeft)
171             return calLeft
172     else:
173         calLeft="X+000"
174         return calLeft
175 def rightWheel(cx, cy):            #compute right wheel pwr/dir and
176     calRight=0                     #format for sending to Max
177     try:
178         calRight=(-cy-cx)
179     except:
180         calRight=0
181     if (calRight==0):
182         calRight="Y+000"
183         return calRight
184     if (calRight >0):
185         if (calRight > 255):
186             calRight = "Y+255"
187             return calRight
188         if (calRight>99):
189             calRight ="Y+"+str(calRight)
190             return calRight
191         if (calRight>9):
192             calRight ="Y+0"+str(calRight)
193             return calRight
194         else:
195             calRight ="Y+00"+str(calRight)
196             return calRight
197     if (calRight < 0):
198         calRight = abs(calRight)
199         if (calRight > 255):
200             calRight = "Y-255"
201             return calRight
202         if (calRight>99):
203             calRight ="Y-"+str(calRight)
204             return calRight
205         if (calRight>9):
206             calRight ="Y-0"+str(calRight)
207             return calRight
208         else:
209             calRight ="Y-00"+str(calRight)
210             return calRight
211     else:
212         calRight="Y+000"
213         return calRight
```

[123:49] : 577   Modified   ANSI   CR+LF   INS   Ready

Exhibit202

105

```python
214
215      def stop ( event):               # issue a stop command
216          SELF.sent="X+000Y+000"       # on button release send STOP robot
217          try:
218              SendQueue.put(SELF.sent)
219              while 1:                  #flush the queue and resend the stop
220                  try:
221                      trash = SendQueue.get_nowait()
222                  except:
223                      break
224              SendQueue.put(SELF.sent)  #makes sure it is sent, do it again
225          except:
226              pass
227          SELF.sysMsg='button release send STOP'
228          updatedisplay.msgFromMax()                   # refresh the display
229
230      def setupCanvas():
231          myCanvas = Canvas( root, width =400, height=300 )
232          myCanvas.grid(column=1,columnspan=3, row=2)
233          myCanvas.configure(cursor="crosshair")
234          myCanvas.bind( "<B1-Motion>", paint )
235          myCanvas.bind("<ButtonRelease-1>",stop)
236          myCanvas.create_line(125, 150, 175, 150, width=1)
237          myCanvas.create_line(225, 150, 275, 150, width=1)
238          myCanvas.create_line(200,  85, 200, 135, width=1)
239          myCanvas.create_line(200, 165, 200, 215, width=1)
240
241      def receiving():   #this will be when receiving communications from Max
242          while True:
243              time.sleep(.1)
244              buffer=''
245              msgLen=0
246              try:
247                  buffer=ser.readline(ser.inWaiting())
248                  msgLen= buffer.__len__()
249              except:
250                  pass
251              if (msgLen >2):
252                  SELF.rec=" "
253                  msgRec = buffer
254                  decoded=msgRec.decode('utf-8')
255                  msgStrip = decoded.strip('\r\n')
256                  SELF.rec=msgStrip
257      #           print(SELF.rec)
258                  if (SELF.rec=='Max ready r234567890'):
259                      SELF.sysMsg='Comm test good'
260                      print ('Comm test good')
261                  if (SELF.rec=='INT'):                #Max's bumber activated
262                      myEvent="<Tkinter.Event>"
263                      stop(myEvent)                    #call stop, send stop/flush queue
264                      SELF.sysMsg='Hit Something STOP'
265                      print('Hit something STOP trash queue')
266                      SELF.INTset=1
267                  updatedisplay.msgFromMax()           # refresh the display
268
269      def sending():       # it uses a separate thread
270          while True:
271              try:
272                  qaction = SendQueue.qsize()          #see if message in queue
273              except:
274                  print('error on get queue size')
275                  qaction=0
276              if (qaction >0):
277                  msgLen=0
278                  msgSend =''
279                  try:
280                      msgSend = SendQueue.get()        #retrieve msg from queue
281                      msgSend = msgSend+"\n"           #append the new line
282                      msgLen = msgSend.__len__()
283                      print 'msgSend length & msg= ',msgLen,' ',msgSend #here to help debug
284                  except:
```

Exhibit203

106

```
285                        print 'error getting queue msg or size'
286            if (msgLen == 11):
287                try:
288                    for i in range (11):
289                        ser.write(msgSend[i])
290                        time.sleep(.1)
291                except:
292                    print 'error on write to serial'
293                    pass                        # keep running
294
295    def threadStart():        #starting child threads
296        recTh=Thread(target=receiving, name='recThread',args=())
297        recTh.setDaemon(True)        # must set all child threads before starting
298        senTh=Thread(target=sending,name='sendThread', args=())
299        senTh.setDaemon(True)
300        try:
301            print'staring recTh'
302            recTh.start()
303        except:
304            print('CRITICAL ERROR starting recThread')
305        try:
306            print 'starting senTh'
307            senTh.start()
308        except:
309            print('CRITICAL ERROR starting sendThread')
310        thCount= threading.active_count()
311        print('# of threads = ',thCount)
312        thNames= threading.enumerate()
313        print (thNames)
314        if (thCount ==3):
315                startSerial()
316
317    def startSerial():
318        global ser
319        ser=serial.Serial()
320        ser.port='com2'
321        ser.baud=9600
322        ser.bytesize=8
323        ser.stopbits=1
324        ser.parity='N'
325        ser.timeout=0
326        ser.xonxoff=0
327        ser.rtscts=0
328        ser.dsrdtr=0
329        print 'ser= ',ser
330
331        try:                        #port should be closed prior to this
332            ser.open()
333            time.sleep(1)
334            print 'Serial Port Open'
335            commCheck()              #run a communications check
336        except OSError as e:
337            formatError="Program\n"+command+"\n could not be run\n"+e.args[1]
338            +"\n Error No= "+str(e.args[0])
339
340
341    def shutdown():
342        print("called shutdown")
343        answer=tkMessageBox.askyesno("EXIT", "Do you really want to quit")
344        if answer==True:
345            thCount= threading.active_count()
346            print('# of threads to stop = ',thCount)
347            thNames= threading.enumerate()
348            print (thNames)
349            while 1:                                #try sending messages in the queue
350                try:
351                    sending = SendQueue.get_nowait()
352                except:
353                    break
354            try:
355                root.quit() #because daemon set 'True' kills child threads also
```

Exhibit204

107

```
356          except:
357              print(" ERROR   could not be terminated")
358
359 def windowsNotepad():
360     osType=platform.system()
361     print osType
362     if (osType=='windows'):
363         try:
364             command = 'C:\WINDOWS\NOTEPAD.EXE'
365             env     = {'FOO': 'bar', 'SystemRoot': os.environ['SystemRoot']}
366             p = subprocess.Popen(command, env=env)
367             p.wait()
368             return
369         except OSError as e:
370             print "Read Error %s: %s\n error no %d"%(command,e.args[1],e.args[0])
371             formatError="Program\n"+command+"\n could not be run\n"+e.args[1]
372             +"\n Error No= "+str(e.args[0])
373             tkMessageBox.showerror("OSError",formatError)
374         except:
375             print("General error opening NOTEPAD.exe")
376     print("Notepad appears to be unavailable on this system")
377
378 def startProNotepad():
379     try:
380         command = "C:\\winAVR-20100110\\pn\\pn.exe" #for 2010 users
381         subprocess.call( [command])
382     except OSError as e:
383         print "Read Error %s: %s\n error no %d"%(command,e.args[1],e.args[0])
384         formatError="Program\n"+command+"\n could not be run\n"+e.args[1]
385         +"\n Error No= "+str(e.args[0])
386         tkMessageBox.showerror("OSError",formatError)
387
388 def showPythonVersion():
389     pyversion=sys.version
390     tkMessageBox.showwarning('Python Version',pyversion)
391
392 def showSystemPlatform():
393     import platform
394     osType=platform.system()
395     osPlatform=platform.win32_ver()
396     osProcessor=platform.processor()
397     tkMessageBox.showwarning('System Information','Operating System: '+ osType +
398         '\nSystem Info:'+osPlatform[0]+
399         '\nRelease: '+osPlatform[1]+
400         '\nService Pack: '+ osPlatform[2]+
401         '\nMultiProcessor: '+osPlatform[3]+
402         '\nProcessor: ' + osProcessor)
403
404 def showRyMax():
405     tkMessageBox.showwarning('RyMax, Inc.','RyMax, Inc.'+
406         '\n web page: www.RyMax.biz'+
407         '\n e-mail: herb@RyMax.biz')
408
409
410
411 def searchPaths():
412     searchwin=Toplevel()
413     searchFrame = LabelFrame(searchwin,text="Python Search Paths",
414         width =100, height=10)
415     searchFrame.grid(column=0, row=0, sticky =Nw)
416     searchBox=Listbox(searchFrame, width=150,height=10)
417     searchBox.grid(column=0, row=0,sticky=Nw)
418     scrollBar = Scrollbar(searchFrame, orient=VERTICAL,command=searchBox.yview)
419     scrollBar.grid(column=1, row=0,sticky=(N,W,E,S))
420     searchBox['yscrollcommand']=scrollBar.set
421
422     myPythonSearch=[]
423     for folder in sys.path:
424         print folder
425         myPythonSearch.append (folder)
426
```

Exhibit205

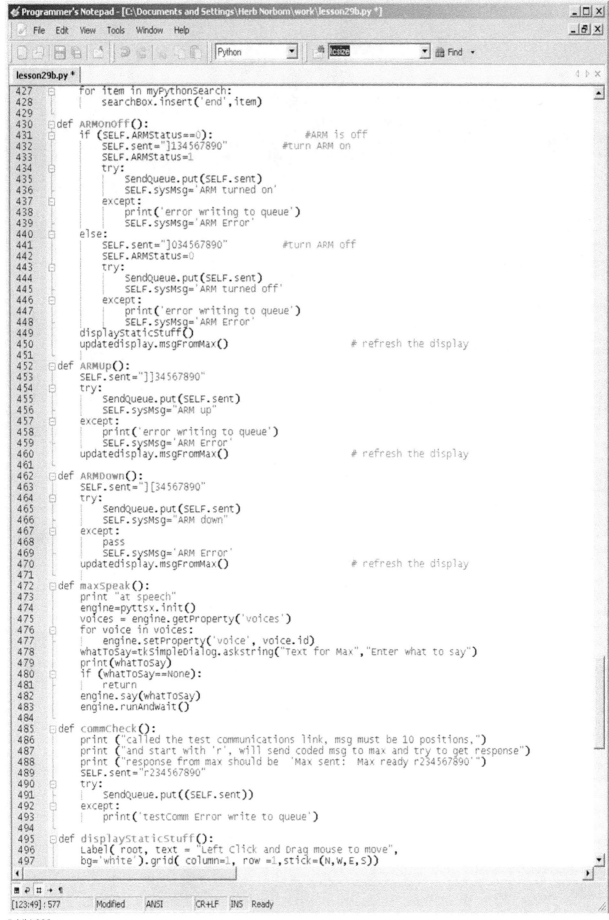

```
427          for item in myPythonSearch:
428              searchBox.insert('end',item)
429
430  def ARMOnOff():
431      if (SELF.ARMStatus==0):              #ARM is off
432          SELF.sent="]134567890"          #turn ARM on
433          SELF.ARMStatus=1
434          try:
435              SendQueue.put(SELF.sent)
436              SELF.sysMsg='ARM turned on'
437          except:
438              print('error writing to queue')
439              SELF.sysMsg='ARM Error'
440      else:
441          SELF.sent="]034567890"          #turn ARM off
442          SELF.ARMStatus=0
443          try:
444              SendQueue.put(SELF.sent)
445              SELF.sysMsg='ARM turned off'
446          except:
447              print('error writing to queue')
448              SELF.sysMsg='ARM Error'
449      displayStaticStuff()
450      updatedisplay.msgFromMax()                    # refresh the display
451
452  def ARMUp():
453      SELF.sent="]]34567890"
454      try:
455          SendQueue.put(SELF.sent)
456          SELF.sysMsg="ARM up"
457      except:
458          print('error writing to queue')
459          SELF.sysMsg='ARM Error'
460      updatedisplay.msgFromMax()                    # refresh the display
461
462  def ARMDown():
463      SELF.sent="][34567890"
464      try:
465          SendQueue.put(SELF.sent)
466          SELF.sysMsg="ARM down"
467      except:
468          pass
469          SELF.sysMsg='ARM Error'
470      updatedisplay.msgFromMax()                    # refresh the display
471
472  def maxSpeak():
473      print "at speech"
474      engine=pyttsx.init()
475      voices = engine.getProperty('voices')
476      for voice in voices:
477          engine.setProperty('voice', voice.id)
478      whatToSay=tkSimpleDialog.askstring("Text for Max","Enter what to say")
479      print(whatToSay)
480      if (whatToSay==None):
481          return
482      engine.say(whatToSay)
483      engine.runAndWait()
484
485  def commCheck():
486      print ("called the test communications link, msg must be 10 positions,")
487      print ("and start with 'r', will send coded msg to max and try to get response")
488      print ("response from max should be  'Max sent:  Max ready r234567890'")
489      SELF.sent="r234567890"
490      try:
491          SendQueue.put((SELF.sent))
492      except:
493          print('testComm Error write to queue')
494
495  def displayStaticStuff():
496      Label( root, text = "Left Click and Drag mouse to move",
497          bg='white').grid( column=1, row =1,stick=(N,W,E,S))
```

Exhibit206

109

```
498
499         robotStatusframe = LabelFrame(root, text="Robot Status",width=20,
500         height=5,cursor="arrow")
501         robotStatusframe.grid(column=0, row =3, sticky=(N,E))
502         Label(robotStatusframe, text= "MSG FROM MAX" ).grid( row=0,sticky=(N,E))
503         Label(robotStatusframe, text= "MSG TO MAX").grid(row=1,sticky=(N,E))
504         Label(robotStatusframe, text= "MSG From System").grid(row=2,sticky=(N,E))
505
506         bFrame = LabelFrame(root,width=100, height=15)
507         bFrame.grid(column=0,columnspan=4, row=0, sticky=(N,W,S))
508         Button(bFrame, text = "MAXSPEAK", fg="white",
509         command = maxSpeak).grid(column=0, row=0)
510         if (SELF.ARMStatus==0):
511             Button(bFrame, text = "ARM OFF", fg="yellow",
512             command=ARMOnOff).grid(column=2, row=0)
513         if (SELF.ARMStatus==1):
514             Button(bFrame, text = "ARM ON", fg="green",
515             command=ARMOnOff).grid(column=2, row=0)
516
517         Button(bFrame, text = "ARMUp", fg="green",
518         command = ARMUp).grid(column=3, row=0)
519         Button(bFrame, text = "ARMDown", fg="green",
520         command = ARMDown).grid(column=4,row=0)
521         Button(bFrame, text = "COMM CHECK", fg="white",
522         command = commCheck).grid(column=5, row=0)
523         Button(bFrame, text = "SHUTDOWN", fg="red",
524         command = shutdown).grid(column=6, row=0)
525 if __name__=='__main__':
526         root = Tk()
527         root.title( "Max Control Center" )
528         root.geometry( "550x450+50+30" ) #width, height, placement on y and  x axis
529         setupCanvas()
530
531 #pull down menu section
532         menubar = Menu(root)
533         root.config(menu=menubar)
534         filemenu = Menu(menubar, tearoff=0)
535         filemenu.add_command(label="Windows Notepad", command=windowsNotepad)
536         filemenu.add_separator()
537         filemenu.add_command(label="Programmer's Notepad", command=startProNotepad)
538         filemenu.add_separator()
539         filemenu.add_separator()
540         filemenu.add_command(label="Exit", command=shutdown)
541         menubar.add_cascade(menu=filemenu, label='File')
542
543         sysMenu=Menu(menubar, tearoff=0)
544         sysMenu.add_command(label="Python version?", command=showPythonVersion)
545         sysMenu.add_command(label="System Platform?", command=showSystemPlatform)
546         sysMenu.add_command(label="Python Search Paths", command=searchPaths)
547         sysMenu.add_command(label="RyMax, Inc. Information?", command=showRyMax)
548         menubar.add_cascade(label="System Info", menu=sysMenu)
549
550 #setup a list box to list our wav and txt files
551         soundFrame = LabelFrame(root, text="Max Sounds",width=20, height=10,
552         cursor="arrow")
553         soundFrame.grid(column=0, row =2, sticky=(N,W,S))
554         soundBox=Listbox(soundFrame, width=20, height=18)
555         soundBox.grid(column=0,row=1,sticky=(N,W,S))
556         scrollBar = Scrollbar(soundFrame, orient=VERTICAL, command=soundBox.yview)
557         scrollBar.grid(column=1,row=1, sticky=(N,E,S))
558         soundBox['yscrollcommand']=scrollBar.set
559         path=SELF.defPath
560         print path
561         soundlist = os.listdir(path)
562 # load the listbox
563         for sound in soundlist:
564             extension = os.path.splitext(sound)[1][1:]
565             if ((extension=='wav') | (extension=='WAV') |(extension=='txt')):
566                 soundBox.insert('end', sound)
567         label1 = Label(soundFrame, text='click to play', width=20, bg='white')
568         label1.grid(column=0, row=0)
```

Exhibit207

110

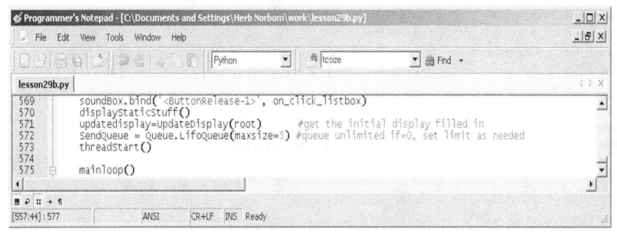

Exhibit208

To speed up the signaling I set the Queue size to 5, less to empty when a STOP is sent. Since we are using the 'LifoQueue' we really care most about the last sent message. I did set up a 'Priority Queue' and there was perhaps a slight improvement, hard to tell at this point. I do think it is worthwhile to implement the 'Priority Queue'. It is a technique that we should know how to use, and as our program gets more complex we may need the capability. Save lesson29b.py as lesson29c.py and make the following changes to the code.

Reference: http://docs.python.org/2/library/queue.html

Line 130 SendQueue.put ((2,SELF.sent))   #write to queue
Line 218 SendQueue.put ((0, SELF.sent))
Line 224 SendQueue.put ((0, SELF.sent))   #makes sure it is sent, do it again

As you can see we send our text and the priority number to the Queue. The Queue returns the data as a tuple, remember those? So we need most of the changes to be made to the sending function. I also wanted to try the empty queue exception. Note all the spacing changes. While I have commented out some of the print lines, you may want to leave them on until you are comfortable. Notice the msgSend becomes a tuple. I ended up moving the value we will transmit to msgSendR.

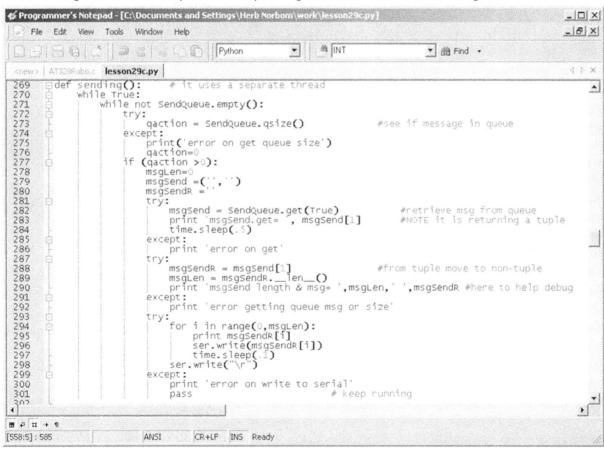

Exhibit209

You will also need to change the ARM functions, note line numbers are changed so adjust accordingly.

Line 443 SendQueue.put (1, SELF.sent)   #ARM Onoff

Line 452 SendQueue.put ((1, SELF.sent))   #ARM Onoff

Line 463 SendQueue.put ((1, SELF.sent))   #ARM Up

Line 473 SendQueue.put ((1, SELF.sent))   #ARM Down

Also need to get the commCheck function.

Line 499 SendQueue.put ((1, SELF.sent))   #commCheck

The set up of the queue also changed.

 Line 580 SendQueue = Queue.PriorityQueue (maxsize=5) #queue grow unlimited=0, set limit if needed

Day Thirty Three - C Program for actual control of Robot

We are going to go back to our C program to begin writing the actual program for controlling the robot. I am going to make a new directory or folder, ATMEGA328Robo, just like before. Copy everything from the ATMEGA328Test to the new directory. Rename the 'AT328serial.c' program to 'AT328Robo.c'. Make the necessary adjustments in the 'Makefile' for the new program name. I suggest using the replace feature of the Programmer's Notepad. Try to compile and run with your Python program, lesson29c.py. Now we will begin our coding on AT328Robo.c.

If possible setup another breadboard as we will need the ports that the LCD is connected to. Just nice to have a breadboard wired up with the LCD.   As we are going to be adding a number of components to the board it is a good idea to use a larger breadboard. In the following schematic you can see that I have made a few changes. The LCD and the resistor that sat behind the voltage regulator have been removed. I added a capacitor, reference D. At this point the size is not too important; you can put in bigger one or multiple smaller ones. I changed the LED and needed a different resistor, G. I also changed the small capacitor, H. You can experiment with different hardware. In the schematic I left the switch, E, in place. You may notice on the picture that I don't have the switch; to program you just need to run PB0 to ground when you want to load a program. In addition to NerdKit here are a few other suppliers that have worked well for me. As a side point on resistors, at this point paying extra dollars for high quality resistors is not needed.

- NerdKit   http://www.nerdkits.com/
- All Electronics   http://allelectronics.com/
- Marlin P. Jones   http://www.mpja.com/
- Mouser Electronics   http://www.mouser.com/Home.aspx
- DigiKey Electronics   http://www.digikey.com/
- MCM Electronics   http://www.mcmelectronics.com/
- Adafruit Industries   http://www.adafruit.com/
- Sure Electronics   http://www.sureelectronics.net/
- Electronix Express   http://www.elexp.com/index.htm
- Atbatt.com   http://www.atbatt.com/sitemap.html

When you are buying some relatively low cost items, resistors, LED's, etc. Buy extras, you will probably end up using them on some project. It is a good idea to have several bread boards of various sizes. For items like the H-Bridge, mosfet's BUY some extra's. It is very easy to fry some of these parts. For your microchip it is also a good idea to have extras. If you hit a point where you cannot get something to work it is possible you have cooked a portion of the chip. If a new chip works, make sure you save the old one as it may be salvaged. Label it as damaged so you don't rip out your hair later trying to make it work.

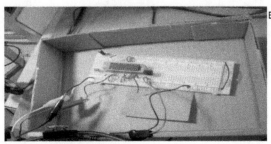
Exhibit210   A picture of the actual setup may be worth a 1000 words.

New Bread Board Diagram

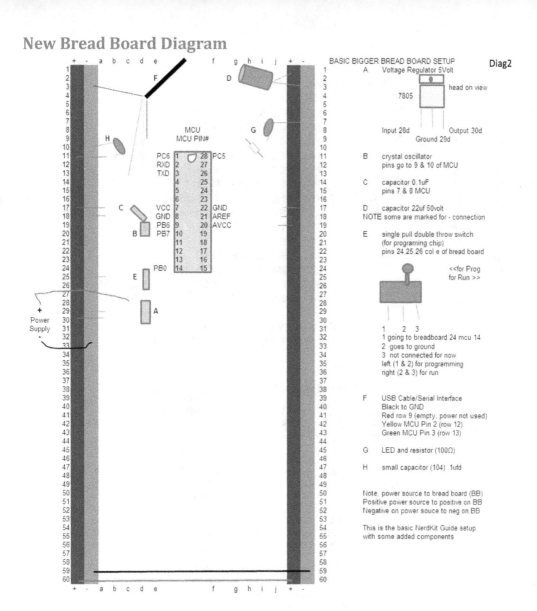

BASIC BIGGER BREAD BOARD SETUP   Diag2

A   Voltage Regulator 5Volt

     7805   head on view

     Input 28d   Output 30d
                  Ground 29d

B   crystal oscillator
     pins go to 9 & 10 of MCU

C   capacitor 0.1uF
     pins 7 & 8 MCU

D   capacitor 22uf 50volt
NOTE some are marked for - connection

E   single pull double throw switch
     (for programing chip)
     pins 24,25,26 col e of bread board

                             <<for Prog
                             for Run >>

     1   2   3
     1 going to breadboard 24 mcu 14
     2 goes to ground
     3 not connected for now
     left (1 & 2) for programming
     right (2 & 3) for run

F   USB Cable/Serial Interface
     Black to GND
     Red row 9 (empty, power not used)
     Yellow MCU Pin 2 (row 12)
     Green MCU Pin 3 (row 13)

G   LED and resistor (100Ω)

H   small capacitor (104) .1ufd

Note. power source to bread board (BB)
Positive power source to positive on BB
Negative on power souce to neg on BB

This is the basic NerdKit Guide setup
with some added components

With your board setup, try to upload the new program, AT328Robo.c and run it with Python lesson29c.py. With everything working we will start changing the program around.

As we just copied the AT328Robo.c program I am just going to delete the following lines, vs. the comment out technique I usually use. Delete in this order lines: 83-110, 77-79, 66. Then delete all the code references to the LCD. This includes the register printouts. Save the program, run the make command, and then run with your Python program. We are going to have two motors for the drive wheels and one motor for the arm. We are going to use PWM, pulse width modulation to drive the motors. NerdKit has excellent tutorials on this subject. I am just going to cover just the basics of what we need for this. Our ATmega328 chip has 8 bit and 16 bit timer/counters for operating our motors. The use of PWM was for me a very intensive learning period. In gaining an understanding of PWM I had many false starts and frustrating days. What PWM basically does is turn a microchip port on and off very rapidly. The on/off time is controlled by how you have set up the registers, counters, and clocks. The power goes on and off so fast that you will not be able to detect the on off in the motors. The longer a pulse is on the faster the motor runs in a nut shell. For the moment we will continue to use our breadboard with the same hardware setup. In place of motors we will use LED's. If you have a very small motor you can use that, but let's get the lights flashing first. To help me understand the new terminology and the interrelation of the registers, vectors, pins, interrupts, etc. I combined as much as I could on the following charts. I originally started these charts for the ATMega168, as the two chips are very similar these should work fine on either chip. To help visualize I have shown the chip with the breadboard references.

	d col	MCU PIN #		g col	
		Bread Board col & row			
PCINT14/RESET) PC6	11	1 28	11	PC5 (ADC5/SCL/PCINT13)	
(PCINT16/RXD) PD0	12	2 27	12	PC4 (ADC4/SDA/PCINT12)	
(PCINT17/TXD) PD1	13	3 26	13	PC3 (ADC3/PCINT11)	
(PCINT18/INT0) PD2	14	4 25	14	PC2 (ADC2/PCINT10)	
8BitPWM (PCINT19/OC2B/INT1) PD3	15	5 24	15	PC1 (ADC1/PCINT9)	
(PCINT20/XCK/T0) PD4	16	6 23	16	PC0 (ADC0/PCINT8)	
VCC	17	7 22	17	GND	
GND	18	8 21	18	AREF (the analog reference to the A/D converter	
(PCINT6/XTAL1/TOSC1) PB6	19	9 20	19	AVCC (analog to digital converter)	
(PCINT7/XTAL2/TOSC2) PB7	20	10 19	20	PB5 (SCK/PCINT5)	
8BitPWM (PCINT21/OC0B/T1) PD5	21	11 18	21	PB4 (MISO/PCINT4)	
8BitPWM (PCINT22/OC0A/AIN0) PD6	22	12 17	22	PB3 (MOSI/OC2A/PCINT3)	8BitPWM
(PCINT23/AIN1) PD7	23	13 16	23	PB2 (SS/OC1B/PCINT2)	16BitPWM
(PCINT0/CLKO/ICP1) PB0	24	14 15	24	PB1 (OC1A/PCINT1)	16BitPWM

For 8 Bit PWM max is 255 or0xFF

For 16 Bit PWM max is 65535 or 0xFFFF

Exhibit210A

Each port pin has three register bits: DDxn,PORTxn,PINxn.

Interrupt Control Register	Pin Change Interrupt	ISR Vector	PCICR BITS	PC INTn	PWM Control	Interrupt Enable Register	PORT DATA Register	DATA BIT R/W driver output	PORT DATA Register	DATA DIRECTION BIT R/W input or output	PORT INPUT PIN R only input value measured	BIT	PIN #	PIN LABEL
PCICR	PCI0	PCINT0_vect	PCIE0	PCINT7		PCMSK0	PORTB	PORTB7	DDRB	DDB7	PINB7	7	10	PB7
PCICR	PCI0	PCINT0_vect	PCIE0	PCINT6		PCMSK0	PORTB	PORTB6	DDRB	DDB6	PINB6	6	9	PB6
PCICR	PCI0	PCINT0_vect	PCIE0	PCINT5		PCMSK0	PORTB	PORTB5	DDRB	DDB5	PINB5	5	19	PB5
PCICR	PCI0	PCINT0_vect	PCIE0	PCINT4		PCMSK0	PORTB	PORTB4	DDRB	DDB4	PINB4	4	18	PB4
PCICR	PCI0	PCINT0_vect	PCIE0	PCINT3	OCR2A	PCMSK0	PORTB	PORTB3	DDRB	DDB3	PINB3	3	17	PB3
PCICR	PCI0	PCINT0_vect	PCIE0	PCINT2	OCR1A	PCMSK0	PORTB	PORTB2	DDRB	DDB2	PINB2	2	16	PB2
PCICR	PCI0	PCINT0_vect	PCIE0	PCINT1	OCR1B	PCMSK0	PORTB	PORTB1	DDRB	DDB1	PINB1	1	15	PB1
PCICR	PCI0	PCINT0_vect	PCIE0	PCINT0		PCMSK0	PORTB	PORTB0	DDRB	DDB0	PINB0	0	14	PB0
						PORTC	PORTC7	DDRC	--		PINC7	7	.	.
PCICR	PCI1	PCINT1_vect	PCIE1	PCINT14		PCMSK1	PORTC	PORTC6	DDRC	DDC6	PINC6	6	1	PC6
PCICR	PCI1	PCINT1_vect	PCIE1	PCINT13		PCMSK1	PORTC	PORTC5	DDRC	DDC5	PINC5	5	28	PC5
PCICR	PCI1	PCINT1_vect	PCIE1	PCINT12		PCMSK1	PORTC	PORTC4	DDRC	DDC4	PINC4	4	27	PC4
PCICR	PCI1	PCINT1_vect	PCIE1	PCINT11		PCMSK1	PORTC	PORTC3	DDRC	DDC3	PINC3	3	26	PC3
PCICR	PCI1	PCINT1_vect	PCIE1	PCINT10		PCMSK1	PORTC	PORTC2	DDRC	DDC2	PINC2	2	25	PC2
PCICR	PCI1	PCINT1_vect	PCIE1	PCINT9		PCMSK1	PORTC	PORTC1	DDRC	DDC1	PINC1	1	24	PC1
PCICR	PCI1	PCINT1_vect	PCIE1	PCINT8		PCMSK1	PORTC	PORTC0	DDRC	DDC0	PINC0	0	23	PC0
PCICR	PCI2	PCINT2_vect	PCIE2	PCINT23		PCMSK2	PORTD	PORTD7	DDRD	DDD7	PIND7	7	13	PD7
PCICR	PCI2	PCINT2_vect	PCIE2	PCINT22	OCR0A	PCMSK2	PORTD	PORTD6	DDRD	DDD6	PIND6	6	12	PD6
PCICR	PCI2	PCINT2_vect	PCIE2	PCINT21	OCR0B	PCMSK2	PORTD	PORTD5	DDRD	DDD5	PIND5	5	11	PD5
PCICR	PCI2	PCINT2_vect	PCIE2	PCINT20		PCMSK2	PORTD	PORTD4	DDRD	DDD4	PIND4	4	6	PD4
PCICR	PCI2	PCINT2_vect	PCIE2	PCINT19	OCR2B	PCMSK2	PORTD	PORTD3	DDRD	DDD3	PIND3	3	5	PD3
PCICR	PCI2	PCINT2_vect	PCIE2	PCINT18		PCMSK2	PORTD	PORTD2	DDRD	DDD2	PIND2	2	4	PD2
PCICR	PCI2	PCINT2_vect	PCIE2	PCINT17		PCMSK2	PORTD	PORTD1	DDRD	DDD1	PIND1	1	3	PD1
PCICR	PCI2	PCINT2_vect	PCIE2	PCINT16		PCMSK2	PORTD	PORTD0	DDRD	DDD0	PIND0	0	2	PD0

All registers and bit references notations "x" letter for port, "n" bit number. PORTB3 (bit 3 in port B)

Exhibit210B

If you have been reading the Data Sheet you will have seen much of the above. The biggest problem with the Data Sheet is that there are over 400 pages with references that jump all over. I hope the above summaries help to show the relationships between the various items. I hope if you now look back at the Data Sheet some of this makes sense. There are good examples out there, try to follow them. We need to move on to our program.

As we will have a number of false starts, I like to save copies of the program as I go. Save the program as AT328Robo2013_03_09works.c or whatever works for you. Just remember that our **make** file loads AT328Robo.c, so do your new work on that. If you really have a disaster, you can copy the saved program back and start from a point that worked.

Pulse Width Modulation (PWM)

We are going to walk through configuring one pin for PWM. Note on the Data Sheet, page 76, that each pin has three resisters bits; DDxn, PORTxn, PINxn. We are going to walk through pin PB3 which we will use for 8 bit PWM. We need to turn on the DDRB Port B Data Direction Register, see page 92.

DDRB | = (1<<PB3);   // this register controls PB pins, here we just set PB3

We also need to set the registers for PWM. This is accomplished in a function we will name pwm_init. In this function we will set clock, pre-scale and PWM mode. To start, look at the Data Sheet pages 94 – 105. We are going to look at TCCR0B for our Timer/Counter Register, page 109. We want to use a prescaling of 8. See page 110. To achieve that prescaling we need to turn on CS01.

TCCR0B = (1<<CS01);

We also need to set the Timer/Counter Control Register B, see page 161 and 162. We are using the prescaling factor of 8. Set the force compare using the CS21 bit.

TCCR2B = (1<<CS21);

These settings allow us to use two Output Compare Registers, OCR2A and OCR2B. We are going to need another Timer/Counter, TCCR0A and TCCR2A set up very similar to the above. Take a look at the Data Sheet and try to set up before looking at the code. While it is hard to tell which LED's are lit in the pictures, the descriptions for the pictures going from left to right are: First picture is for forward; both green LED's are lit. Second picture is for reverse; both red LED's are lit. Third picture is for sharp left turn the right green and the left red LED's are lit. The fourth picture is for sharp right turn the left green and the right red LED's are lit.

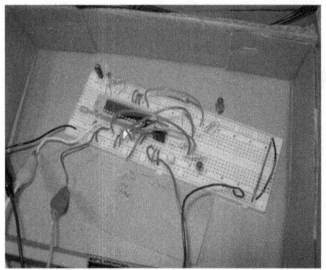
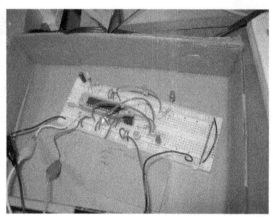

Exhibits 211 & 212

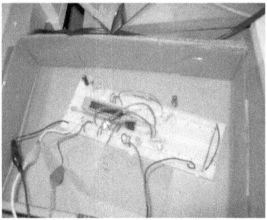
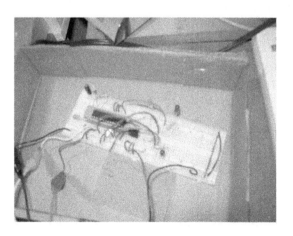

Exhibits 213 & 214

As you run the program you should see the intensity of the LED's change as power is increased. The code as shown in the following flashes the PC5 LED when a USART message is received. When you have everything running you can comment that line out for improved performance. I was originally going to put color photographs in the book. Cost considerations ended that plan. I left the four pictures in the book, even though it is very difficult to tell what lights are on. The complete C source code is shown in the following. See the website, www.rymax.biz, for color pictures.

```
1   /*for ATMega328 Herb Norbom, RyMax, Inc.3/14/2013
2   for communications using serial port at 9600 BAUD via Hyper Termianal or Putty
3   program will also work with our Python program lesson29c.py
4   to microchip with various displays on LCD    add PWM and motor controls
5   for personal hobby use only, include references to RyMax Inc.
6    for resale or commercial use contact RyMax, Inc. for written persmission.
7   */
8   #define F_CPU 14745600
9   #include <stdio.h>
10  #include <stdlib.h>
11  #include <avr/io.h>
12  #include <avr/interrupt.h>
13  #include <avr/pgmspace.h>
14  #include <inttypes.h>
15  #include <string.h>
16  #include "../libnerdkits/io_328p.h"
17  #include "../libnerdkits/delay.h"
18  #include "../libnerdkits/uart.h"
19
20  volatile int i=0;                   //use as counter/incrementer
21  volatile char tcread[13];           //variable that receives from PC
22  volatile int speedX=0;              //speed  Left Motor
23  volatile int speedY=0;              //speed  Right Motor
24  volatile int stspeedX[5];           //get prelim string speed
25  volatile int stspeedY[5];           //get prelim string speed
26
27  void pwm_init() {
28      /*for drive motors using 8 bit timers for PWM, MAX is 255
29          OCR0A & OCR0B & OCR2B & OCR2A
30          clock 0 for PD5 & PD6 Timer\Counter Control Register A   */
31      TCCR0A = (1<<COM0A1)|(1<<COM0B1)|(1<<WGM01)|(1<<WGM00);
32      TCCR0B =(1<<CS01); //prescale clk 8 use for OCR0A and OCR0B
33      //CLOCK 2 for PB3 and PD3
34      TCCR2A = (1<<COM2A1)|(1<<COM2B1)|(1<<WGM21)|(1<<WGM20);
35      TCCR2B =(1<<CS21); //prescale clk 8 use for OCR2A and OCR2B
36      //combo of WGM20,21,22 sets to FAST PWM mode 7, see page 162
37  }
38
39  void flash_led()
40      {
41      PORTC |= (1<<PC5);                  // turn on LED signal ready and received
42      delay_ms(20);                       //delay  20 milliseconds light on
43      PORTC &= ~(1<<PC5);                 // turn off LED
44      }
45
46  void motorcontrol()         //MOTOR COMMAND PROCESSIONS FUNCTUION
47      {
48  //ALL STOP
49      if((speedX==0)&&(speedY==0)){
50          OCR0B=0;        //OFF PD5   fwd  RIGHT MOTOR
51          OCR2B=0;        //OFF PD3   fwd  LEFT MOTOR
52          OCR2A=0;        //OFF PB3   rev  RIGHT MOTOR
53          OCR0A=0;        //OFF PD6   rev  LEFT MOTOR
54          DDRB |=(0<<PB3); //PB3 Right rev  OCR2A  OFF
55          DDRD |=(0<<PD6); //PD6 Left  rev  OCR0A  OFF
56          DDRD |=(0<<PD5); //PD5 Right fwd  OCR0B  OFF
57          DDRD |=(0<<PD3); //PD3 Left  fwd  OCR2B  OFF
58          /*                          PORT ON        PORT OFF
59              X+      FWD LEFT         OCR2B PD3       OCR0A PD6
60              Y+      FWD RIGHT        OCR0B PD5       OCR2A PB3
61              X-      REV LEFT         OCR0A PD6       OCR2B PD3
62              Y-      REV RIGHT        OCR2A PB3       OCR0B PD5
63          for direction control  +speed is fwd  -speed is reverse
64          X is left motor    Y is right motor
65          max speed for 8 bit port is 255 which is what this is using,
66          limit set from PC program */
67      }
```

Exhibit215

Programmer's Notepad - [C:\Documents and Settings\Herb Norbom\My Documents\NERDKIT\Code\Sample328\ATMEGA328Robo\A... ☐☐☒

File   Edit   View   Tools   Window   Help   _ ☐ ☒

☐☐☐☐☐☐☐ ☐☐☐☐☐☐ │C / C++   ▼│ ☐│   ▼│ ☷ Find ▼

<new>   AT328Robo.c   ◁ ▷ ✕

```
68      //FWD with left or right dependent on speeds
69              if((speedX > 0) && (speedY > 0))   //go fwd  want PD5 & PD3 on
70                                                 // want PB3 & PD6 off
71                  {
72                  DDRB |=(0<<PB3);    //PB3 Right rev  OCR2A Y-    OFF
73                  DDRD |=(0<<PD6);    //PD6 Left  rev  OCR0A X-    OFF
74                  DDRD |=(1<<PD5);    //PD5 Right fwd  OCR0B Y+    ON
75                  DDRD |=(1<<PD3);    //PD3 Left  fwd  OCR2B X+    ON
76                  OCR0A = OCR2A = 0;
77                  OCR2B=speedX;       //speed  Left FwD
78                  OCR0B=speedY;       //speed  RIGHT  FWD
79                  }
80      //REV with left or right dependent on speeds
81              if((speedX<0)&&(speedY<0))    // go rev want PB3 & PD6 on
82                                            //want PD5 & PD3 off
83                  {
84                  DDRD |=(0<<PD3);    //PD3 Left  fwd OCR2B X+    OFF
85                  DDRD |=(0<<PD5);    //PD5 Right fwd OCR0B Y+    OFF
86                  DDRD |=(1<<PD6);    //PD6 Left  rev OCR0A X-    ON
87                  DDRB |=(1<<PB3);    //PB3 Right rev OCR2A Y-    ON
88                  OCR2B = OCR0B =0;
89                  OCR0A=speedX*-1;        //speed PD6 Left  Rev
90                  OCR2A=speedY*-1;        //speed right Rev
91                  }
92      //SHARPER Right Turn with FWD on left motor and REV on right motor
93              if((speedX>0)&&(speedY<0))     // left motor fwd, right motor rev
94                  {
95                  DDRD |=(0<<PD5);    //PD5 Right fwd OCR0B Y+    OFF
96                  DDRD |=(0<<PD6);    //PD6 Left  rev OCR0A X-    OFF
97                  DDRB |=(1<<PB3);    //PB3 Right rev OCR2A Y-    ON
98                  DDRD |=(1<<PD3);    //PD3 Left  fwd OCR2B X+    ON
99                  OCR0A = OCR0B =0;
100                 OCR2A=speedY*-1;        //speed right Rev
101                 OCR2B=speedX;       //speed  Left FwD
102                 }
103     //LEFT Turn with FWD on right motor and REV on left motor
104             if((speedX<0)&&(speedY>0))     // right motor fwd, left motor rev
105                 {
106                 DDRB |=(0<<PB3);    //PB3 Right rev OCR2A Y-    OFF
107                 DDRD |=(0<<PD3);    //PD3 Left  fwd OCR2B X+    OFF
108                 DDRD |=(1<<PD5);    //PD5 Right fwd OCR0B Y+    ON
109                 DDRD |=(1<<PD6);    //PD6 Left  rev OCR0A X-    ON
110                 OCR2A = OCR2B =0;
111                 OCR0B=speedY;       //speed  RIGHT  FWD
112                 OCR0A=speedX*-1;        //speed PD6 Left  Rev
113                 }
114         }
115
116     ISR(USART_RX_vect)
117         {
118         flash_led();                //flash,interrupt fired have msg, take out when working good
119         for (i=0;i<6;i++)
120             {
121             stspeedX[i]=' ';
122             stspeedY[i]=' ';
123             }
124         for (i=0;i<14;i++)                              //clear variable
125             {
126             tcread[i]= ' ';
127             }
128         char sign[]="-";
129         scanf_P(PSTR("%12s"),&tcread);              // read from uart receiver
130         printf_P(PSTR("Max says %s\r\n"),tcread);       //send to uart
131         if(tcread[0]=='r')
132             {
133                 //do nothing as sent msg back in above to be interperted on PC
134             }
```

Exhibit216

117

```
135         if(tcread[0]=='X')          //for LEFT MOTOR
136            {
137                stspeedx[1]=tcread[2]-'0';  //strip off end, convert tosingle digit decimal
138                stspeedx[2]=tcread[3]-'0';
139                stspeedx[3]=tcread[4]-'0';
140                speedx= stspeedx[1]*100+stspeedx[2]*10+stspeedx[3];
141                if (speedx >255){    //PWM limit exceeded
142                   speedx =0;        //some kind of error set speed = 0
143                   }
144                if (tcread[1] == sign[0]){     //TCREAD[1] HAS THE SIGN FOR X
145                   speedx=speedx*-1;       //make it negative
146                   }
147            }
148         if(tcread[5]=='Y')          //for RIGHT MOTOR
149            {
150                stspeedy[1]=tcread[7]-'0';
151                stspeedy[2]=tcread[8]-'0';
152                stspeedy[3]=tcread[9]-'0';
153                speedy= stspeedy[1]*100+stspeedy[2]*10+stspeedy[3];
154                if (speedy >255){
155                   speedy =0;        //some kind of error set speed = 0
156                   }
157                if (tcread[6] == sign[0]){   //TCREAD[6] HAS THE SIGN FOR Y
158                   speedy=speedy*-1;        //make it negative
159                   }
160            }
161         motorcontrol();
162      }
163
164 int main() {
165      cli();                  //stop the interrupt detection while loading
166      pwm_init();             //setup PWM
167      uart_init();            //start serial port and uart stream
168      FILE uart_stream = FDEV_SETUP_STREAM(uart_putchar, uart_getchar, _FDEV_SETUP_RW);
169      stdin = stdout = &uart_stream;
170      UBRR0L = (1<<6 | 1<<4 | 1<<3 | 1<<2 | 1<<1 | 1<<0);   //BAUD 9600,Data Sheet 195-203
171      UBRR0H = 0;
172      UCSR0B |= (1<<RXCIE0); // enable uart RX RECEIVE Interrupt page 196
173      DDRC |= (1<<PC5);      // ready port LED signal-for valid receive and startup
174      delay_ms(500);         // pause to let you watch a little better
175      flash_led();           // flash ready signal
176      sei();                 //turn interrupt handler on
177
178 while(1) {
179                    //JUST A LOOP TO KEEP IT ALL RUNNING
180 }
181      return 0;
182 }
```

Exhibit217

Some observations from running our Python and C program follow:

- We will need to work on some speed issues in Python, for now when you are moving the mouse around- go a little slow. I am running the Python program on a somewhat ancient PC, at least by computer standards. Watch the control panel for send and receive messages and you will see the lag. Also watch the light flash on the breadboard for when a message is received. Not to mention the lag in lights changing colors.

- Think about what our robot would do if communications were lost. At this point it would just continue executing the last set of commands.

- I found that the microchip program needs to be running prior to starting the Python program. Why do you think that is? We may want to look at that.

- On the microchip as we change X and Y direction I am setting the compare value to zero and turning off the port. Try playing with different combinations and see the results. You need to know compare settings and port on/off settings.

- We went through some extra steps on the ports that we will be taking out later.

Day Thirty Four - Physical Bumper

I want to add the code to our C program for activation of the bumper. We already have the code in place for Python. Take a look at the receiving function. On our microchip we will use PC4 as our interrupt. Insert the following code into AT328Robo.c right before turning on the interrupt handler currently on line 176.

```
//for bumper interrupt      see Data Sheet pages 70 - 74
        DDRC &= ~ (1<<PC4);        //make PC4 input pin
        PORTC |= (1<<PC4);         //turn on pullup resistor
        PCICR |= (1<<PCIE1);       //setup interrupt value 1 turns on 0 turns off
        PCMSK1 |= (1<<PCINT12); // mask other pins so only PC4 works on interrupt
```
We also need to add the code for handling the interrupt. Add the following with the other procedures. I will put it at line 116 after the motor control procedure.

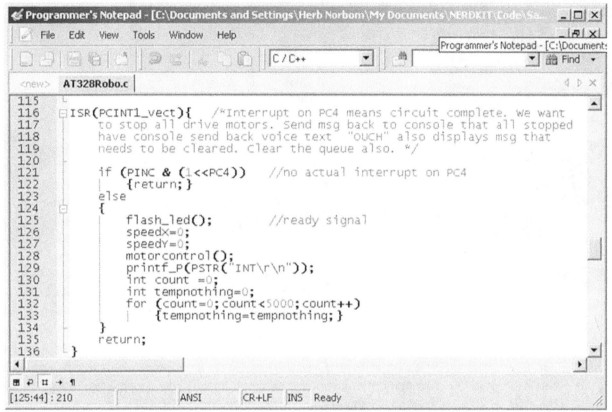

Exhibit218   Refer to the Data Sheet for more information.

Locate PC4 on your ATMega328 and you see that it is pin 27. On the breadboard it is connected to row 12 and columns f – g. To see if it works we are going to complete the circuit by connecting a wire to the breadboard and then just touching the other end to the ground on the breadboard. DO NOT PLUG in just touch. If you have the focus on the control panel you should see the message appear indicating an interrupt. You may have to click on the control panel to hear the message and to clear the message box. This is a little rough, but when running the actual robot it does work better. At least you get the idea and we prove the logic.

H-Bridge

Now that we have the logic down we need to refine our hardware for the motor control. The simplest way I found to do this was with a chip called the H-bridge. I am using the ST L293D. Make sure you get the Data Sheet. There are a number of different H-bridges on the market. There are differences.   While we have not built the robot yet the following will complete the electronics side. For testing if you have some small motors from toys or hand held fans they will work well. As for the auxiliary power supply I show it as 9V, but that will vary for you depending on your motor choice. If you are using some small motors reduce the auxiliary voltage. A 9 volt battery, a voltage regulator or a voltage divider can be used. Many DC motors will run on various voltages, just at different speeds. Don't run too long if not sure, watch for signs of overheating. If you detect the ozone smell shut down the power quickly. It is very easy to burn up a chip at this point. If your microchip reboots when you start the motor, check your wiring first. If everything is correct you may need to add some additional capacitors. Depending on the size of the capacitor you may want to add 3 or 4. If the reboot problem stops, you can reduce the number if you want. Remember when a motor starts up it can draw a strong current. Capacitors hold a charge, so even after you shut off the external power there is power in your circuit. Ground yourself and the board. If you don't have motors you can improvise with the LED's, but you will need more because LED's are not bidirectional for current flow. In place of the H-Bridge you could use a series of mosfet's.   I found the low cost H-Bridge much simpler to use. Make sure you select an H-Bridge that has internal clamp diodes to prevent inductive flyback effect from the motors. When a motor suddenly stops a voltage in the opposite direction can occur, you need to prevent this, hence the clamp diodes. In the pictures that follow you will note the inclusion of the H-Bridge, an extra voltage regulator, an additional power source, extra capacitors and two salvaged motors.

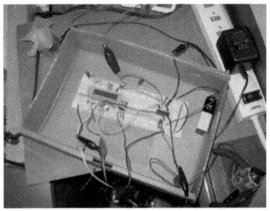 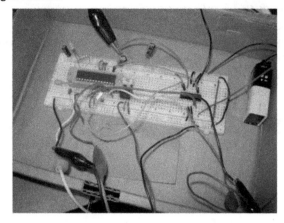

Exhibits 219 & 220

 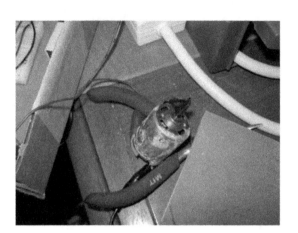

Exhibits 221 & 222

The motors are very different. I put tape on the drive shaft of the right motor to help me see it run. Before you go too far with your motors, try giving them some direct power from a battery that you plan to use as the auxiliary power supply. Depending on your motors you may see that the PWM levels, X and Y, values need to be above a level before the motors will start, these are at about 90. As we get our robot working we can go back and adjust the X Y factors in either Python or the C program. I plan to do it in the Python program. You may also notice that the motors run for a bit after the stop command. As our robot is going to use a motor with a gear box this may not be an issue. As we progress we will evaluate. The power level on our board is increasing and we are adding capacitors. The short possibilities increase in severity. Capacitors hold a charge, even after you turn the power off. Get used to grounding yourself and the board to discharge any build up. I cannot stress enough that we are at a point where frying a chip is easy. For example if you have conflicting ports on with high compare values a motor turned on for forward and backward can quickly fry the H-Bridge. If you reverse the auxiliary power supply connections you will fry the H-Bridge and probably your microchip. The following diagram shows the basic wiring. The diagram includes the bumper and servo. While I know the actual wiring works, there is the possibility of something moving as I drew the diagram, so don't use blind faith, think it through. I found in using the ST H-Bridge that I did not need to enable the pins 1 and 9. This may not be true for other H-Bridges.

Bread Board Diagram with H-Bridge and Motors

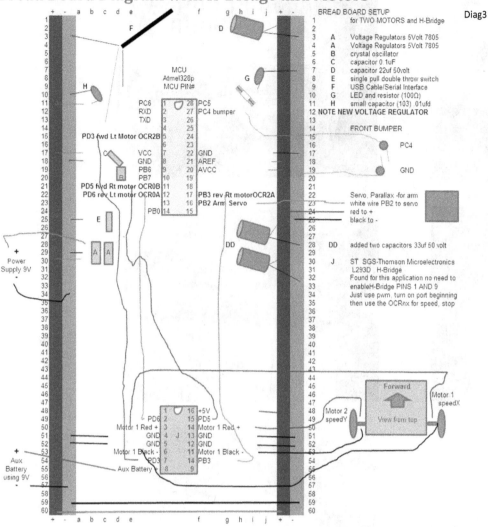

There is an excellent tool for designing your circuits, CircuitLab© at www.circuitlab.com.

Day Thirty Five - Building the Physical Robot

You have been very patient and I hope you have learned a bunch. Are you ready to build your robot? You can spend as much money as you want, but I tend to be well shall we say thrifty. Let me talk a little about Max. Max is a simple prototype designed to prove concepts, not to look pretty. Max's frame is a salvaged metal case from a cable or satellite control box. The two drive motors are 24 VDC with wheels and built in gearboxes. I purchased them for about $9.00 each. You will want drive motors with gearboxes. I had connectors around so I used those, as I wanted to be able to take Max apart easily. The front wheel is a swivel caster wheel that I had lying around. The arm is driven by a small stepper motor. The arm itself is just a small piece of wood. The bumper is a wood strip on screws with springs and a contact wire. The contact wire is striped ordinary household gauge 10 to 12. You are ready, Go ahead and assemble your robot. We will still need to add the stepper motor control, the wireless communications, and the camera with speaker to the robot. You will see in the pictures that I have gone ahead and soldered the components onto a solder board, I suggest you wait a bit before taking that step. As you can see in the pictures there are a lot of wires. I hope as you look at this you can visualize your board. When you get to the point of soldering a board I strongly suggest that you put the H-Bridge and the microchip in a suitable holder that allows you to remove and replace the chip. In the picture you may note that there is a wireless communications device in place, we will talk about that in a moment. You will also see a number of wires to nowhere. All I can say is that I knew in the future that I would want to connect to other ports on the microchip. I did not have some extra connectors to place on the platform. So I just put some wires in place. Auxiliary power and the primary microchip power are from 9 volt and 12 volt AC to DC transformers while I am testing.

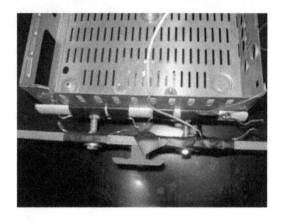

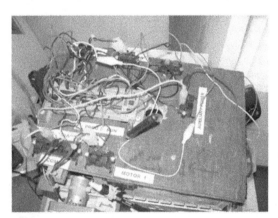

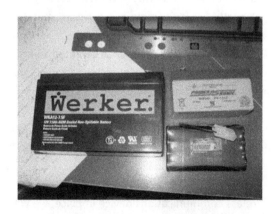

Max1 & 8

The batteries ride in the metal case. A 9.6 volt battery powers the microchip and arm servo. The large 12 volt 7.6Ah battery is for the soon to be added camera. The 12 volt 1.4Ah battery is for the drive motors. While the drive motors can take up to 24 volts, I decided to stick with the 12 volt battery at this point. For your robot you will need to evaluate the hardware specifications, and consider your future needs. The magnificent wooden arm is driven by a parallax standard servo. Whichever servo you choose make sure you get the data sheet. There are excellent tutorials on the web about servo's or stepper motors. I am asking you to do your homework and not just rely on the setting I show in the program for running the servo. As the project progressed I have found that I needed to make numerous changes to the C program and to the Python program. What we had worked, but not really well. Once we added more power and motors the weakness were quickly revealed.

Day Thirty Six - Running Smoother

C Improved Motor Control

Let's make the changes to the C program first. Make sure you save a copy of the program prior to making these extensive changes. The biggest change is to the motor control function. I decided to take out the PORT on off and just turn the motor ports on when program starts. The motor ports are always on just the current flow or PWM is controlled by the compare values. I took a better look at the logic and decided it was simpler to work with if I treated each motor independently. Once we put the robot on the ground to run we may make some additional changes.

Servo Control

The code for turning on/off the arm servo and for moving it has been added. The NerdKit tutorial on servo control is a good starting place to gain understanding of the controls needed. In very simplistic terms servo control is done by the recurring sending of a pulse and the length of time the pulse is on. Our servo needs a signal every 20ms to maintain a position. When the servo is on it draws power to maintain position. The length of the pulse that is sent every 20ms determines the servo's position. In the AT328Robo.c program we use a 16 bit PWM pin to control and send the pulse. Complete code for AT328Robo.c follows. After you complete the changes and upload the program wait until you make the changes to the Python program before running.

C / C++   ▼   print   ▼   Find ▼

<new>   AT328Robo.c   ◁ ▷ X

```
1   /*for ATMega328 Herb Norbom, RyMax, Inc.3/18/2013   add stepper motor control
2   for communications using serial port at 9600 BAUD via Hyper Termianal or Putty
3   program will also work with our Python program lesson29c.py
4   to microchip with various displays on LCD   add PWM and motor controls
5   for personal hobby use only, include references to RyMax Inc.
6    for resale or commercial use contact RyMax, Inc. for written persmission.
7   */
8   #define F_CPU 14745600
9   #include <stdio.h>
10  #include <stdlib.h>
11  #include <avr/io.h>
12  #include <avr/interrupt.h>
13  #include <avr/pgmspace.h>
14  #include <inttypes.h>
15  #include <string.h>
16  #include "../libnerdkits/io_328p.h"
17  #include "../libnerdkits/delay.h"
18  #include "../libnerdkits/uart.h"
19
20  volatile int i=0;              //use as counter/incrementer
21  volatile char tcread[13];      //variable that receives from PC
22  volatile int speedX=0;         //speed  Left Motor
23  volatile int speedY=0;         //speed  Right Motor
24  volatile int stspeedX[5];      //get prelim string speed
25  volatile int stspeedY[5];      //get prelim string speed
26  volatile uint16_t pos = 1765;  //move Arm to start postion
27
28  //ARM CONTROL SETTINGS
29  void pwm_Fset(uint16_t x) {
30      OCR1B = x;  }
31
32  #define PWM_ARMmin 1650     // For ARM servo
33  #define PWM_ARMmax 4325     //for parallax std servo 900-0005
34  #define PWM_ARMstart 1765   //pulse seting for positions
35          |   |   |   |   |  //center would be 2765
36
37  void pwm_init() {
38      /*for drive motors using 8 bit timers for PWM, MAX is 255
39          OCR0A & OCR0B & OCR2B & OCR2A
40          clock 0 for PD5 & PD6 Timer\Counter Control Register A  */
41      TCCR0A = (1<<COM0A1)|(1<<COM0B1)|(1<<WGM01)|(1<<WGM00);
42      TCCR0B =(1<<CS01); //prescale clk 8 use for OCR0A and OCR0B
43      //CLOCK 2 for PB3 and PD3
44      TCCR2A = (1<<COM2A1)|(1<<COM2B1)|(1<<WGM21)|(1<<WGM20);
45      TCCR2B =(1<<CS21); //prescale clk 8 use for OCR2A and OCR2B
46      //combo of WGM20,21,22 sets to FAST PWM mode 7, see page 162
47
48  //SERVO   setup Timer1 for Fast PWM mode, 16-bit, MODE 15
49      // COM1B1 -- for non-inverting output
50      // WGM13, WGM12, WGM11, WGM10 -- for Fast PWM with OCR1A as TOP value
51      // CS11 -- for CLK/8 prescaling
52      OCR1A = 36864; //need for arm servo  signal every 20 ms
53      // sets PWM to repeat pulse every 20.0ms   see page 134 - 137
54      pwm_Fset(PWM_ARMstart);
55      TCCR1A = (1<<COM1B1) | (1<<WGM11) | (1<<WGM10);
56      TCCR1B = (1<<WGM13) | (1<<WGM12) | (1<<CS11);
57  /*  we are using a prescale of 8
58      14745600/8 = 1843200
```

Exhibit223

124

Programmer's Notepad - [C:\Documents and Settings\Herb Norbom\My Documents\NERDKIT\Code\Sample328\ATMEGA328R...

File   Edit   View   Tools   Window   Help

C / C++   ▼   print   ▼   Find ▼

<new>   AT328Robo.c

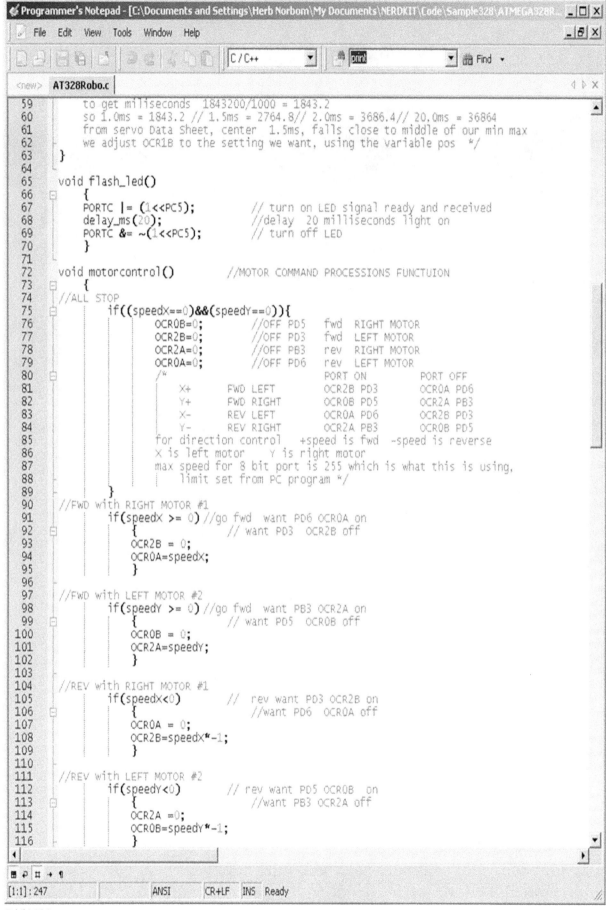

```
59         to get milliseconds   1843200/1000 = 1843.2
60         so 1.0ms = 1843.2 // 1.5ms = 2764.8// 2.0ms = 3686.4// 20.0ms = 36864
61         from servo Data Sheet, center  1.5ms, falls close to middle of our min max
62         we adjust OCR1B to the setting we want, using the variable pos   */
63      }
64
65    void flash_led()
66        {
67        PORTC |= (1<<PC5);          // turn on LED signal ready and received
68        delay_ms(20);               //delay  20 milliseconds light on
69        PORTC &= ~(1<<PC5);         // turn off LED
70        }
71
72    void motorcontrol()           //MOTOR COMMAND PROCESSIONS FUNCTUION
73        {
74    //ALL STOP
75           if((speedX==0)&&(speedY==0)){
76                  OCR0B=0;         //OFF PD5   fwd   RIGHT MOTOR
77                  OCR2B=0;         //OFF PD3   fwd   LEFT MOTOR
78                  OCR2A=0;         //OFF PB3   rev   RIGHT MOTOR
79                  OCR0A=0;         //OFF PD6   rev   LEFT MOTOR
80                  /*                        PORT ON           PORT OFF
81                    X+     FWD LEFT      OCR2B PD3         OCR0A PD6
82                    Y+     FWD RIGHT     OCR0B PD5         OCR2A PB3
83                    X-     REV LEFT      OCR0A PD6         OCR2B PD3
84                    Y-     REV RIGHT     OCR2A PB3         OCR0B PD5
85                  for direction control   +speed is fwd  -speed is reverse
86                  X is left motor    Y is right motor
87                  max speed for 8 bit port is 255 which is what this is using,
88                      limit set from PC program */
89                  }
90    //FWD with RIGHT MOTOR #1
91           if(speedX >= 0) //go fwd  want PD6 OCR0A on
92                  {            // want PD3   OCR2B off
93              OCR2B = 0;
94              OCR0A=speedX;
95                  }
96
97    //FWD with LEFT MOTOR #2
98           if(speedY >= 0) //go fwd  want PB3 OCR2A on
99                  {            // want PD5   OCR0B off
100             OCR0B = 0;
101             OCR2A=speedY;
102                 }
103
104   //REV with RIGHT MOTOR #1
105          if(speedX<0)      //  rev want PD3 OCR2B on
106                 {           //want PD6  OCR0A off
107             OCR0A = 0;
108             OCR2B=speedX*-1;
109                 }
110
111   //REV with LEFT MOTOR #2
112          if(speedY<0)      // rev want PD5 OCR0B  on
113                 {           //want PB3 OCR2A off
114             OCR2A =0;
115             OCR0B=speedY*-1;
116                 }
```

125

Programmer's Notepad - [C:\Documents and Settings\Herb Norbom\My Documents\NERDKIT\Code\Sample328\ATMEGA328R...

File   Edit   View   Tools   Window   Help

C / C++   print   Find

<new>   AT328Robo.c

```
117         }
118
119    ISR(PCINT1_vect){   /*Interrupt on PC4 means circuit complete. We want
120         to stop all drive motors. Send msg back to console that all stopped
121         have console send back voice text  "OUCH" for speaker on MAX.
122         Displays msg on PC that needs to be cleared. Clear the queue also. */
123
124         if (PINC & (1<<PC4))    //no actual interrupt on PC4
125            {return;}
126         else
127         {
128             flash_led();          //ready signal
129             speedX=0;
130             speedY=0;
131             motorcontrol();
132             printf_P(PSTR("INT\r\n"));
133             int count =0;
134             int tempnothing=0;
135             for (count=0;count<5000;count++)
136                {tempnothing=tempnothing; }
137         }
138         return;
139    }
140    ISR(USART_RX_vect)
141         {
142             flash_led();              //flash,interrupt fired have msg
143             speedX=0;
144             speedY=0;
145             for (i=0;i<6;i++)
146                {
147                    stspeedX[i]=' ';
148                    stspeedY[i]=' ';
149                }
150             for (i=0;i<14;i++)                            //clear variable
151                {
152                    tcread[i]= ' ';
153                }
154             char sign[]="-";
155
156             scanf_P(PSTR("%s"),tcread);              // read from uart receiver
157             printf_P(PSTR("Max says %s \r\n"),tcread);    //send to uart
158             if(tcread[0]=='r')
159                {
160                    //do nothing, sent msg back in above to be interperted on PC
161                }
162             if(tcread[0]=='x')              //for LEFT MOTOR
163                {
164                    stspeedX[1]=tcread[2]-'0'; //strip off end, convert to single
165                    stspeedX[2]=tcread[3]-'0'; //    digit decimal
166                    stspeedX[3]=tcread[4]-'0';
167                    speedX= stspeedX[1]*100+stspeedX[2]*10+stspeedX[3];
168                    if (speedX >255){   //PWM limit exceeded
169                        speedX =0;      //some kind of error set speed = 0
170                        }
171                    if (tcread[1] == sign[0]){    //TCREAD[1] HAS THE SIGN FOR X
172                        int temp =speedX;
173                        speedX=temp*-1;    //make it negative
174                        }
```

Exhibit225

126

```
175                          }
176              if(tcread[5]=='Y')            //for RIGHT MOTOR
177                  {
178                       stspeedY[1]=tcread[7]-'0';
179                       stspeedY[2]=tcread[8]-'0';
180                       stspeedY[3]=tcread[9]-'0';
181                       speedY= stspeedY[1]*100+stspeedY[2]*10+stspeedY[3];
182                       if (speedY >255){
183                          speedY =0;       //some kind of error set speed = 0
184                          }
185                       if (tcread[6] == sign[0]){   //TCREAD[6] HAS THE SIGN FOR Y
186                          int temp = speedY;
187                          speedY=temp*-1;     //make it negative
188                          }
189  //        printf_P(PSTR("spX= %i   spy= %i\r\n"),speedX, speedY);       //for debuging
190                  }
191              if(tcread[0]==']')
192                  {
193                  if(tcread[1]=='1')
194                      {
195                      printf_P(PSTR("Max ARM ready %s\r\n"),tcread);
196                      DDRB |= (1<<PB2); //servo on ARM
197                      pwm_Fset(PWM_ARMstart);
198                      pos =PWM_ARMstart;
199                      }
200                  if(tcread[1]=='0')
201                      {
202                      printf_P(PSTR("Max ARM STOP %s\r\n"),tcread);
203                      DDRB &= ~(1<<PB2); //servo OFF for ARM
204                      delay_ms(500);
205                      }
206                  if(tcread[1]==']') pos+=25;
207                  if(tcread[1]=='[') pos-=25;
208                  //check limits for the servo
209                  if(pos >= PWM_ARMmax) pos = PWM_ARMmax;
210                  if(pos <= PWM_ARMmin) pos = PWM_ARMmin;
211                  pwm_Fset(pos);
212                  printf_P(PSTR("ATM Pos %i\r\n"),pos);
213                  }
214              motorcontrol();
215          }
216
217  int main() {
218      cli();                  //stop the interrupt detection while loading
219      pwm_init();             //setup PWM
220      uart_init();            //start serial port and uart stream
221      FILE uart_stream = FDEV_SETUP_STREAM(uart_putchar, uart_getchar, _FDEV_SETUP_RW);
222      stdin = stdout = &uart_stream;
223      UBRR0L = (1<<6 | 1<<4 | 1<<3 | 1<<2 | 1<<1 | 1<<0);//BAUD 9600,Data Sheet 195-203
224      UBRR0H = 0;
225      UCSR0B |= (1<<RXCIE0); // enable uart RX RECEIVE Interrupt page 196
226      DDRB |=(1<<PB3);        //PB3 on Right Motor rev
227      DDRD |=(1<<PD5);        //PD5 on Left Motor fwd
228      DDRD |=(1<<PD6);        //PD6 on Left Motor rev
229      DDRD |=(1<<PD3);        //PD3 on Right Motor fwd
230
231      DDRC |= (1<<PC5);       // ready port LED signal-for valid receive and startup
232      delay_ms(2500);         // pause to CHARGE capacitors
```

Exhibit226

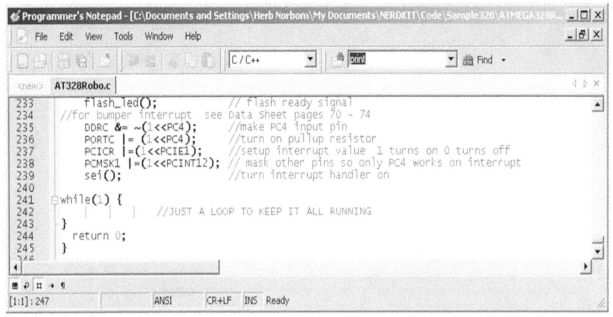

```
233      flash_led();              // flash ready signal
234  //for bumper interrupt  see Data Sheet pages 70 - 74
235      DDRC &= ~(1<<PC4);        //make PC4 input pin
236      PORTC |= (1<<PC4);        //turn on pullup resistor
237      PCICR |=(1<<PCIE1);       //setup interrupt value  1 turns on 0 turns off
238      PCMSK1 |=(1<<PCINT12);    // mask other pins so only PC4 works on interrupt
239      sei();                    //turn interrupt handler on
240
241  while(1) {
242    │    │    │      //JUST A LOOP TO KEEP IT ALL RUNNING
243  }
244    return 0;
245  }
```

Exhibit227

Python Running Smoother

Now we need to make a number of changes to the Python program lesson29c.py. Save lesson29c.py as lesson29d.py. The first changes were made to the paint function.

- I moved our adjustment factor for events to the first assignments to cx and cy, lines 88 and 89. I also added a multiplication factor of 2 to enable the quicker jump in PWM and ease of position of the mouse on the canvas.
- Line 114 changed to SELF.INTset=0
- On lines 122 and 123 I took out the adjustment centering factors. I also changed the order of the variables.
  - Line 139 calLeft = (-cy-cx)
  - Line 178 calRight=(-cy+cx)
- The error description on line 132 was changed to be a little more general. I generally forget to change the line number reference. Just naming the function should be enough description.
- I inserted on line 142 return calLeft. (Note if you are making these changes I have adjusted line reference accordingly for the following references.)
- On line 185 insert return calRight, line numbers adjusted accordingly.
- Line 253 I changed the msgLen to 1 vs. 2
- Line 260 changed the comm test to 'Max says r2 '   (Note space after the 2)
- Line 442 changed the SELF.sent to "]1"
- Line 451 changed the SELF.sent to "]0"
- Line 463 changed the SELF.sent to "]]"
- Line 473 changed the SELF.sent to "]["
- For commCheck function
  - I took out line 496 (left a blank line to keep numbering consistent)
  - Changed line 497 to print ("called the test communications,")
  - Changed line 498 to print ("response from Max should be 'Max says r2 '")
  - Changed line 499 to SELF.sent="r2"
- Line 524 added a space to text "ARM ON "vs. The current "ARM ON". Space is after ON to keep buttons same size
- Line 527 added two qualifiers "repeatdelay=500, repeatinterval=300"   (Now when you hold down the button the command repeats. Note with our queue setting not very effective, but we may want to adjust the queue size)
- Line 527 added two qualifiers "repeatdelay=500 , repeatinterval=300"

We will still have adjustments, for example, our bumper sends multiple interrupt signals we will need to add a de-bounce routine on the C program. The message box for displaying obstacle does not display until after you try to move robot again.   Our random message for the bumper starts with the same message each time. We need to provide a seed factor that is not static. Minor inconveniences, I am sure we will find more pressing issues. There are two issues that I want to address now.

Queue Improvements

The first issue is our queue. Our PC via the mouse events loads the queue very quickly. I am going to put in a test to see if the queue is full. If the queue is full we will not write to it. We only need this test in the paint function as that is where the direction and speed control is loaded into the queue. Assuming changes mentioned above have been made. Add the following code to the lines shown. Also, adjusted the queue size. SendQueue = Queue.PriorityQueue(maxsize=5).

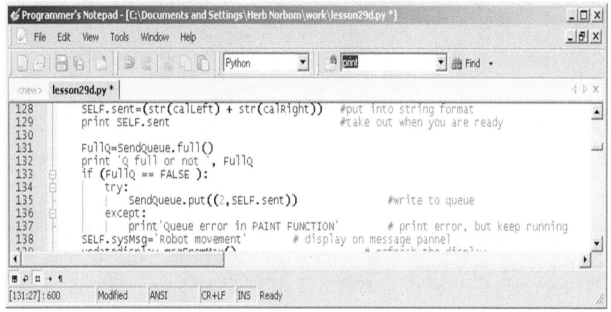

```
128     SELF.sent=(str(calLeft) + str(calRight))    #put into string format
129     print SELF.sent                             #take out when you are ready
130
131     FullQ=SendQueue.full()
132     print 'Q full or not ', FullQ
133     if (FullQ == FALSE ):
134         try:
135             SendQueue.put((2,SELF.sent))                #write to queue
136         except:
137             print'Queue error in PAINT FUNCTION'        # print error, but keep running
138     SELF.sysMsg='Robot movement'        # display on message pannel
```

Exhibit228

Minimum PWM values

The second issue deals with our motors. You may have noticed the motor does not start until a PWM value of approximately 70 in my case is reached. The microchip is sending commands to start the motor as soon as the value is greater than 0. We are using juice and applying torque to the motors, but not moving. For your motors you may need to set different values. I want to leave the PWM at 0 until a true start point for the motors is achieved.

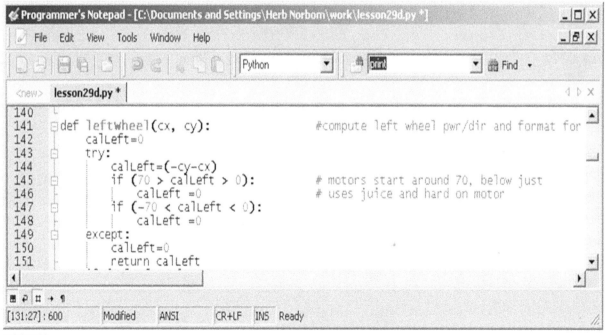

```
140
141     def leftwheel(cx, cy):               #compute left wheel pwr/dir and format for
142         calLeft=0
143         try:
144             calLeft=(-cy-cx)
145             if (70 > calLeft > 0):       # motors start around 70, below just
146                 calLeft =0               # uses juice and hard on motor
147             if (-70 < calLeft < 0):
148                 calLeft =0
149         except:
150             calLeft=0
151         return calLeft
```

Exhibit229

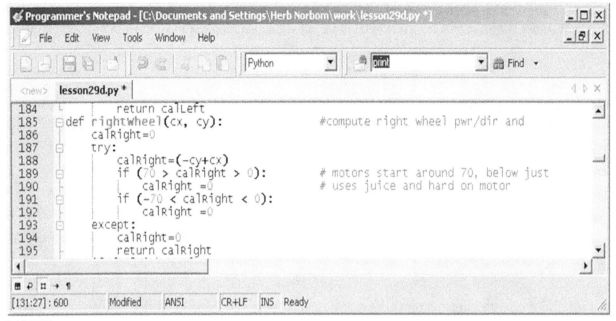
Exhibit230

Random Function Improvement

Before giving you the complete Python code I want to fix our random message generator by adding a seed value. If we use a portion of 'time' as a seed, we should get a random number.

- Line 20 from time import gmtime, strftime
  - See http://docs.python.org/2/library/time.html for explanation

- Line 99   random.seed=time.strftime("%S", gmtime())   #insert as a new line, this is getting seconds and using as a seed for generating a random number.

I think we have covered enough code changes for now. Here is the complete code for lesson29d.py.

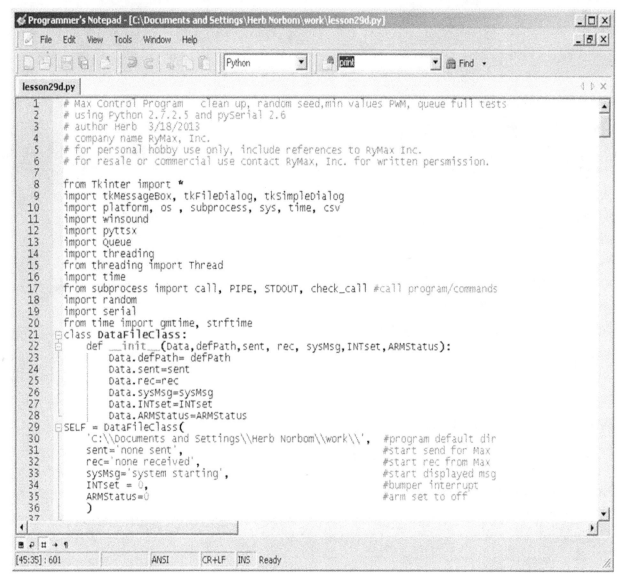

```python
# Max Control Program   clean up, random seed,min values PwM, queue full tests
# using Python 2.7.2.5 and pySerial 2.6
# author Herb  3/18/2013
# company name RyMax, Inc.
# for personal hobby use only, include references to RyMax Inc.
# for resale or commercial use contact RyMax, Inc. for written persmission.

from Tkinter import *
import tkMessageBox, tkFileDialog, tkSimpleDialog
import platform, os , subprocess, sys, time, csv
import winsound
import pyttsx
import Queue
import threading
from threading import Thread
import time
from subprocess import call, PIPE, STDOUT, check_call #call program/commands
import random
import serial
from time import gmtime, strftime
class DataFileClass:
    def __init__(Data,defPath,sent, rec, sysMsg,INTset,ARMStatus):
        Data.defPath= defPath
        Data.sent=sent
        Data.rec=rec
        Data.sysMsg=sysMsg
        Data.INTset=INTset
        Data.ARMStatus=ARMStatus
SELF = DataFileClass(
    'C:\\Documents and Settings\\Herb Norbom\\work\\',   #program default dir
    sent='none sent',                                    #start send for Max
    rec='none received',                                 #start rec from Max
    sysMsg='system starting',                            #start displayed msg
    INTset = 0,                                          #bumper interrupt
    ARMStatus=0                                          #arm set to off
    )
```

Exhibit231

131

```python
38  class UpdateDisplay:                    #display messages
39      def __init__(DISP, root):
40          DISP.robotStatusDataframe = LabelFrame(root, text="***Max Comm Robot Data***")
41          DISP.robotStatusDataframe.config(width=25, cursor="arrow")
42          DISP.robotStatusDataframe.grid(column=1, row=3, sticky=(N,W))
43
44          DISP.fromMax = StringVar()
45          DISP.fromMax.set(SELF.rec)
46          DISP.msgRec = Label(DISP.robotStatusDataframe, textvariable=DISP.fromMax)
47          DISP.msgRec.grid(column=0,row=1,sticky=(N,W,E,S))
48
49          DISP.toMax = StringVar()
50          DISP.toMax.set(SELF.sent)
51          DISP.msgSend = Label(DISP.robotStatusDataframe, textvariable=DISP.toMax)
52          DISP.msgSend.grid(column=0,row=2,sticky=(N,W,E,S))
53
54          DISP.systemMsg= StringVar()
55          DISP.systemMsg.set(SELF.sysMsg)
56          DISP.sysMsg = Label(DISP.robotStatusDataframe, textvariable=DISP.systemMsg)
57          DISP.sysMsg.grid(column=0,row=3, sticky=(N,W,E,S))
58
59      def msgFromMax(DISP):                #when info changes this is the called function
60          DISP.fromMax.set(SELF.rec)
61          DISP.toMax.set(SELF.sent)
62          DISP.systemMsg.set(SELF.sysMsg)
63  #       print "at msgFromMax ", SELF.rec
64
65  def on_click_listbox(event):
66      index = soundBox.curselection()      # get selected line index
67      soundFile = soundBox.get(index)      # get the line's text
68      label1.configure(text=soundFile)     # show selected text in label
69      path=SELF.defPath                    # use our class defined path
70      if soundFile != None:
71          extension = os.path.splitext(soundFile)[1][1:]
72          print (extension)
73          if ((extension=='wav') | (extension=='WAV')):   # this is the or | connector
74              winsound.PlaySound(str(path)+soundFile,0)
75          if(extension=='txt'):
76              engine=pyttsx.init()
77              voices = engine.getProperty('voices')
78              for voice in voices:
79                  engine.setProperty('voice', voice.id)
80              with open(str(path)+soundFile) as f:
81                  for line in f:
82                      engine.say(line)
83                      engine.runAndWait()
84
85  def paint( event ):
86      cx=cy=0
87      try:
88          cx=(event.x-200)*2
89          cy=(event.y-150)*2
90      except:
91          cx=0                             # if something not working want to
92          cy=0                             # set mouse event location to (0,0)
93      if (SELF.INTset==1):                 #Max's bumper was pressed
94          print("whats up")
95          engine=pyttsx.init()
96          voices = engine.getProperty('voices')
97          for voice in voices:
98              engine.setProperty('voice', voice.id)
99              random.seed=time.strftime("%S", gmtime()) #use seconds as seed
100             ranNumber=random.choice([1,2,3,4,5])
101             if (ranNumber==1):
102                 engine.say('OUCH that hurt')
103             if (ranNumber==2):
104                 engine.say("who's driving this bus?")
105             if (ranNumber==3):
106                 engine.say('Do not touch me')
107             if (ranNumber==4):
108                 engine.say('Go away')
```

Exhibit232

132

```python
109            if (ranNumber==5):
110                engine.say('Move it or loose it')
111            engine.runAndWait()
112        status= tkMessageBox.askyesno("Bumper","Obstacle removed?\n(%s) " % ranNumber)
113        print status
114        if (status== True): #from message box if obstacle removed YES
115            SELF.INTset=0
116            cx=0
117            cy=0
118        else:
119            cx=0
120            cy=0
121
122        try:
123            calLeft=leftwheel(cx, cy)        #power and direction of left wheel
124            calRight=rightwheel(cx,cy)       #power and direction of right wheel
125        except:
126            print 'error on Max speed calLeft= ', calLeft, 'calRight= ',calRight
127            calLeft='X+000'                  #if error want to set power to 0
128            calRight='Y+000'
129        SELF.sent=(str(calLeft) + str(calRight))   #put into string format
130        print SELF.sent                            #take out when you are ready
131
132        FullQ=SendQueue.full()
133        print 'Q full or not ', FullQ
134        if (FullQ == FALSE ):
135            try:
136                SendQueue.put((2,SELF.sent))            #write to queue
137            except:
138                print'Queue error in PAINT FUNCTION'     # print error, but keep running
139        SELF.sysMsg='Robot movement'        # display on message pannel
140        updatedisplay.msgFromMax()                      # refresh the display
141
142 def leftwheel(cx, cy):                  #compute left wheel pwr/dir and format for
143     calLeft=0
144     try:
145         calLeft=(-cy-cx)
146         if (70 > calLeft > 0):          # motors start around 70, below just
147             calLeft =0                  # uses juice and hard on motor
148         if (-70 < calLeft < 0):
149             calLeft =0
150     except:
151         calLeft=0
152         return calLeft
153     if (calLeft==0):
154         calLeft=str("X+000")
155         return calLeft
156     if (calLeft >0):
157         if (calLeft > 255):
158             calLeft = str("X+255")
159             return calLeft
160         if (calLeft>99):
161             calLeft ="X+"+str(calLeft)
162             return calLeft
163         if (calLeft>9):
164             calLeft ="X+0"+str(calLeft)
165             return calLeft
166         else:
167             calLeft ="X+00"+str(calLeft)
168             return calLeft
169     if (calLeft < 0):
170         calLeft = abs(calLeft)          #GET ABSOLUTE VALUE
171         if (calLeft > 255):
172             calLeft = str("X-255")
173             return calLeft
174         if (calLeft>99):
175             calLeft ="X-"+str(calLeft)
176             return calLeft
177         if (calLeft>9):
178             calLeft ="X-0"+str(calLeft)
179             return calLeft
```

Exhibit233

133

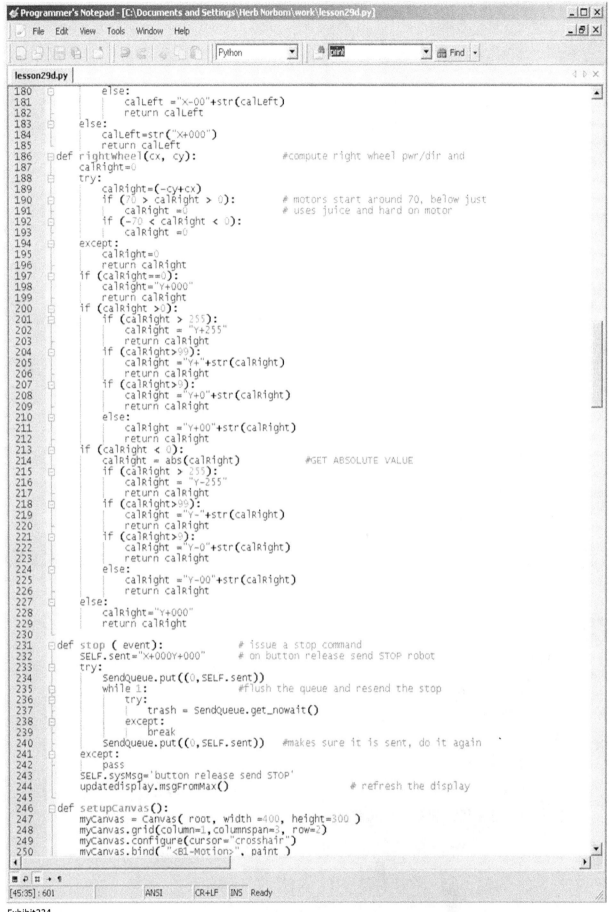

```
180                 else:
181                     calLeft ="X-00"+str(calLeft)
182                     return calLeft
183         else:
184             calLeft=str("X+000")
185             return calLeft
186  def rightWheel(cx, cy):              #compute right wheel pwr/dir and
187      calRight=0
188      try:
189          calRight=(-cy+cx)
190          if (70 > calRight > 0):       # motors start around 70, below just
191              calRight =0               # uses juice and hard on motor
192          if (-70 < calRight < 0):
193              calRight =0
194      except:
195          calRight=0
196          return calRight
197      if (calRight==0):
198          calRight="Y+000"
199          return calRight
200      if (calRight >0):
201          if (calRight > 255):
202              calRight = "Y+255"
203              return calRight
204          if (calRight>99):
205              calRight ="Y+"+str(calRight)
206              return calRight
207          if (calRight>9):
208              calRight ="Y+0"+str(calRight)
209              return calRight
210          else:
211              calRight ="Y+00"+str(calRight)
212              return calRight
213      if (calRight < 0):
214          calRight = abs(calRight)          #GET ABSOLUTE VALUE
215          if (calRight > 255):
216              calRight = "Y-255"
217              return calRight
218          if (calRight>99):
219              calRight ="Y-"+str(calRight)
220              return calRight
221          if (calRight>9):
222              calRight ="Y-0"+str(calRight)
223              return calRight
224          else:
225              calRight ="Y-00"+str(calRight)
226              return calRight
227      else:
228          calRight="Y+000"
229          return calRight
230
231  def stop ( event):              # issue a stop command
232      SELF.sent="X+000Y+000"      # on button release send STOP robot
233      try:
234          SendQueue.put((0,SELF.sent))
235          while 1:                #flush the queue and resend the stop
236              try:
237                  trash = SendQueue.get_nowait()
238              except:
239                  break
240          SendQueue.put((0,SELF.sent))   #makes sure it is sent, do it again
241      except:
242          pass
243      SELF.sysMsg='button release send STOP'
244      updatedisplay.msgFromMax()                  # refresh the display
245
246  def setupCanvas():
247      myCanvas = Canvas( root, width =400, height=300 )
248      myCanvas.grid(column=1,columnspan=3, row=2)
249      myCanvas.configure(cursor="crosshair")
250      myCanvas.bind( "<B1-Motion>", paint )
```

Exhibit234

134

```python
251        myCanvas.bind("<ButtonRelease-1>",stop)
252        myCanvas.create_line(125, 150, 175, 150, width=1)
253        myCanvas.create_line(225, 150, 275, 150, width=1)
254        myCanvas.create_line(200,  85, 200, 135, width=1)
255        myCanvas.create_line(200, 165, 200, 215, width=1)
256
257    def receiving():   #this will be when receiving communications from Max
258        while True:
259            time.sleep(.1)
260            buffer=''
261            msgLen=0
262            try:
263                buffer=ser.readline(ser.inwaiting())
264                msgLen= buffer.__len__()
265            except:
266                pass
267            if (msgLen >1):
268                SELF.rec=" "
269                msgRec = buffer
270                decoded=msgRec.decode('utf-8')
271                msgStrip = decoded.strip('\r\n')
272                SELF.rec=msgStrip
273    #           print(SELF.rec)
274                if (SELF.rec=='Max says r2 '):            #note space after r2
275                    SELF.sysMsg='Comm test good'
276                    print ('Comm test good')
277                if (SELF.rec=='INT'):                     #Max's bumber activated
278                    myEvent="<Tkinter.Event>"
279                    stop(myEvent)                         #call stop, send stop/flush queue
280                    SELF.sysMsg='Hit Something STOP'
281                    print('Hit something STOP trash queue')
282                    SELF.INTset=1
283                updatedisplay.msgFromMax()                    # refresh the display
284
285    def sending():      # it uses a separate thread
286        while True:
287            while not SendQueue.empty():
288                try:
289                    qaction = SendQueue.qsize()          #see if message in queue
290                except:
291                    print('error on get queue size')
292                    qaction=0
293                if (qaction >0):
294                    msgLen=0
295                    msgSend =('','')
296                    msgSendR =''
297                    try:
298                        msgSend = SendQueue.get(True)        #retrieve msg from queue
299                        print 'msgSend.get= ', msgSend[1]    #NOTE it is returning a tuple
300                        time.sleep(.5)
301                    except:
302                        print 'error on get'
303                    try:
304                        msgSendR = msgSend[1]                #from tuple move to non-tuple
305                        msgLen = msgSendR.__len__()
306    #                   print 'msgSend length & msg= ',msgLen,' ',msgSendR #here to help debug
307                    except:
308                        print 'error getting queue msg or size'
309                    try:
310                        for i in range(0,msgLen):
311    #                       print msgSendR[i]
312                            ser.write(msgSendR[i])
313                            time.sleep(.1)
314                        ser.write("\r")
315                    except:
316                        print 'error on write to serial'
317                        pass                            # keep running
318
319    def threadStart():       #starting child threads
320        recTh=Thread(target=receiving, name='recThread',args=())
321        recTh.setDaemon(True)        # must set all child threads before starting
```

[45:35] : 601   ANSI   CR+LF   INS   Ready

Exhibit235

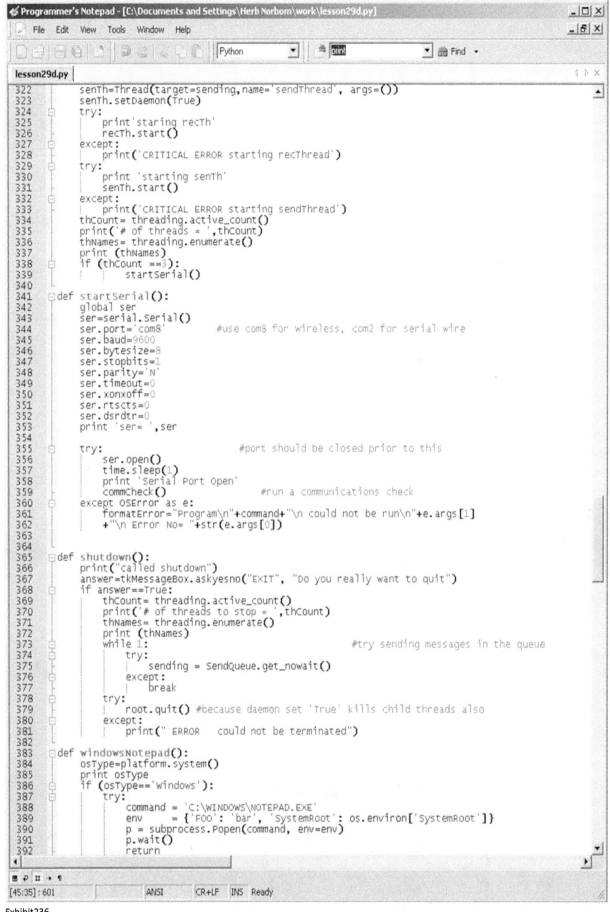

```
322        senTh=Thread(target=sending,name='sendThread', args=())
323        senTh.setDaemon(True)
324        try:
325            print'staring recTh'
326            recTh.start()
327        except:
328            print('CRITICAL ERROR starting recThread')
329        try:
330            print 'starting senTh'
331            senTh.start()
332        except:
333            print('CRITICAL ERROR starting sendThread')
334        thCount= threading.active_count()
335        print('# of threads = ',thCount)
336        thNames= threading.enumerate()
337        print (thNames)
338        if (thCount ==3):
339            startSerial()
340
341    def startSerial():
342        global ser
343        ser=serial.Serial()
344        ser.port='com8'            #use com8 for wireless, com2 for serial wire
345        ser.baud=9600
346        ser.bytesize=8
347        ser.stopbits=1
348        ser.parity='N'
349        ser.timeout=0
350        ser.xonxoff=0
351        ser.rtscts=0
352        ser.dsrdtr=0
353        print 'ser= ',ser
354
355        try:                        #port should be closed prior to this
356            ser.open()
357            time.sleep(1)
358            print 'Serial Port Open'
359            commCheck()              #run a communications check
360        except OSError as e:
361            formatError="Program\n"+command+"\n could not be run\n"+e.args[1]
362            +"\n Error No= "+str(e.args[0])
363
364
365    def shutdown():
366        print("called shutdown")
367        answer=tkMessageBox.askyesno("EXIT", "Do you really want to quit")
368        if answer==True:
369            thCount= threading.active_count()
370            print('# of threads to stop = ',thCount)
371            thNames= threading.enumerate()
372            print (thNames)
373            while 1:                                #try sending messages in the queue
374                try:
375                    sending = SendQueue.get_nowait()
376                except:
377                    break
378            try:
379                root.quit() #because daemon set 'True' kills child threads also
380            except:
381                print(" ERROR   could not be terminated")
382
383    def windowsNotepad():
384        osType=platform.system()
385        print osType
386        if (osType=='windows'):
387            try:
388                command = 'C:\WINDOWS\NOTEPAD.EXE'
389                env     = {'FOO': 'bar', 'SystemRoot': os.environ['SystemRoot']}
390                p = subprocess.Popen(command, env=env)
391                p.wait()
392                return
```

Exhibit236

136

```
393         except OSError as e:
394             print "Read Error %s: %s\n error no %d"%(command,e.args[1],e.args[0])
395             formatError="Program\n"+command+"\n could not be run\n"+e.args[1]
396             +"\n Error No= "+str(e.args[0])
397             tkMessageBox.showerror("OSError",formatError)
398         except:
399             print("General error opening NOTEPAD.exe")
400     print("Notepad appears to be unavailable on this system")
401
402 def startProNotepad():
403     try:
404         command = "C:\\winAVR-20100110\\pn\\pn.exe" #for 2010 users
405         subprocess.call( [command])
406     except OSError as e:
407         print "Read Error %s: %s\n error no %d"%(command,e.args[1],e.args[0])
408         formatError="Program\n"+command+"\n could not be run\n"+e.args[1]
409         +"\n Error No= "+str(e.args[0])
410         tkMessageBox.showerror("OSError",formatError)
411
412 def showPythonVersion():
413     pyVersion=sys.version
414     tkMessageBox.showwarning('Python Version',pyVersion)
415
416 def showSystemPlatform():
417     import platform
418     osType=platform.system()
419     osPlatform=platform.win32_ver()
420     osProcessor=platform.processor()
421     tkMessageBox.showwarning('System Information','Operating System: '+ osType +
422         '\nSystem Info:'+osPlatform[0]+
423         '\nRelease: '+osPlatform[1]+
424         '\nService Pack: '+ osPlatform[2]+
425         '\nMultiProcessor: '+osPlatform[3]+
426         '\nProcessor: ' + osProcessor)
427
428 def showRyMax():
429     tkMessageBox.showwarning('RyMax, Inc.','RyMax, Inc.'+
430         '\n web page: www.RyMax.biz'+
431         '\n e-mail: herb@RyMax.biz')
432
433
434
435 def searchPaths():
436     searchwin=Toplevel()
437     searchFrame = LabelFrame(searchwin,text="Python Search Paths",
438     width =100, height=10)
439     searchFrame.grid(column=0, row=0, sticky =Nw)
440     searchBox=Listbox(searchFrame, width=150,height=10)
441     searchBox.grid(column=0, row=0,sticky=NW)
442     scrollBar = Scrollbar(searchFrame, orient=VERTICAL,command=searchBox.yview)
443     scrollBar.grid(column=1, row=0,sticky=(N,W,E,S))
444     searchBox['yscrollcommand']=scrollBar.set
445
446     myPythonSearch=[]
447     for folder in sys.path:
448         print folder
449         myPythonSearch.append (folder)
450
451     for item in myPythonSearch:
452         searchBox.insert('end',item)
453
454 def ARMOnoff():
455     if (SELF.ARMStatus==0):                    #ARM is off
456         SELF.sent="]1"          #turn ARM on
457         SELF.ARMStatus=1
458         try:
459             SendQueue.put((1,SELF.sent))          #ARM Onoff
460             SELF.sysMsg='ARM turned on'
461         except:
462             print('error writing to queue')
463             SELF.sysMsg='ARM Error'
```

[415:1] : 601   ANSI   CR+LF   INS   Ready

Exhibit237

```python
464            else:
465                SELF.sent="]0"              #turn ARM off
466                SELF.ARMStatus=0
467                try:
468                    SendQueue.put((1,SELF.sent))     #ARM OnOff
469                    SELF.sysMsg='ARM turned off'
470                except:
471                    print('error writing to queue')
472                    SELF.sysMsg='ARM Error'
473            displayStaticStuff()
474            updatedisplay.msgFromMax()                  # refresh the display
475
476    def ARMUp():
477        SELF.sent="]]"
478        try:
479            SendQueue.put((1,SELF.sent))                #ARM Up
480            SELF.sysMsg="ARM up"
481        except:
482            print('error writing to queue')
483            SELF.sysMsg='ARM Error'
484        updatedisplay.msgFromMax()                  # refresh the display
485
486    def ARMDown():
487        SELF.sent="]["
488        try:
489            SendQueue.put((1,SELF.sent))                #ARM Down
490            SELF.sysMsg="ARM down"
491        except:
492            pass
493            SELF.sysMsg='ARM Error'
494        updatedisplay.msgFromMax()                  # refresh the display
495
496    def maxSpeak():
497    #    print "at speech"
498        engine=pyttsx.init()
499        voices = engine.getProperty('voices')
500        for voice in voices:
501            engine.setProperty('voice', voice.id)
502        whatToSay=tkSimpleDialog.askstring("Text for Max","Enter what to say")
503    #    print(whatToSay)
504        if (whatToSay==None):
505            return
506        engine.say(whatToSay)
507        engine.runAndWait()
508
509    def commCheck():
510
511        print ("called the test communications,")
512        print ("response from max should be   'Max says r2 '")
513        SELF.sent="r2"
514        try:
515            SendQueue.put((1,SELF.sent))        #commCheck
516        except:
517            print('testComm Error write to queue')
518
519    def displayStaticStuff():
520        Label( root, text = "Left Click and Drag mouse to move",
521            bg='white').grid( column=1, row =1,stick=(N,W,E,S))
522
523        robotStatusframe = LabelFrame(root, text="Robot Status",width=20,
524            height=5,cursor="arrow")
525        robotStatusframe.grid(column=0, row =3, sticky=(N,E))
526        Label(robotStatusframe, text= "MSG FROM MAX" ).grid( row=0,sticky=(N,E))
527        Label(robotStatusframe, text= "MSG TO MAX").grid(row=1,sticky=(N,E))
528        Label(robotStatusframe, text= "MSG From System").grid(row=2,sticky=(N,E))
529
530        bFrame = LabelFrame(root,width=100, height=15)
531        bFrame.grid(column=0, columnspan=4, row=0, sticky=(N,W,S))
532        Button(bFrame, text = "MAXSPEAK", fg="white",
533            command = maxSpeak).grid(column=0, row=0)
534        if (SELF.ARMStatus==0):
```

Exhibit238

138

```
535         Button(bFrame, text = "ARM OFF", fg="yellow",
536            command=ARMOnOff).grid(column=2, row=0)
537     if (SELF.ARMStatus==1):
538         Button(bFrame, text = "ARM ON ", fg="green",    #note extra space end of text
539            command=ARMOnOff).grid(column=2, row=0)
540
541     Button(bFrame, text = "ARMUp", fg="green",repeatdelay=500,repeatinterval=300,
542       command = ARMUp).grid(column=3, row=0)
543     Button(bFrame, text = "ARMDown", fg="green",repeatdelay=500,repeatinterval=300,
544       command = ARMDown).grid(column=4,row=0)
545     Button(bFrame, text = "COMM CHECK", fg="white",
546       command = commCheck).grid(column=5, row=0)
547     Button(bFrame, text = "SHUTDOWN", fg="red",
548       command = shutdown).grid(column=6, row=0)
549  if __name__=='__main__':
550     root = Tk()
551     root.title( "Max Control Center" )
552     root.geometry( "550x450+50+30" ) #width, height, placement on y and  x axis
553     setupCanvas()
554
555  #pull down menu section
556     menubar = Menu(root)
557     root.config(menu=menubar)
558     filemenu = Menu(menubar, tearoff=0)
559     filemenu.add_command(label="Windows Notepad", command=windowsNotepad)
560     filemenu.add_separator()
561     filemenu.add_command(label="Programmer's Notepad", command=startProNotepad)
562     filemenu.add_separator()
563     filemenu.add_separator()
564     filemenu.add_command(label="Exit", command=shutdown)
565     menubar.add_cascade(menu=filemenu, label='File')
566
567     sysMenu=Menu(menubar, tearoff=0)
568     sysMenu.add_command(label="Python version?", command=showPythonVersion)
569     sysMenu.add_command(label="System Platform?", command=showSystemPlatform)
570     sysMenu.add_command(label="Python Search Paths", command=searchPaths)
571     sysMenu.add_command(label="RyMax, Inc. Information?", command=showRyMax)
572     menubar.add_cascade(label="System Info", menu=sysMenu)
573
574  #setup a list box to list our wav and txt files
575     soundFrame = LabelFrame(root, text="Max Sounds",width=20, height=10,
576       cursor="arrow")
577     soundFrame.grid(column=0, row =2, sticky=(N,W,S))
578     soundBox=Listbox(soundFrame, width=20, height=18)
579     soundBox.grid(column=0,row=1,sticky=(N,W,S))
580     scrollBar = Scrollbar(soundFrame, orient=VERTICAL, command=soundBox.yview)
581     scrollBar.grid(column=1,row=1, sticky=(N,E,S))
582     soundBox['yscrollcommand']=scrollBar.set
583     path=SELF.defPath
584     print path
585     soundlist = os.listdir(path)
586  # load the listbox
587     for sound in soundlist:
588         extension = os.path.splitext(sound)[1][1:]
589         if ((extension=='wav') | (extension=='WAV') |(extension=='txt')):
590            soundBox.insert('end', sound)
591     label1 = Label(soundFrame, text='click to play', width=20, bg='white')
592     label1.grid(column=0, row=0)
593     soundBox.bind('<ButtonRelease-1>', on_click_listbox)
594     displayStaticStuff()
595     updatedisplay=UpdateDisplay(root)        #get the initial display filled in
596     SendQueue = Queue.PriorityQueue(maxsize=5) #queue grow unlimited=0, set limit as needed
597     threadStart()
598
599     mainloop()
```

Exhibit239

For our next step we need to add the wireless communications to the robot and the PC.

Day Thirty Seven - Going Wireless

I am going to cover what I used for wireless communications and to some extent why I went with it. I purchased from Sure Electronics a Wireless RF Transceiver 431-470. I believe the price was around $43. This gets you two mini half-duplex Wireless Transceiver 431-470MHz GFSK Data Transfer devices, Number RMB-CM12111.

Web site: http://www.sureelectronics.net/goods.php?id=1053

This device has a maximum speed of 9600 bps, which is the real reason we have been working at that speed. I have the device connected to the USB port using a USB/SERIAL converter. I also purchased the converter from Sure Electronics; under that site's keywords enter UC001. Price about $12. CP2102 USB/TTL/RS232 Serial Port Converter Communications Module (DB-UC001), Part number MB-CM13112. The converter came with a mini USB Cable. (If you want I believe the NerdKit USB Serial converter cable should work.) Both of the Sure Electronics products have worked well for me. I found documentation to be weak, but with digging, adequate. The Serial Port Converter has transmit and receive lights, their flashing helped a lot in getting things going. At the time I searched for components I found this option to be the best priced. That may have changed. Wiring is not difficult, just be aware that in some respects it is like dealing with a null modem. There are many alternatives available for your communications. As you can see from the pictures on the PC side I used a bread board to plug in the Wireless Transceiver. On the robot side I plugged the Wireless Transceiver into a socket from which I could easily remove it.

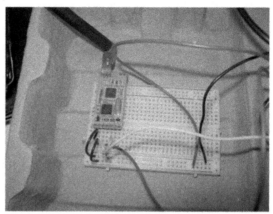

Max9-11

You can leave the robot on the external power supplies, but give the robot wireless communications a test. I have set up com8 for the wireless communications.

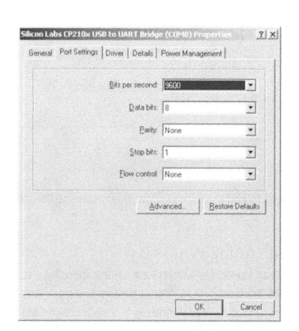

Exhibits 240 & 241

While bench testing I leave the USB serial converter cable and the wireless connected to the robot. Even though they use the same pins on the microchip, you can load programs and then run the robot using the wireless. Remember, before you get too frustrated; check your lesson29d.py serial settings. We had set it for com2; you will need to change if using com8. You can leave your settings in the 'make file' as they were.

Wireless Diagram

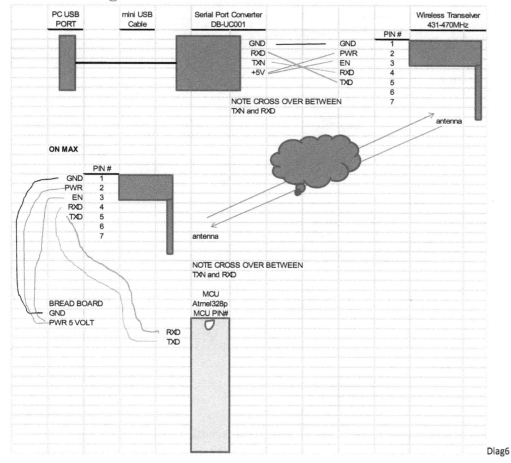

Diag6

Day Thirty Eight – Battery Voltage

With our wireless communications working the last item I want to add is the camera, but I decided it would be nice if you had a way to measure the battery voltage. So we are going to add that. We will need to add code to both the Python program and the C program, not to mention we need to construct a voltage divider. Let's do the hardware first and you can use a multimeter to check the voltage. The on-line site for CircuitLab is a good first step to design your circuit. www.circuitlab.com

Voltage Divider

In the following we are looking at three separate voltage measurement circuits. I have them all on one board. You can use a bread board for this project. I wanted three separate voltage dividers as I plan on having three batteries. (MCU, drive, camera) Also for a starting point I computed values expecting to use batteries in the 12volt to 9 volt range. The AREF site is after the voltage regulator.

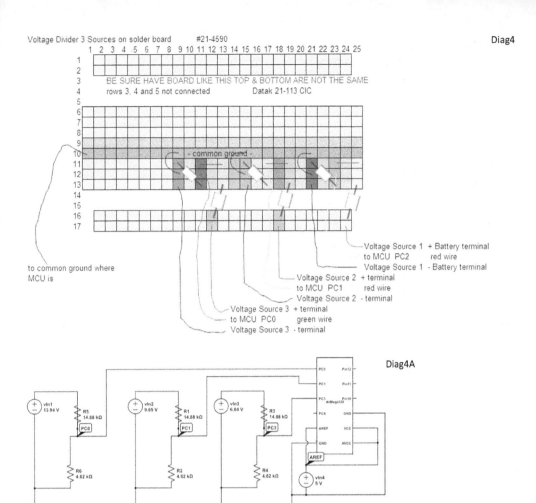

Voltage Divider 3 Sources on solder board   #21-4590   Diag4

BE SURE HAVE BOARD LIKE THIS TOP & BOTTOM ARE NOT THE SAME
rows 3, 4 and 5 not connected   Datak 21-113 CIC

- common ground -

to common ground where
MCU is

Voltage Source 1 + Battery terminal
to MCU PC2   red wire
Voltage Source 1 - Battery terminal

Voltage Source 2 + terminal
to MCU PC1   red wire
Voltage Source 2 - terminal

Voltage Source 3 + terminal
to MCU PC0   green wire
Voltage Source 3 - terminal

Diag4A

PC0 =3.3V
PC1 =2.3V
PC3 = 1.4V
AREF=5.0V

There is a lot of information available on the web for voltage dividers. We have to keep in mind what the maximum input voltage to a pin is for our microchip. We want to have a safety margin so we never exceed the input limit to our microchip. In the diagram you can see that I am using just two resistor sizes. If you play with a design using a circuit simulator you can substitute various resistor sizes and determine the appropriate sizes for your circuit. In the above circuit I measured the resistance of the resistors and the actual voltage of the batteries using the multimeter. Try using Ohm's and Kitchhoff's laws. For Ohm's law: V=I * R (V=Voltage, I=Current, R=Resistance).   In summary, Kitchhoff's circuit law states that the sum of voltage drops across each component in the circuit equal the supply voltage. For our simple circuit the formula you can use is   Vout = R2/ (R1 + R2) * Vin. Substituting our values into the formula you get the following.

Resistor values in Ω			Vin*R2/(R1+R2)=Vout		Diag4B
	Our Variables		Substution	Result	
Vin	R1	R2		Vout	
13.94	4.62	14.88	13.94*14.88/(4.62+14.88)=	3.3	
9.65	4.62	14.88	9.65*14.88/(4.62+14.88)=	2.3	
6.04	4.62	14.88	6.04*14.88/(4.62+14.88)=	1.4	

A quick note on the resistors, I am using economical ones, as you might expect, that is why I used the multimeter to get the true resistance. The R1 is a 15kΩ with a 10% margin, so the 14.88Ω is within the tolerance range. The R2 is a 4.7kΩ with a 10% margin, so the 4.62Ω is within the tolerance range.

The twisted pairs of black and red go to the batteries, red to +, black to -.   I connected these to the terminal connectors on the robot right where the battery connects. From right to left the yellow, green and black wires go to the microchip ports PC0, PC1 and PC2. The black wire, on left side goes to the board ground.   You can build your circuit with just one voltage divider to get the idea. Test the voltage with a battery prior to hooking to the microchip pin. The microchip pin 21 is the AREF and if you have been following the diagrams from way back it is already connected to the regulated 5.0 volt power supply. I am going to connect the right most voltage divider circuit to my 9.0 volt battery that powers the microchip and to PC0 and to ground. In the diagram that follows I am showing just the one voltage divider going to PC0 and the 9Volt power supply. As you can see the diagrams are getting a little crowded. Once again, see www.rymax.biz for color pictures.

Bread Board with Voltage Divider

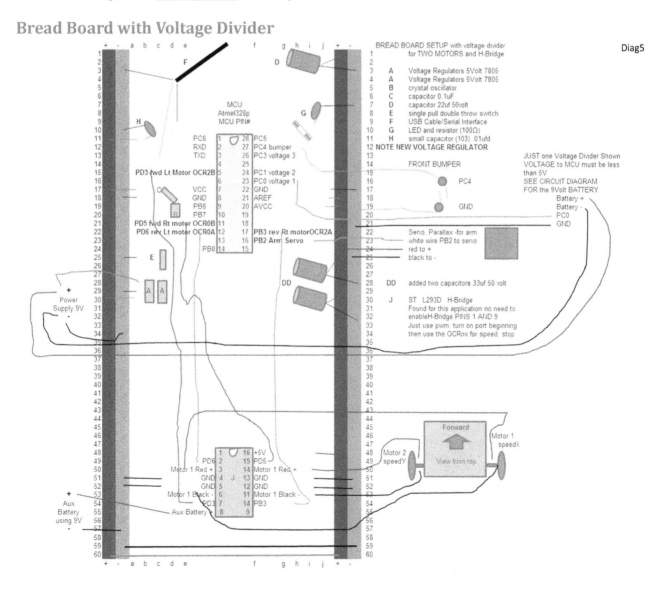

Voltage Divider Code for C Program

Let us change the C program AT328Robo.c first. After the motor control function insert the following code. We will need to call a function to setup the registers. Insert in the main section after the DDRC enable line: ADMUX_init ();. We will add two new functions, void ADMUX_init () and unint16_t register_read () after our motor control function. Before setting up the registers take a look at the ATmega328 data sheet, pages 262-266. Take a look at the code that is shown in the following and match back to the data sheet and visualize what is going on. Also take a look back at the pin out for the ATMega328, note ADC0 is for PC0.

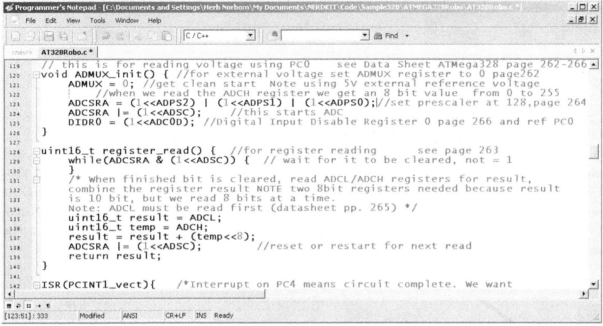

Exhibit242

We also need to capture our input from the PC requesting a voltage read. Add the following code to the ISR (USARTRX_vect) function. We are going to take 5 separate voltage readings and display the voltage back on the PC. These voltage readings can only be considered reasonably accurate; they are not exact by any means. But we really don't care too much about that; we just want an approximation as to the juice left. We are working with a 10 bit number. When you get to the step on calculating the voltage you need to ponder just why we are doing what we do. How I tend to think of what is happening is that we are measuring elapsed time. A 10 bit number has 2^10 possibilities or 1,024 as output values. We know our voltage has to be greater than 0, and smaller than our reference value of 5Volts (otherwise a real problem). We are comparing our voltage in to the reference value of 5 volts. So if our voltage in is 5 volts our value would be 1,024 and 1,024/1,024 = 1 times our voltage-in of 5 gives us 5 volts. If our computed factor was 512 then 512/1,024= .5 times our voltage in of 5 gives us 2.5 volts. The next line of our code is adjusting our voltage by a factor of 4.29. That factor is what I calculated our program needs to use for a more accurate reading.

Exhibit243

Voltage Reading Python Program

Save the Python lesson29d.py as lesson30.py. We will add a menu item for getting the voltage and displaying it in our communication box. The results will also print in the DOS window. Make the following changes to our program. After the commCheck function, at approximately 519 add the following:

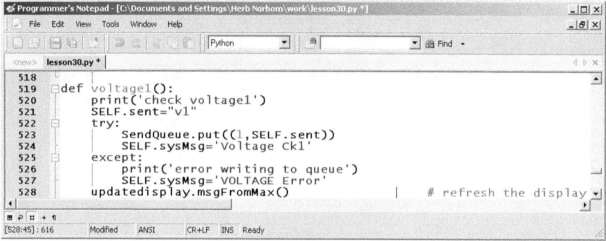

Exhibit244

We are also adding a menu category and item, code as follows.

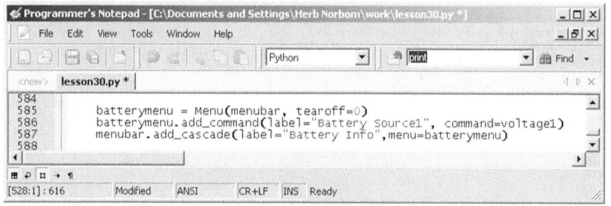

Exhibit245

You can go ahead and add the other two battery voltage checks if you like. You would also need to add appropriate code to AT328Robo.c for getting the other voltages. I have to warn you that these voltage checks drain power even when you are not checking. While it is neat to know the voltage it may be better to leave this feature off your final robot and just use a multimeter to check the battery voltage.

Day Thirty Nine – Lost Communications

Before we add our camera we need to think once again about what Max would do if communications were lost. If Max was moving, Max would just continue as no stop signal would be received. Try it for yourself, start Max moving then unplug the USB communications wire. Let's fix that by putting a timer on Max that says if no communication received in x seconds stop this runaway train. The complete C code is shown in the following. Note line 27 where I set up a counter. When we receive a communication, reset the counter to zero, line 166. I put the safety stop in the 'while loop'. As we lost communication, in theory I did not send a message back to the PC. However, you will probably notice if you stop moving the mouse a stop order will be issued. You can work with the messaging and timing as you like. To improve performance I also took the flash signal out of the communications loop.

Final C program Source Code

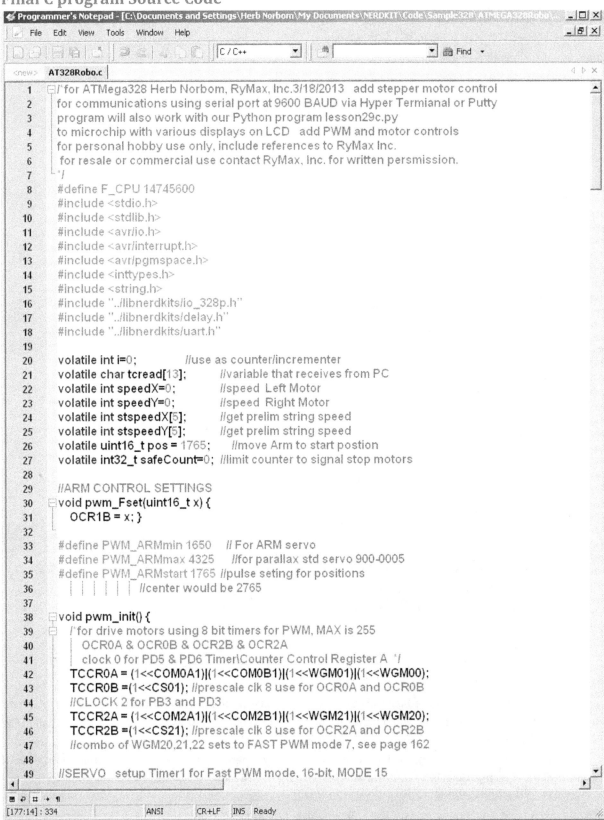

```c
/* for ATMega328 Herb Norbom, RyMax, Inc.3/18/2013   add stepper motor control
 for communications using serial port at 9600 BAUD via Hyper Termianal or Putty
 program will also work with our Python program lesson29c.py
 to microchip with various displays on LCD   add PWM and motor controls
 for personal hobby use only, include references to RyMax Inc.
 for resale or commercial use contact RyMax, Inc. for written persmission.
 */
#define F_CPU 14745600
#include <stdio.h>
#include <stdlib.h>
#include <avr/io.h>
#include <avr/interrupt.h>
#include <avr/pgmspace.h>
#include <inttypes.h>
#include <string.h>
#include "../libnerdkits/io_328p.h"
#include "../libnerdkits/delay.h"
#include "../libnerdkits/uart.h"

volatile int i=0;          //use as counter/incrementer
volatile char tcread[13];      //variable that receives from PC
volatile int speedX=0;      //speed  Left Motor
volatile int speedY=0;      //speed  Right Motor
volatile int stspeedX[5];     //get prelim string speed
volatile int stspeedY[5];     //get prelim string speed
volatile uint16_t pos = 1765;    //move Arm to start postion
volatile int32_t safeCount=0;  //limit counter to signal stop motors

//ARM CONTROL SETTINGS
void pwm_Fset(uint16_t x) {
    OCR1B = x; }

#define PWM_ARMmin 1650    // For ARM servo
#define PWM_ARMmax 4325     //for parallax std servo 900-0005
#define PWM_ARMstart 1765 //pulse seting for positions
               //center would be 2765


void pwm_init() {
    /* for drive motors using 8 bit timers for PWM, MAX is 255
      OCR0A & OCR0B & OCR2B & OCR2A
      clock 0 for PD5 & PD6 Timer\Counter Control Register A */
    TCCR0A = (1<<COM0A1)|(1<<COM0B1)|(1<<WGM01)|(1<<WGM00);
    TCCR0B =(1<<CS01); //prescale clk 8 use for OCR0A and OCR0B
    //CLOCK 2 for PB3 and PD3
    TCCR2A = (1<<COM2A1)|(1<<COM2B1)|(1<<WGM21)|(1<<WGM20);
    TCCR2B =(1<<CS21); //prescale clk 8 use for OCR2A and OCR2B
    //combo of WGM20,21,22 sets to FAST PWM mode 7, see page 162

    //SERVO   setup Timer1 for Fast PWM mode, 16-bit, MODE 15
```

Exhibit246

146

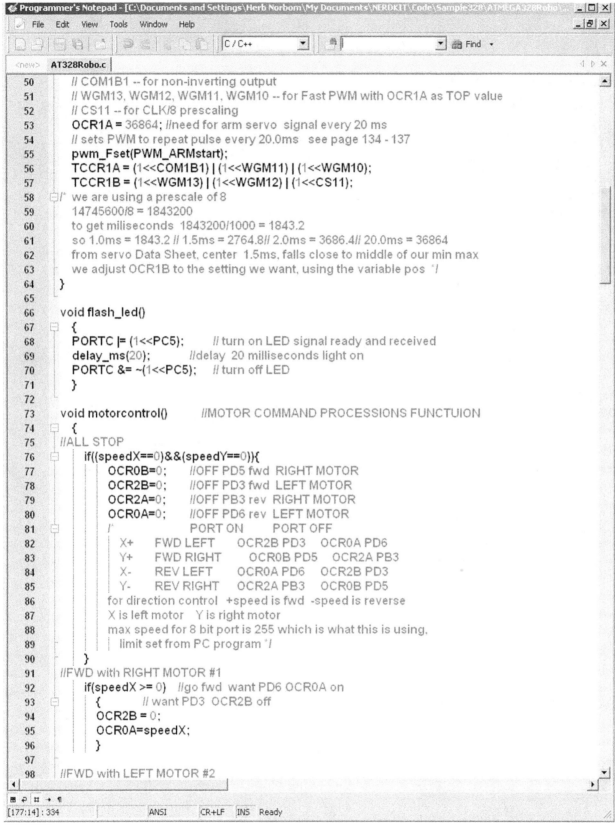

```
50        // COM1B1 -- for non-inverting output
51        // WGM13, WGM12, WGM11, WGM10 -- for Fast PWM with OCR1A as TOP value
52        // CS11 -- for CLK/8 prescaling
53        OCR1A = 36864; //need for arm servo  signal every 20 ms
54        // sets PWM to repeat pulse every 20.0ms   see page 134 - 137
55        pwm_Fset(PWM_ARMstart);
56        TCCR1A = (1<<COM1B1) | (1<<WGM11) | (1<<WGM10);
57        TCCR1B = (1<<WGM13) | (1<<WGM12) | (1<<CS11);
58    /* we are using a prescale of 8
59        14745600/8 = 1843200
60        to get miliseconds  1843200/1000 = 1843.2
61        so 1.0ms = 1843.2 // 1.5ms = 2764.8// 2.0ms = 3686.4// 20.0ms = 36864
62        from servo Data Sheet, center  1.5ms, falls close to middle of our min max
63        we adjust OCR1B to the setting we want, using the variable pos  */
64    }
65
66    void flash_led()
67    {
68        PORTC |= (1<<PC5);        // turn on LED signal ready and received
69        delay_ms(20);           //delay  20 milliseconds light on
70        PORTC &= ~(1<<PC5);    // turn off LED
71    }
72
73    void motorcontrol()          //MOTOR COMMAND PROCCESSIONS FUNCTUION
74    {
75    //ALL STOP
76        if((speedX==0)&&(speedY==0)){
77            OCR0B=0;      //OFF PD5 fwd  RIGHT MOTOR
78            OCR2B=0;      //OFF PD3 fwd  LEFT MOTOR
79            OCR2A=0;      //OFF PB3 rev  RIGHT MOTOR
80            OCR0A=0;      //OFF PD6 rev  LEFT MOTOR
81            /*               PORT ON        PORT OFF
82            X+    FWD LEFT      OCR2B PD3   OCR0A PD6
83            Y+    FWD RIGHT      OCR0B PD5   OCR2A PB3
84            X-    REV LEFT      OCR0A PD6   OCR2B PD3
85            Y-    REV RIGHT     OCR2A PB3   OCR0B PD5
86            for direction control   +speed is fwd  -speed is reverse
87            X is left motor   Y is right motor
88            max speed for 8 bit port is 255 which is what this is using,
89            limit set from PC program */
90        }
91    //FWD with RIGHT MOTOR #1
92        if(speedX >= 0)   //go fwd  want PD6 OCR0A on
93        {            // want PD3  OCR2B off
94        OCR2B = 0;
95        OCR0A=speedX;
96        }
97
98    //FWD with LEFT MOTOR #2
```

Exhibit247

147

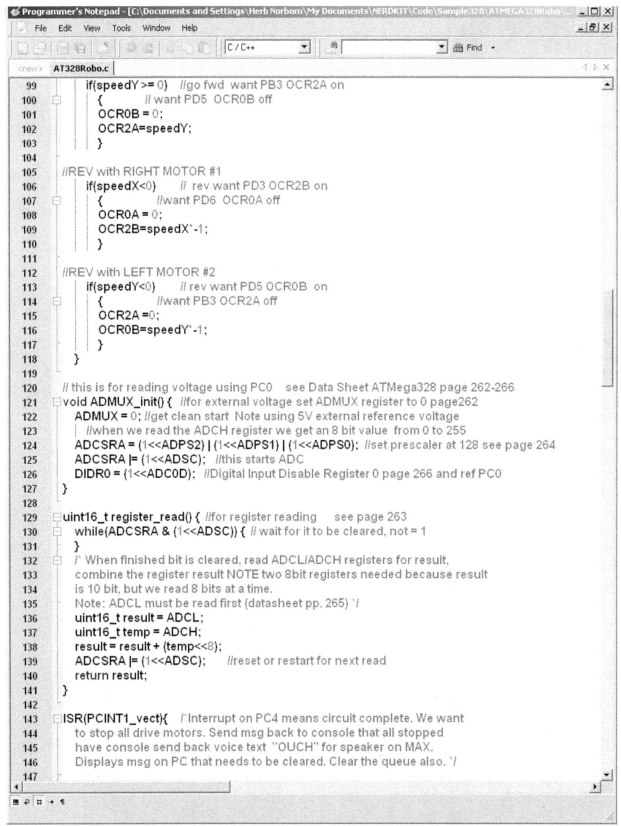

Programmer's Notepad – [C:\Documents and Settings\Herb Norbom\My Documents\NERDKIT\Code\Sample328\ATMEGA328Robo\...

File   Edit   View   Tools   Window   Help

C / C++   Find ▾

<new>   AT328Robo.c

```c
99        if(speedY >= 0)   //go fwd  want PB3 OCR2A on
100       {          // want PD5  OCR0B off
101       OCR0B = 0;
102       OCR2A=speedY;
103       }
104
105   //REV with RIGHT MOTOR #1
106       if(speedX<0)      // rev want PD3 OCR2B on
107       {          //want PD6  OCR0A off
108       OCR0A = 0;
109       OCR2B=speedX*-1;
110       }
111
112   //REV with LEFT MOTOR #2
113       if(speedY<0)      // rev want PD5 OCR0B  on
114       {          //want PB3 OCR2A off
115       OCR2A =0;
116       OCR0B=speedY*-1;
117       }
118     }
119
120    // this is for reading voltage using PC0    see Data Sheet ATMega328 page 262-266
121   void ADMUX_init() { //for external voltage set ADMUX register to 0 page262
122      ADMUX = 0; //get clean start  Note using 5V external reference voltage
123       //when we read the ADCH register we get an 8 bit value  from 0 to 255
124      ADCSRA = (1<<ADPS2) | (1<<ADPS1) | (1<<ADPS0); //set prescaler at 128 see page 264
125      ADCSRA |= (1<<ADSC);   //this starts ADC
126      DIDR0 = (1<<ADC0D); //Digital Input Disable Register 0 page 266 and ref PC0
127   }
128
129   uint16_t register_read() { //for register reading     see page 263
130      while(ADCSRA & (1<<ADSC)) { // wait for it to be cleared, not = 1
131      }
132      /* When finished bit is cleared, read ADCL/ADCH registers for result,
133      combine the register result NOTE two 8bit registers needed because result
134      is 10 bit, but we read 8 bits at a time.
135      Note: ADCL must be read first (datasheet pp. 265) */
136      uint16_t result = ADCL;
137      uint16_t temp = ADCH;
138      result = result + (temp<<8);
139      ADCSRA |= (1<<ADSC);     //reset or restart for next read
140      return result;
141   }
142
143   ISR(PCINT1_vect){   /*Interrupt on PC4 means circuit complete. We want
144      to stop all drive motors. Send msg back to console that all stopped
145      have console send back voice text "OUCH" for speaker on MAX.
146      Displays msg on PC that needs to be cleared. Clear the queue also. */
147
```

Exhibit248

148

Programmer's Notepad - [C:\Documents and Settings\Herb Norbom\My Documents\NERDKIT\Code\Sample328\ATMEGA328Robo\...

File   Edit   View   Tools   Window   Help

C / C++   Find

<new>   AT328Robo.c

```
148    if (PINC & (1<<PC4))  //no actual interrupt on PC4
149      {return;}
150    else
151    {
152      flash_led();      //ready signal
153      speedX=0;
154      speedY=0;
155      motorcontrol();
156      printf_P(PSTR("INT\r\n"));
157      int count =0;
158      int tempnothing=0;
159      for (count=0;count<5000;count++)
160        {tempnothing=tempnothing;}
161    }
162    return;
163  }
164  ISR(USART_RX_vect)
165  {
166      safeCount=0;        //have signal so reset counter
167      speedX=0;
168      speedY=0;
169      for (i=0;i<6;i++)
170        {
171        stspeedX[i]=' ';
172        stspeedY[i]=' ';
173        }
174      for (i=0;i<14;i++)              //clear variable
175        {
176        tcread[i]=' ';
177        }
178      char sign[]="-";
179
180      scanf_P(PSTR("%s"),tcread);          // read from uart receiver
181      printf_P(PSTR("Max says %s \r\n"),tcread);    //send to uart
182      if(tcread[0]=='r')
183        {
184          //do nothing, sent msg back in above to be interperted on PC
185        }
186      if((tcread[0]=='v')&&(tcread[1]=='1'))    //voltage check 1 PC0
187        {
188        ADMUX=0;        //set to read PC0, internal voltage ref off
189        ADCSRA |= (1<<ADEN); //page 263  enables ADC  write a 0 to it to turn off
190        for (i=0;i<5;i++)
191          {
192          uint16_t last_read = 0;
193          double this_voltage = 0.0;
194          last_read = register_read(); //returns result
195          this_voltage = (last_read/1024.0)*5.0;
196          this_voltage = this_voltage * 4.29;
```

Exhibit249

149

Programmer's Notepad - [C:\Documents and Settings\Herb Norbom\My Documents\NERDKIT\Code\Sample328\ATMEGA328Robo\...
File   Edit   View   Tools   Window   Help

C / C++   Find

<new>   AT328Robo.c

```
197          printf_P(PSTR("Volt1= %2.2f\r\n"),this_voltage);
198          delay_ms(500); //allow time to read display on PC
199        }
200        ADCSRA &=~(1<<ADEN);   // turn off ADC
201        }
202
203     if((tcread[0]=='v')&&(tcread[1]=='2'))      //voltage check 2 PC1
204        {
205        ADMUX=0;  //make sure internal ref voltage off
206        ADMUX |=(1<<ADMUX);             //set to read PC1
207        ADCSRA |= (1<<ADEN); //page 263  enables ADC  write a 0 to it to turn off
208        for (i=0;i<5;i++)
209        {
210          uint16_t last_read = 0;
211          double this_voltage = 0.0;
212          last_read = register_read(); //returns result
213          this_voltage = (last_read/1024.0)*5.0;
214          this_voltage = this_voltage * 4.29;
215          printf_P(PSTR("Volt2= %2.2f\r\n"),this_voltage);
216          delay_ms(500); //allow time to read display on PC
217        }
218        ADCSRA &=~(1<<ADEN);   // turn off ADC
219        }
220
221     if((tcread[0]=='v')&&(tcread[1]=='3'))      //voltage check 3 PC2
222        {
223        ADMUX=0;          //make sure internal ref voltage off
224        ADMUX |=(2<<ADMUX);             //set to read PC2
225        ADCSRA |= (1<<ADEN); //page 263  enables ADC  write a 0 to it to turn off
226        for (i=0;i<5;i++)
227        {
228          uint16_t last_read = 0;
229          double this_voltage = 0.0;
230          last_read = register_read(); //returns result
231          this_voltage = (last_read/1024.0)*5.0;
232          this_voltage = this_voltage * 4.29;
233          printf_P(PSTR("Volt3= %2.2f\r\n"),this_voltage);
234          delay_ms(500); //allow time to read display on PC
235        }
236        ADCSRA &=~(1<<ADEN);   // turn off ADC
237        }
238
239     if(tcread[0]=='X')          //for LEFT MOTOR
240        {
241          stspeedX[1]=tcread[2]-'0';  //strip off end, convert to single
242          stspeedX[2]=tcread[3]-'0';  //  digit decimal
243          stspeedX[3]=tcread[4]-'0';
244          speedX= stspeedX[1]*100+stspeedX[2]*10+stspeedX[3];
245          if (speedX >255){   //PWM limit exceeded
```

Exhibit250

150

Programmer's Notepad - [C:\Documents and Settings\Herb Norbom\My Documents\NERDKIT\Code\Sample328\ATMEGA328Robo\...

File   Edit   View   Tools   Window   Help

C / C++   Find

<new>   AT328Robo.c

```
246          speedX =0;      //some kind of error set speed = 0
247          }
248       if (tcread[1] == sign[0]){      //TCREAD[1] HAS THE SIGN FOR X
249          int temp =speedX;
250          speedX=temp`-1;      //make it negative
251          }
252       }
253    if(tcread[5]=='Y')      //for RIGHT MOTOR
254       {
255          stspeedY[1]=tcread[7]-'0';
256          stspeedY[2]=tcread[8]-'0';
257          stspeedY[3]=tcread[9]-'0';
258          speedY= stspeedY[1]`100+stspeedY[2]`10+stspeedY[3];
259          if (speedY >255){
260             speedY =0;      //some kind of error set speed = 0
261             }
262          if (tcread[6] == sign[0]){      //TCREAD[6] HAS THE SIGN FOR Y
263             int temp = speedY;
264             speedY=temp`-1;      //make it negative
265             }
266 //    printf_P(PSTR("spX= %i  spy= %i\r\n"),speedX, speedY);      //for debuging
267       }
268    if(tcread[0]==']')
269       {
270       if(tcread[1]=='1')
271          {
272          printf_P(PSTR("Max ARM ready %s\r\n"),tcread);
273          DDRB |= (1<<PB2); //servo on ARM
274          pwm_Fset(PWM_ARMstart);
275          pos =PWM_ARMstart;
276          }
277       if(tcread[1]=='0')
278          {
279          printf_P(PSTR("Max ARM STOP %s\r\n"),tcread);
280          DDRB &= ~(1<<PB2);   //servo OFF for ARM
281          delay_ms(500);
282          }
283       if(tcread[1]==']') pos+=25;
284       if(tcread[1]=='[') pos-=25;
285       //check limits for the servo
286       if(pos >= PWM_ARMmax) pos = PWM_ARMmax;
287       if(pos <= PWM_ARMmin) pos = PWM_ARMmin;
288       pwm_Fset(pos);
289       printf_P(PSTR("ATM Pos %i\r\n"),pos);
290       }
291    motorcontrol();
292    }
293
294 int main() {
```

Exhibit250A

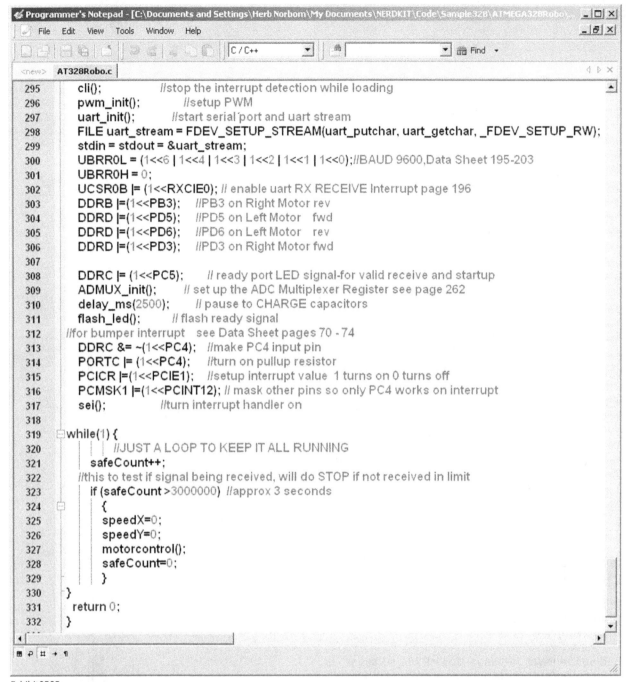

```
295    cli();              //stop the interrupt detection while loading
296    pwm_init();         //setup PWM
297    uart_init();        //start serial port and uart stream
298    FILE uart_stream = FDEV_SETUP_STREAM(uart_putchar, uart_getchar, _FDEV_SETUP_RW);
299    stdin = stdout = &uart_stream;
300    UBRR0L = (1<<6 | 1<<4 | 1<<3 | 1<<2 | 1<<1 | 1<<0);//BAUD 9600,Data Sheet 195-203
301    UBRR0H = 0;
302    UCSR0B |= (1<<RXCIE0); // enable uart RX RECEIVE Interrupt page 196
303    DDRB |=(1<<PB3);    //PB3 on Right Motor rev
304    DDRD |=(1<<PD5);    //PD5 on Left Motor   fwd
305    DDRD |=(1<<PD6);    //PD6 on Left Motor   rev
306    DDRD |=(1<<PD3);    //PD3 on Right Motor fwd
307
308    DDRC |= (1<<PC5);        // ready port LED signal-for valid receive and startup
309    ADMUX_init();       // set up the ADC Multiplexer Register see page 262
310    delay_ms(2500);     // pause to CHARGE capacitors
311    flash_led();        // flash ready signal
312 //for bumper interrupt   see Data Sheet pages 70 - 74
313    DDRC &= ~(1<<PC4);  //make PC4 input pin
314    PORTC |= (1<<PC4);  //turn on pullup resistor
315    PCICR |=(1<<PCIE1); //setup interrupt value  1 turns on 0 turns off
316    PCMSK1 |=(1<<PCINT12); // mask other pins so only PC4 works on interrupt
317    sei();              //turn interrupt handler on
318
319 while(1) {
320            //JUST A LOOP TO KEEP IT ALL RUNNING
321        safeCount++;
322    //this to test if signal being received, will do STOP if not received in limit
323        if (safeCount >3000000) //approx 3 seconds
324        {
325        speedX=0;
326        speedY=0;
327        motorcontrol();
328        safeCount=0;
329        }
330 }
331    return 0;
332 }
```

Exhibit250B
Unless another wonderful idea occurs to me this should be our last update to the program AT328Robo.c.

Day Forty – Camera and Speakers

Driving Max around without being in the same room is fun. You can drive your pets wild too.   Just be careful that they don't destroy your robot. When I started this project I envisioned the robot camera using the same wireless communications that we have been using. That is not practical; band width alone will bring about a rapid end. The camera I purchased is the Foscam Model Fi8918W. Information on the camera is available at the following site. http://foscam.us/products/foscam-fi8918w-wireless-ip-camera-11.html?gclid=CLz408-ImLYCFYI-MgodOU4AZA. This camera comes with its own control panel, night vision, speaker and microphone. I run it over my wireless network from a NetGear® wireless router.   Getting it running was a little bit of a challenge. You really need to plug in with Ethernet connection prior to going wireless. From my research on the web it appears there are clones out there that are not quite up to par. Do your homework and get the real thing. The real one is probably no more expensive than a clone. After you have the wired connection working, get the wireless connection up and running. I expect you are going to curse at the speaker and the microphone before long. They do work, maybe not perfect but they are ok.   I expect you will need to adjust the PC volume controls for the speakers and the microphone to be able to hear anything.   What drove me crazy was my desire to send sounds from my Max Control Panel to the camera. This desire drove me nuttier than I already was. The solution turned out not to be not too complicated. Basically you want to call the PC camera control panel from within our Max Control Panel.

The camera needs 5 volts of power and 300mA. I use the 12 volt battery with <u>three voltage regulators</u> and large heat sinks to get down to the 5 volts. Make a **completely separate electrical circuit** from our robots existing systems.   Get everything for the camera running off the AC power converter first. When you change over to battery make sure the infrared is off unless you really want it on. Go ahead and save lesson30.py as finalcontrol.py. We are going to add just a little code to the program, as we really just want to call the camera control program. We will use the button widget to call the IPCamera Tool. You can add speakers to the camera for more volume. There is an output jack on the back of the camera. I found a small pair of speakers at one of the discount stores for a couple of bucks that had a battery amplifier built-in. Or go wild, you can buy or build a small amplifier or add speakers that need another power supply. Needless to say lots of choices. The speakers shown run on two AAA batteries.

MaxSpeakers

Max13- 15

Exhibit251

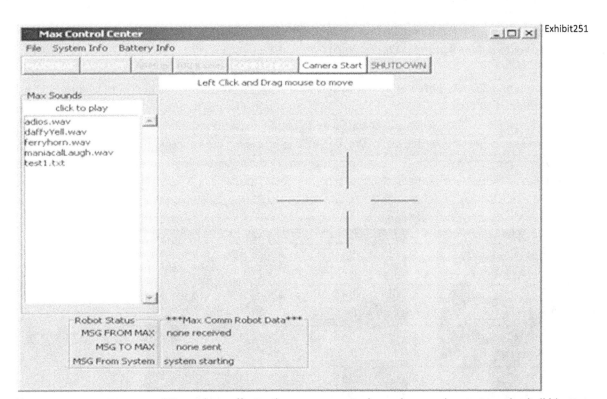

You may want to turn your PC speakers off. On the camera control panel remember to turn the 'talk' button on, found under the Visitor menu.

I thought at one time that I could run the camera off a 6.6 volt 4.0Ah battery. I could not get it to work. The camera needs a lot of juice. With the 12 volt 7.5Ah battery the camera works over the wireless connection. As you can see in the circuit I set up for the voltage regulator on a separate bread board. The BB uses three voltage regulators and you probably noticed the wings on the regulators. There is a lot of heat generated so these are my homemade heat sinks. I am not sure how long the camera can run off the battery, I am expecting a few hours, which is more than enough for my purposes here. While I like the camera, I am going to be looking for something with the same capabilities but needing less power.

The following is the complete and final for now Python source code. We need one more module for the sound to work correctly. Insert "import win32api" on line 21. Note new code lines 531 – 538 and 569 – 570. Notice in the camera function that I gave the complete path to the IPCamera start program. While I have not tried this with other cameras it could work with appropriate changes.

Final Python program complete Source Code

```
1    # Max Control Program    add camera
2    # using Python 2.7.2.5 and pySerial 2.6
3    # author Herb  3/20/2013
4    # company name RyMax, Inc.
5    # for personal hobby use only, include references to RyMax Inc.
6    # for resale or commercial use contact RyMax, Inc. for written persmission.
7
8    from Tkinter import *
9    import tkMessageBox, tkFileDialog, tkSimpleDialog
10   import platform, os , subprocess, sys, time, csv
11   import winsound          #windows sound playing module
12   import pyttsx            #text to speech module
13   import Queue
14   import threading
15   from threading import Thread
16   import time
17   from subprocess import call, PIPE, STDOUT, check_call #call program/commands
18   import random
19   import serial
20   from time import gmtime, strftime
21   import win32api         #need for sound to amplify
22   class DataFileClass:
23       def __init__(Data,defPath,sent, rec, sysMsg,INTset,ARMStatus):
24           Data.defPath= defPath
25           Data.sent=sent
26           Data.rec=rec
27           Data.sysMsg=sysMsg
28           Data.INTset=INTset
29           Data.ARMStatus=ARMStatus
30   SELF = DataFileClass(
31       'C:\\Documents and Settings\\Herb Norbom\\work\\',  #program default dir
32       sent='none sent',                            #start send for Max
33       rec='none received',                         #start rec from Max
34       sysMsg='system starting',                    #start displayed msg
35       INTset = 0,                                  #bumper interrupt
36       ARMStatus=0                                  #arm set to off
37       )
38
39   class UpdateDisplay:              #display messages
40       def __init__(DISP, root):
41           DISP.robotStatusDataframe = LabelFrame(root, text="***Max Comm Robot Data***")
42           DISP.robotStatusDataframe.config(width=25, cursor="arrow")
43           DISP.robotStatusDataframe.grid(column=1, row =3, sticky=(N,W))
44
45           DISP.fromMax = StringVar()
46           DISP.fromMax.set(SELF.rec)
47           DISP.msgRec = Label(DISP.robotStatusDataframe, textvariable=DISP.fromMax)
48           DISP.msgRec.grid(column=0,row=1,sticky=(N,W,E,S))
49
50           DISP.toMax = StringVar()
51           DISP.toMax.set(SELF.sent)
52           DISP.msgSend = Label(DISP.robotStatusDataframe, textvariable=DISP.toMax)
53           DISP.msgSend.grid(column=0,row=2,sticky=(N,W,E,S))
54
55           DISP.systemMsg= StringVar()
56           DISP.systemMsg.set(SELF.sysMsg)
57           DISP.sysMsg = Label(DISP.robotStatusDataframe, textvariable=DISP.systemMsg)
58           DISP.sysMsg.grid(column=0,row=3, sticky=(N,W,E,S))
59
60       def msgFromMax(DISP):                  #when info changes this is the called function
61           DISP.fromMax.set(SELF.rec)
62           DISP.toMax.set(SELF.sent)
63           DISP.systemMsg.set(SELF.sysMsg)
64   #        print "at msgFromMax ", SELF.rec
```

Exhibit252

155

File   Edit   View   Tools   Window   Help

Python ▼   on_click_listbox ▼   Find ▼

<new>   finalControl.py

```python
65
66  def on_click_listbox(event):
67      index = soundBox.curselection()        # get selected line index
68      soundFile = soundBox.get(index)        # get the line's text
69      label1.configure(text=soundFile)       # show selected text in label
70      path=SELF.defPath                      # use our Class defined path
71      if soundFile != None:
72          extension = os.path.splitext(soundFile)[1][1:]
73          print (extension)
74          if ((extension=='wav') | (extension=='WAV')):   # this is the or  | connector
75              winsound.PlaySound(str(path)+soundFile,0)
76          if(extension=='txt'):
77              engine=pyttsx.init()
78              voices = engine.getProperty('voices')
79              for voice in voices:
80                  engine.setProperty('voice', voice.id)
81              with open(str(path)+soundFile) as f:
82                  for line in f:
83                      engine.say(line)
84                      engine.runAndWait()
85
86  def paint( event ):
87      cx=cy=0
88      try:
89          cx=(event.x-200)*2
90          cy=(event.y-150)*2
91      except:
92          cx=0                               # if something not working want to
93          cy=0                               # set mouse event location to (0,0)
94      if (SELF.INTset==1):                   #Max's bumper was pressed
95          print("whats up")
96          engine=pyttsx.init()
97          voices = engine.getProperty('voices')
98          for voice in voices:
99              engine.setProperty('voice', voice.id)
100             random.seed=time.strftime("%S", gmtime()) #use seconds as seed
101             ranNumber=random.choice([1,2,3,4,5])
102             if (ranNumber==1):
103                 engine.say('OUCH that hurt')
104             if (ranNumber==2):
105                 engine.say("who's driving this bus?")
106             if (ranNumber==3):
107                 engine.say('Do not touch me')
108             if (ranNumber==4):
109                 engine.say('Go away')
110             if (ranNumber==5):
111                 engine.say('Move it or loose it')
112             engine.runAndWait()
113         status= tkMessageBox.askyesno("Bumper","Obstacle removed?\n(%s) " % ranNumber)
114         print status
115         if (status== True): #from message box if obstacle removed YES
116             SELF.INTset=0
117             cx=0
118             cy=0
119         else:
120             cx=0
121             cy=0
122
123     try:
124         calLeft=leftwheel(cx, cy)          #power and direction of left wheel
125         calRight=rightwheel(cx,cy)         #power and direction of right wheel
126     except:
127         print 'error on Max speed calLeft= ', calLeft, 'calRight= ',calRight
128         calLeft='X+000'                    #if error want to set power to 0
129         calRight='Y+000'
130     SELF.sent=(str(calLeft) + str(calRight))   #put into string format
131     print SELF.sent                        #take out when you are ready
132
133     FullQ=SendQueue.full()
```

■ ₽ ⊞ → ¶

[21:1] : 629   ANSI   CR+LF   INS   44 character(s) selected.

Exhibit253

156

```python
134         print 'Q full or not ', FullQ
135         if (FullQ == FALSE ):
136             try:
137                 SendQueue.put((2,SELF.sent))                #write to queue
138             except:
139                 print'Queue error in PAINT FUNCTION'        # print error, but keep running
140         SELF.sysMsg='Robot movement'            # display on message pannel
141         updatedisplay.msgFromMax()                  # refresh the display
142
143     def leftwheel(cx, cy):                  #compute left wheel pwr/dir and format for
144         calLeft=0
145         try:
146             calLeft=(-cy-cx)
147             if (70 > calLeft > 0):          # motors start around 70, below just
148                 calLeft =0                  # uses juice and hard on motor
149             if (-70 < calLeft < 0):
150                 calLeft =0
151         except:
152             calLeft=0
153             return calLeft
154         if (calLeft==0):
155             calLeft=str("X+000")
156             return calLeft
157         if (calLeft >0):
158             if (calLeft > 255):
159                 calLeft = str("X+255")
160                 return calLeft
161             if (calLeft>99):
162                 calLeft ="X+"+str(calLeft)
163                 return calLeft
164             if (calLeft>9):
165                 calLeft ="X+0"+str(calLeft)
166                 return calLeft
167             else:
168                 calLeft ="X+00"+str(calLeft)
169                 return calLeft
170         if (calLeft < 0):
171             calLeft = abs(calLeft)          #GET ABSOLUTE VALUE
172             if (calLeft > 255):
173                 calLeft = str("X-255")
174                 return calLeft
175             if (calLeft>99):
176                 calLeft ="X-"+str(calLeft)
177                 return calLeft
178             if (calLeft>9):
179                 calLeft ="X-0"+str(calLeft)
180                 return calLeft
181             else:
182                 calLeft ="X-00"+str(calLeft)
183                 return calLeft
184         else:
185             calLeft=str("X+000")
186             return calLeft
187     def rightwheel(cx, cy):                 #compute right wheel pwr/dir and
188         calRight=0
189         try:
190             calRight=(-cy+cx)
191             if (70 > calRight > 0):         # motors start around 70, below just
192                 calRight =0                 # uses juice and hard on motor
193             if (-70 < calRight < 0):
194                 calRight =0
195         except:
196             calRight=0
197             return calRight
198         if (calRight==0):
199             calRight="Y+000"
200             return calRight
201         if (calRight >0):
202             if (calRight > 255):
```

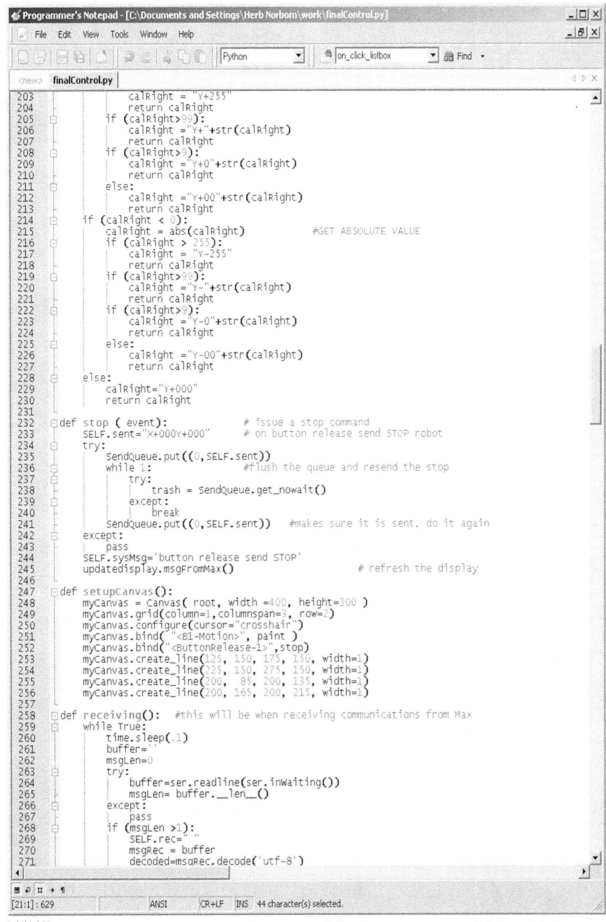

File   Edit   View   Tools   Window   Help

```
Python        ▼     on_click_listbox     ▼     Find   ▼
```

<new>   finalControl.py

```python
203             calRight = "Y+255"
204             return calRight
205         if (calRight>99):
206             calRight ="Y+"+str(calRight)
207             return calRight
208         if (calRight>9):
209             calRight ="Y+0"+str(calRight)
210             return calRight
211         else:
212             calRight ="Y+00"+str(calRight)
213             return calRight
214     if (calRight < 0):
215         calRight = abs(calRight)                    #GET ABSOLUTE VALUE
216         if (calRight > 255):
217             calRight = "Y-255"
218             return calRight
219         if (calRight>99):
220             calRight ="Y-"+str(calRight)
221             return calRight
222         if (calRight>9):
223             calRight ="Y-0"+str(calRight)
224             return calRight
225         else:
226             calRight ="Y-00"+str(calRight)
227             return calRight
228     else:
229         calRight="Y+000"
230         return calRight
231
232 def stop ( event):              # issue a stop command
233     SELF.sent="X+000Y+000"      # on button release send STOP robot
234     try:
235         SendQueue.put((0,SELF.sent))
236         while 1:                    #flush the queue and resend the stop
237             try:
238                 trash = SendQueue.get_nowait()
239             except:
240                 break
241         SendQueue.put((0,SELF.sent))    #makes sure it is sent, do it again
242     except:
243         pass
244     SELF.sysMsg='button release send STOP'
245     updatedisplay.msgFromMax()                      # refresh the display
246
247 def setupCanvas():
248     myCanvas = Canvas( root, width =400, height=300 )
249     myCanvas.grid(column=1,columnspan=3, row=2)
250     myCanvas.configure(cursor="crosshair")
251     myCanvas.bind( "<B1-Motion>", paint )
252     myCanvas.bind("<ButtonRelease-1>",stop)
253     myCanvas.create_line(125, 150, 175, 150, width=1)
254     myCanvas.create_line(225, 150, 275, 150, width=1)
255     myCanvas.create_line(200,  85, 200, 135, width=1)
256     myCanvas.create_line(200, 165, 200, 215, width=1)
257
258 def receiving():    #this will be when receiving communications from Max
259     while True:
260         time.sleep(.1)
261         buffer=''
262         msgLen=0
263         try:
264             buffer=ser.readline(ser.inWaiting())
265             msgLen= buffer.__len__()
266         except:
267             pass
268         if (msgLen >1):
269             SELF.rec=" "
270             msgRec = buffer
271             decoded=msgRec.decode('utf-8')
```

[21:1] : 629   ANSI   CR+LF   INS   44 character(s) selected.

Exhibit255

158

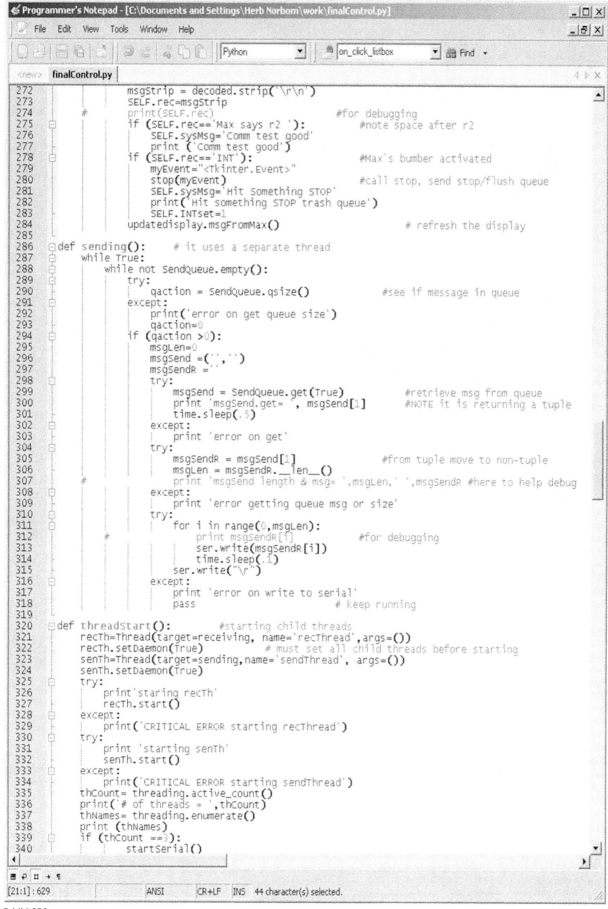

```python
272             msgStrip = decoded.strip('\r\n')
273             SELF.rec=msgStrip
274    #        print(SELF.rec)                    #for debugging
275             if (SELF.rec=='Max says r2 '):         #note space after r2
276               SELF.sysMsg='Comm test good'
277               print ('Comm test good')
278             if (SELF.rec=='INT'):                  #Max's bumber activated
279               myEvent="<Tkinter.Event>"
280               stop(myEvent)                        #call stop, send stop/flush queue
281               SELF.sysMsg='Hit Something STOP'
282               print('Hit something STOP trash queue')
283               SELF.INTset=1
284             updatedisplay.msgFromMax()                   # refresh the display
285
286  def sending():      # it uses a separate thread
287      while True:
288          while not SendQueue.empty():
289              try:
290                  qaction = SendQueue.qsize()             #see if message in queue
291              except:
292                  print('error on get queue size')
293                  qaction=0
294              if (qaction >0):
295                  msgLen=0
296                  msgSend =('','')
297                  msgSendR =''
298                  try:
299                      msgSend = SendQueue.get(True)         #retrieve msg from queue
300                      print 'msgSend.get= ', msgSend[1]      #NOTE it is returning a tuple
301                      time.sleep(.5)
302                  except:
303                      print 'error on get'
304                  try:
305                      msgSendR = msgSend[1]              #from tuple move to non-tuple
306                      msgLen = msgSendR.__len__()
307    #                 print 'msgSend length & msg= ',msgLen,' ',msgSendR #here to help debug
308                  except:
309                      print 'error getting queue msg or size'
310                  try:
311                      for i in range(0,msgLen):
312    #                     print msgSendR[i]                #for debugging
313                          ser.write(msgSendR[i])
314                          time.sleep(.1)
315                      ser.write("\r")
316                  except:
317                      print 'error on write to serial'
318                      pass                         # keep running
319
320  def threadStart():          #starting child threads
321      recTh=Thread(target=receiving, name='recThread',args=())
322      recTh.setDaemon(True)           # must set all child threads before starting
323      senTh=Thread(target=sending,name='sendThread', args=())
324      senTh.setDaemon(True)
325      try:
326          print'staring recTh'
327          recTh.start()
328      except:
329          print('CRITICAL ERROR starting recThread')
330      try:
331          print 'starting senTh'
332          senTh.start()
333      except:
334          print('CRITICAL ERROR starting sendThread')
335      thCount= threading.active_count()
336      print('# of threads = ',thCount)
337      thNames= threading.enumerate()
338      print (thNames)
339      if (thCount ==3):
340          startSerial()
```

[21:1] : 629   ANSI   CR+LF INS 44 character(s) selected.

Exhibit256

159

```python
341     L
342     def startSerial():
343         global ser
344         ser=serial.Serial()
345         ser.port='com8'           #use com8 for wireless, com2 for serial wire
346         ser.baud=9600
347         ser.bytesize=8
348         ser.stopbits=1
349         ser.parity='N'
350         ser.timeout=0
351         ser.xonxoff=0
352         ser.rtscts=0
353         ser.dsrdtr=0
354         print 'ser= ',ser
355
356         try:                      #port should be closed prior to this
357             ser.open()
358             time.sleep(1)
359             print 'Serial Port Open'
360             commCheck()           #run a communications check
361         except OSError as e:
362             formatError="Program\n"+command+"\n could not be run\n"+e.args[1]
363             +"\n Error No= "+str(e.args[0])
364
365
366     def shutdown():
367         print("called shutdown")
368         answer=tkMessageBox.askyesno("EXIT", "Do you really want to quit")
369         if answer==True:
370             thCount= threading.active_count()
371             print('# of threads to stop = ',thCount)
372             thNames= threading.enumerate()
373             print (thNames)
374             while 1:                              #try sending messages in the queue
375                 try:
376                     sending = SendQueue.get_nowait()
377                 except:
378                     break
379             try:
380                 root.quit() #because daemon set 'True' kills child threads also
381             except:
382                 print(" ERROR   could not be terminated")
383
384     def windowsNotepad():
385         osType=platform.system()
386         print osType
387         if (osType=='windows'):
388             try:
389                 command = 'C:\WINDOWS\NOTEPAD.EXE'
390                 env    = {'FOO': 'bar', 'SystemRoot': os.environ['SystemRoot']}
391                 p = subprocess.Popen(command, env=env)
392                 p.wait()
393                 return
394             except OSError as e:
395                 print "Read Error %s: %s\n error no %d"%(command,e.args[1],e.args[0])
396                 formatError="Program\n"+command+"\n could not be run\n"+e.args[1]
397                 +"\n Error No= "+str(e.args[0])
398                 tkMessageBox.showerror("OSError",formatError)
399             except:
400                 print("General error opening NOTEPAD.exe")
401         print("Notepad appears to be unavailable on this system")
402
403     def startProNotepad():
404         try:
405             command = "C:\\WinAVR-20100110\\pn\\pn.exe" #for 2010 users
406             subprocess.call( [command])
407         except OSError as e:
408             print "Read Error %s: %s\n error no %d"%(command,e.args[1],e.args[0])
409             formatError="Program\n"+command+"\n could not be run\n"+e.args[1]
```

Exhibit257

160

```
410                +"\n Error No= "+str(e.args[0])
411                tkMessageBox.showerror("OSError",formatError)
412
413     def showPythonVersion():
414         pyversion=sys.version
415         tkMessageBox.showwarning('Python Version',pyversion)
416
417     def showSystemPlatform():
418         import platform
419         osType=platform.system()
420         osPlatform=platform.win32_ver()
421         osProcessor=platform.processor()
422         tkMessageBox.showwarning('System Information','Operating System: '+ osType +
423             '\nSystem Info:'+osPlatform[0]+
424             '\nRelease: '+osPlatform[1]+
425             '\nService Pack: '+ osPlatform[2]+
426             '\nMultiProcessor: '+osPlatform[3]+
427             '\nProcessor: ' + osProcessor)
428
429     def showRyMax():
430         tkMessageBox.showwarning('RyMax, Inc.','RyMax, Inc.'+
431             '\n web page: www.RyMax.biz'+
432             '\n e-mail: herb@RyMax.biz')
433
434
435
436     def searchPaths():
437         searchWin=Toplevel()
438         searchFrame = LabelFrame(searchWin,text="Python Search Paths",
439         width =100, height=10)
440         searchFrame.grid(column=0, row=0, sticky =NW)
441         searchBox=Listbox(searchFrame, width=150,height=10)
442         searchBox.grid(column=0, row=0,sticky=NW)
443         scrollBar = Scrollbar(searchFrame, orient=VERTICAL,command=searchBox.yview)
444         scrollBar.grid(column=1, row=0,sticky=(N,W,E,S))
445         searchBox['yscrollcommand']=scrollBar.set
446
447         myPythonSearch=[]
448         for folder in sys.path:
449             print folder
450             myPythonSearch.append (folder)
451
452         for item in myPythonSearch:
453             searchBox.insert('end',item)
454
455     def ARMonoff():
456         if (SELF.ARMStatus==0):                    #ARM is off
457             SELF.sent="]1"          #turn ARM on
458             SELF.ARMStatus=1
459             try:
460                 SendQueue.put((1,SELF.sent))        #ARM Onoff
461                 SELF.sysMsg='ARM turned on'
462             except:
463                 print('error writing to queue')
464                 SELF.sysMsg='ARM Error'
465         else:
466             SELF.sent="]0"          #turn ARM off
467             SELF.ARMStatus=0
468             try:
469                 SendQueue.put((1,SELF.sent))     #ARM Onoff
470                 SELF.sysMsg='ARM turned off'
471             except:
472                 print('error writing to queue')
473                 SELF.sysMsg='ARM Error'
474         displayStaticStuff()
475         updatedisplay.msgFromMax()                         # refresh the display
476
477     def ARMUp():
478         SELF.sent="]]"
```

[546:29] : 629   ANSI   CR+LF   INS   Ready

Exhibit258

File   Edit   View   Tools   Window   Help

Python ▾   on_click_listbox ▾   Find ▾

<new>   finalControl.py

```python
479         try:
480             SendQueue.put((1,SELF.sent))                #ARM Up
481             SELF.sysMsg="ARM up"
482         except:
483             print('error writing to queue')
484             SELF.sysMsg='ARM Error'
485         updatedisplay.msgFromMax()                      # refresh the display
486
487     def ARMDown():
488         SELF.sent="][" 
489         try:
490             SendQueue.put((1,SELF.sent))                #ARM Down
491             SELF.sysMsg="ARM down"
492         except:
493             pass
494             SELF.sysMsg='ARM Error'
495         updatedisplay.msgFromMax()                      # refresh the display
496
497     def maxSpeak():
498     #   print "at speech"
499         engine=pyttsx.init()
500         voices = engine.getProperty('voices')
501         for voice in voices:
502             engine.setProperty('voice', voice.id)
503         whatToSay=tkSimpleDialog.askstring("Text for Max","Enter what to say")
504     #   print(whatToSay)
505         if (whatToSay==None):
506             return
507         engine.say(whatToSay)
508         engine.runAndWait()
509
510     def commCheck():
511
512         print ("called the test communications,")
513         print ("response from max should be  'Max says r2 '")
514         SELF.sent="r2"
515         try:
516             SendQueue.put((1,SELF.sent))        #commCheck
517         except:
518             print('testComm Error write to queue')
519
520     def voltage1():
521         print('check voltage1')
522         SELF.sent="v1"
523         try:
524             SendQueue.put((1,SELF.sent))
525             SELF.sysMsg='Voltage Ck1'
526         except:
527             print('error writing to queue')
528             SELF.sysMsg='VOLTAGE Error'
529         updatedisplay.msgFromMax()                      # refresh the display
530
531     def cameraStart():
532         try:
533             subprocess.Popen('c:/windows/system32/ipcamera.exe')
534             SELF.sysMsg ='Camera started'
535         except:
536             print('ERROR IP Camera Program not found')
537             SELF.sysMsg='ERROR IP Camera Program not found'
538         updatedisplay.msgFromMax()
539
540
541     def displayStaticStuff():
542         Label( root, text = "Left Click and Drag mouse to move",
543         bg='white').grid( column=1, row =1,stick=(N,W,E,S))
544
545         robotStatusframe = LabelFrame(root, text="Robot Status",width=20,
546         height=5,cursor="arrow")
547         robotStatusframe.grid(column=0, row =3, sticky=(N,E))
```

[538:37] : 629   ANSI   CR+LF   INS   260 character(s) selected.

Exhibit259

162

```python
548         Label(robotStatusframe, text= "MSG FROM MAX" ).grid( row=0,sticky=(N,E))
549         Label(robotStatusframe, text= "MSG TO MAX").grid(row=1,sticky=(N,E))
550         Label(robotStatusframe, text= "MSG From System").grid(row=2,sticky=(N,E))
551
552         bFrame = LabelFrame(root,width=100, height=15)
553         bFrame.grid(column=0,columnspan=4, row=0, sticky=(N,W,S))
554         Button(bFrame, text = "MAXSPEAK", fg="white",
555         command = maxSpeak).grid(column=0, row=0)
556         if (SELF.ARMStatus==0):
557             Button(bFrame, text = "ARM OFF", fg="yellow",
558             command=ARMOnOff).grid(column=2, row=0)
559         if (SELF.ARMStatus==1):
560             Button(bFrame, text = "ARM ON ", fg="green",   #note extra space end of text
561             command=ARMOnOff).grid(column=2, row=0)
562
563         Button(bFrame, text = "ARMUp", fg="green",repeatdelay=500,repeatinterval=300,
564         command = ARMUp).grid(column=3, row=0)
565         Button(bFrame, text = "ARMDown", fg="green",repeatdelay=500,repeatinterval=300,
566         command = ARMDown).grid(column=4,row=0)
567         Button(bFrame, text = "COMM CHECK", fg="white",
568         command = commCheck).grid(column=5, row=0)
569         Button(bFrame, text = "Camera Start", fg="black",bg="white",
570         command = cameraStart).grid(column=6, row=0)
571         Button(bFrame, text = "SHUTDOWN", fg="red",
572         command = shutdown).grid(column=7, row=0)
573 if __name__=='__main__':
574         root = Tk()
575         root.title( "Max Control Center" )
576         root.geometry( "550x450+50+30" ) #width, height, placement on y and  x axis
577         setupCanvas()
578
579 #pull down menu section
580         menubar = Menu(root)
581         root.config(menu=menubar)
582         filemenu = Menu(menubar, tearoff=0)
583         filemenu.add_command(label="Windows Notepad", command=windowsNotepad)
584         filemenu.add_separator()
585         filemenu.add_command(label="Programmer's Notepad", command=startProNotepad)
586         filemenu.add_separator()
587         filemenu.add_separator()
588         filemenu.add_command(label="Exit", command=shutdown)
589         menubar.add_cascade(menu=filemenu, label='File')
590
591         sysMenu=Menu(menubar, tearoff=0)
592         sysMenu.add_command(label="Python version?", command=showPythonVersion)
593         sysMenu.add_command(label="System Platform?", command=showSystemPlatform)
594         sysMenu.add_command(label="Python Search Paths", command=searchPaths)
595         sysMenu.add_command(label="RyMax, Inc. Information?", command=showRyMax)
596         menubar.add_cascade(label="System Info", menu=sysMenu)
597
598         batterymenu = Menu(menubar, tearoff=0)
599         batterymenu.add_command(label="Battery Source1", command=voltage1)
600         menubar.add_cascade(label="Battery Info",menu=batterymenu)
601
602 #setup a list box to list our wav and txt files
603         soundFrame = LabelFrame(root, text="Max Sounds",width=20, height=10,
604         cursor="arrow")
605         soundFrame.grid(column=0, row =2, sticky=(N,W,S))
606         soundBox=Listbox(soundFrame, width=20, height=18)
607         soundBox.grid(column=0,row=1,sticky=(N,W,S))
608         scrollBar = Scrollbar(soundFrame, orient=VERTICAL, command=soundBox.yview)
609         scrollBar.grid(column=1,row=1, sticky=(N,E,S))
610         soundBox['yscrollcommand']=scrollBar.set
611         path=SELF.defPath
612         print path
613         soundlist = os.listdir(path)
614 # load the listbox
615         for sound in soundlist:
616             extension = os.path.splitext(sound)[1][1:]
```

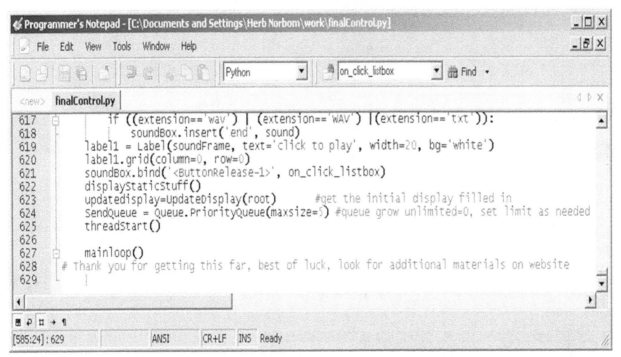

```
617        if ((extension=='wav') | (extension=='WAV') |(extension=='txt')):
618            soundBox.insert('end', sound)
619        label1 = Label(soundFrame, text='click to play', width=20, bg='white')
620        label1.grid(column=0, row=0)
621        soundBox.bind('<ButtonRelease-1>', on_click_listbox)
622        displayStaticStuff()
623        updatedisplay=UpdateDisplay(root)       #get the initial display filled in
624        SendQueue = Queue.PriorityQueue(maxsize=5) #queue grow unlimited=0, set limit as needed
625        threadStart()
626
627        mainloop()
628    # Thank you for getting this far, best of luck, look for additional materials on website
629
```

Exhibit261

I have continued playing with the Queue size and have set it down to maxsize=3. I still am not happy with the stop response time. I hope you continue to work with the programs and try to increase the response times. I am not sure if there would be an improvement or not, but try a regular Queue and adjust the size there too.

The End or the Beginning

I hope that you have learned a lot and had some fun. You can add many types of sensors to your project. You can even add additional microprocessors and external storage. The technology is advancing at an unbelievable rate. Depending on enclosures you make for your robot you might want to consider putting in a temperature gauge. The options are increasing in number and capabilities and in many cases the prices are falling. I hope to have more information available for you on the web site. On the web site I will be offering instructions on upgrading your code to Python 3.x. If there is interest I will also setup a forum and other services. In another stage of this project, look out, I may have another book in me, I am looking at using the Raspberry Pi in connection with the ATMega328. You might want some of Max's vital statistics. Weight approximately 6.4 kg or 14 lbs (including all the batteries). Approximate size length 13", width 12", height 15" to top of camera. Pulse is strong at 14,745,600. Temperature rising, age 1 month+, IQ =0.0001. Keep having fun.

When you get around to soldering a board I recommend you buy some connectors for building out the pins on the microchips. Ideally you would have a connector for each pin that could support a device. As a final note, be careful, as voltages increase, so do the risks. Visit the web site www.rymax.biz for additional information. I would like to learn from your experience, you can e-mail me at herb@rymax.biz.

Max16-19

Cost and Possible Parts List

Approximate Cost of MAX			
PART DESCRIPTION	QTY	APPROXIMATE COST $	NOTES
Metal Chassis Frame	1	0	salvaged
Drive Motors with gear box	2	18	wheels were included
Stepper Motor -Parallax Standard Servo (#900-00005)	1	15	
Front Caster	1	0	salvaged
Original NerdKit	1	80	
Extra ATMega328p	1	7	with boot loader installed
Extra Voltage Regulators	5	3	
H- Bridge	1	4	
Various Capacitors		10	
Various Resistors		10	
Various Extra Wire		3	
scrap wood		0	salvaged
Various connectors		10	salvaged
solder board and/or breadboard			many options you decide
Battery - 9.6Volt Rechargeable	1	15	Note you can just use simple one
Battery - 12Volt/1.4AH Sealed Rechargeable	1	14	for drive motors
Battery - 12Volt/7.5AH Sealed Rechargeable	1	25	for camera (salvaged from old UPS)
Foscam Fi8910W	1	90	
Auxiliary Speaker	1	4	includes 2 AAA batteries
Serial Port Converter DB-UC001	1	12	
Wireless Transceiver 431-470MHz	1	43	2 per set
	Total	363	
			add as appropriate tax and shipping

Salvaged parts are shown at zero cost or estimated
As you can see the price adds up very quickly. The camera and battery add weight and cost. If money is tight leave off for now or shop around for used/different parts.